Pollution Control and Energy Needs

Pollution Control and Energy Needs

Robert M. Jimeson and Roderick S. Spindt, *Editors*

A symposium co-sponsored

by the Division of Fuel Chemistry

and the Division of Petroleum

Chemistry at the 164th Meeting

of the American Chemical Society,

New York, N.Y., Aug. 29–30, 1972.

ADVANCES IN CHEMISTRY SERIES **127**

AMERICAN CHEMICAL SOCIETY

WASHINGTON, D. C.   1973

6 28.5
P 77

ADCSAJ 127 1-251 (1973)

Library of Congress Catalog Card No. 73-92108

ISBN 8412-0190-0

PRINTED IN THE UNITED STATES OF AMERICA

Advances in Chemistry Series

Robert F. Gould, *Editor*

FOREWORD

ADVANCES IN CHEMISTRY SERIES was founded in 1949 by the American Chemical Society as an outlet for symposia and collections of data in special areas of topical interest that could not be accommodated in the Society's journals. It provides a medium for symposia that would otherwise be fragmented, their papers distributed among several journals or not published at all. Papers are refereed critically according to ACS editorial standards and receive the careful attention and processing characteristic of ACS publications. Papers published in ADVANCES IN CHEMISTRY SERIES are original contributions not published elsewhere in whole or major part and include reports of research as well as reviews since symposia may embrace both types of presentation.

CONTENTS

PREFACE

Currently two issues are pervasive national concerns. One is the adequate, reliable supply of all forms of energy; the other is the protection of environmental values. These concerns are interrelated. Each influences the other, and frequently the Nation's environmental goals conflict with its energy demands. Although the public is acutely aware that a damaged ecology is not in its interest, it still expects the material benefits of advanced technology and the ready availability of energy. A balance is required to enhance the total quality of life.

To achieve this balance, the public—which includes all segments of producers and consumers—must come to grips with the alternatives and provide a workable expression of the public interest. Understanding the complex interplay among the various factors is important if an equitable relationship is to be achieved between the energy and environmental issues. Efforts of science, industry, and government must continue to develop the needed technology and energy resources.

The American Chemical Society Symposium on Environmental Pollution Control which was held in New York City during August 1972 examined the energy–environmental situation to place in perspective all important, interrelated factors. It also strove to guide and to catalyze scientific and technological activities into forms that will mitigate the conflict. Although no one energy type or technology is expected to resolve the problem completely, the papers presented exposed the merits of various technologies that may lessen it. The achievement of environmental goals will depend on industry's ability to transform the technological information into working realities, on government's formulation and enforcement of realistic regulations, and on the public's clear expression of the quality of life desired. To these ends the Symposium was directed. The papers were presented in three main sessions. The first focused on the energy and primary fuel situation expected in the 1970's and the environmental impact of its development and use. The second assessed the technologies and their ability to provide fuels that would meet environmental regulations. The final session appraised the effectiveness of various stack control processes. The salient papers of the three sessions are contained in this volume.

Total national primary energy demand of all forms is expected to increase dramatically over the next 20 years. The Nation's projected gas supplies cannot meet current projections of demand. Domestic production is expected to peak in the 1970's and decline thereafter. Supplementary sources like pipeline imports, liquefied natural gas, synthetic gas from coal, and gas from Alaska will be increasingly important.

The Nation has many years of coal resources available. Unfortunately most of the energy demand is in the East where environmentally acceptable reserves of coal are least abundant. The dislocations caused by the demand for naturally occurring low sulfur coal along with uncertainties of nuclear power generation, oil imports, environmental pressures, and success of stack gas control technology has fostered unsettled conditions in an industry working with the Nation's largest energy resource base.

Domestic production of crude oil and condensate peaked in 1970. For over a year now market demand pro-ration has been essentially lifted, and wells have been operating at maximum production, short of reservoir damage. Nevertheless domestic production since then has been lower in each succeeding year. Development of Prudhoe Bay in Alaska along with other discoveries in the Arctic and the lower 48 states will be needed to hold U.S. crude production near current levels. The remaining U.S. oil supply must come from foreign oil. In 1972 these imports accounted for 29% of the total oil supply and 12.5% of total energy consumption. U.S. oil imports are projected to triple by 1980. The Middle East contains about 70% of the free world's proved reserves. Since crude oil production in areas outside the Persian Gulf cannot meet world needs, most of the additional imports into the U.S. and other countries must come from this region. Since Middle East oil is typically high in sulfur, it must be hydrodesulfurized to meet U.S. environmental regulations.

The growth of electrical energy is expected to be much greater than that of primary energy. This trend is the result of a persistent demand by the public for a clean, convenient, and reliable source of energy which is available instantaneously. Energy conservation is often lauded as a panacea to expanding demand: however such practices appear unrealistic since the items which could be controlled are those which use little energy. For example, although some would give up an electric toothbrush, very few would sacrifice their washing machines, electric range, electric iron or even their air conditioning. New members of the expanding population will also demand these conveniences.

Electricity is the cleanest energy at the point of use. It is sought by many relatively small energy users to satisfy environmental restrictions. In essence they transfer their environmental problems to the electric generating stations.

Analyses of the requirements for quality fossil fuels to meet environmental regulations in electric power generation indicate that low sulfur coal and fuel oil supplies fall short. Adequate and reliable stack gas scrubbing technology to permit the combustion of high sulfur fuels in large boilers is not yet widely realized. A few prototype scrubbers have been constructed and operated for limited periods in conjunction with large utility boilers. However, sufficient quantities of stack scrubbers are not expected to meet all the needs. Even so, a large waste of by-product disposal problem and risk of water pollution are associated with scrubbers. Furthermore scrubbing costs are continually rising.

The protection of the public health and welfare is a prime consideration of environmental regulations, and the Clean Air Amendments of 1970 require that ambient air standards be established for this protection. However the emission regulations as they stand are too stringent to be practical. They require that the scarce low sulfur fuels be used all the time when actually wind currents and other meteorological conditions diffuse emissions and leave the ambient air well within the standards 90% of the time. The consequence is a large, immediate demand for limited supplies of high quality fuels. Models have been developed to relate emissions and their impact on air ambient quality under various meteorological conditions. Their use in analyzing local situations enables emission regulations that will simultaneously attain air quality goals and mitigate the fuels crisis.

Basically, there are only two ways to resolve the sulfur emission problem. First, a fuel (natural, desulfurized, or synthetic) low enough in sulfur to meet regulations can be utilized, or secondly, a high sulfur fuel can be burned with sufficient removal of sulfur oxides from their flue gases.

Coal can be made environmentally acceptable for combustion by removal of its mineral and sulfur content. New technology for this is proceeding along two patterns. In one approach pyritic and organic sulfur are chemically removed from coal. In the other approach, coal is dispersed in a solvent, the organic sulfur compounds are hydrodesulfurized, and the mineral matter containing pyritic sulfur is filtered from the liquid coal solution. Coal can also be processed to other forms of fuel that meet environmental regulations. It can be hydrogenated to an oil, or it can be converted to char by processes with a potential for producing low sulfur fuel.

The desulfurization of heavy fuel oil is generally categorized as direct or indirect. Feedstocks for the direct process can be a whole crude, top crude, an atmospheric residuum, or a vacuum residuum. The indirect process for desulfurization is similar to the direct process except that it is applied to a vacuum gas oil fraction, after which the desulfurized product is blended with either an undesulfurized vacuum residuum, a desulfurized vacuum residuum, a naturally occurring low-sulfur crude oil, or a combination of these. A number of processes are commercially available. The selection of a desulfurization process depends largely upon the nature of the available feed stock and the desired sulfur level of the fuel-oil pool. Key properties with important influence on the technology are: sulfur level, metals content, Conradson carbon, asphaltene concentration, nitrogen content, and oil viscosity. Most of these affect the economics and consumptive use of hydrogen. Many hydrodesulfurization processes feature a fixed bed type of catalytic reactor where liquid feed is contacted with the hydrogen-rich recycled gas under elevated pressures and temperatures.

The catalyst is keyed to most of the hydrodesulfurization processes and tailored for a specific oil. Some catalysts can tolerate deposition of large quantities of heavy metals while maintaining high desulfurization activities. Other catalysts need plugging protection against suspended salts and particulates in the feedstock. To protect fixed-bed catalysts these sediments are removed before they enter the desulfurization reactor.

The H-Oil ebulating reactor bed is unique. It overcomes the problems encountered in hydrosulfurization of residual oil and fixed-bed catalytic reactors. In the H-Oil process the feedstock is mixed with the hydrogen gas, and both enter the bottom of the reactor. The catalyst comprising the bed is finely divided. The upward liquid velocity is sufficient to keep the catalyst expanded and moving. The circulating motion eliminates the need for adding hydrogen quench at various levels along the reactor as is done with fixed-bed units. Since any solids in the feed pass through the expanded bed, the reactor does not plug. The catalyst is replaced continuously in small quantities to maintain steady-state activity. Uniform activity can be maintained while processing a varying metals content feedstock.

The second general method of resolving the sulfur emission problem involves removal of sulfur oxides from flue gases emanating from the combustion of high sulfur fuels.

Flue gas desulfurization systems are classified in two general categories. One group involves throwaway product systems where sulfur product (untreated or treated) is disposed of as a landfill. The other group produces saleable products such as sulfuric acid, elemental sulfur or, as in Japan, gypsum for wallboard and sodium sulfite for paper mills.

Scrubbing processes use various removal media including limestone, lime, dolomite, magnesium carbonate, sodium carbonate, ammonia, molten carbonate, or activated carbon.

Many processes simultaneously remove other pollutants such as particulates and nitrogen oxide. Some processes are tailored to remove more than one pollutant.

Since the formation of nitrogen oxides in the flue gas is a strong function of the combustion system, its control is possible by combustion modification. For example, burner design and methods of introducing air for combustion have a pronounced effect on the formation of nitrogen oxides. Thus, the relationship of the various factors and their effect on nitrogen oxide formation in different fuel combustion furnaces is important in designing new equipment and refashioning existing units to meet nitrogen oxide emission standards.

This volume will stimulate the thoughts of anyone responsible for the future energy and environmental needs of the country. Most specifically the subject is addressed to persons who conscientiously struggle to abate air pollution generated by combustion processes; to executives, engineers, and consultants of private organizations who must undertake corporate action to comply with environmental control requirements; to state, local, and federal pollution control officials who must implement plans and develop further policies to ensure environmental quality without sacrificing the energy needs and values of society; and to members of environmental interest groups and the public working for a pragmatically balanced energy–environment policy. Finally, the study will help to direct researchers involved in most aspects of the energy and environmental control field.

Robert M. Jimeson

Washington, D.C.
September 1973

The Gas Supplies of the United States—
Present and Future

GORDON K. ZARESKI

Bureau of Natural Gas, Federal Power Commission, Washington, D.C. 20426

Forecasted natural gas availability from 1971 to 1990 indicates the Nation's supply will be inadequate to meet projected demand. Domestic production is expected to peak at about 25 trillion cubic feet (Tcf) in the mid-seventies and decline slowly thereafter, while demand could reach 46 Tcf in 1990. Supplemental sources of gas, including pipeline imports, liquefied natural gas, synthetic gas from coal, and gas from Alaska, will be required to ameliorate indigenous supply deficiencies. Expected volumes of gas from these supplemental sources may total 4.6 and 11.5 Tcf annually by 1980 and 1990, respectively, and by 1990 could provide about 40% of the Nation's gas consumption. Nevertheless, total gas supply will be insufficient to meet projected demand, and a continuing supply–demand imbalance is expected.

The growth of natural gas service in the United States between 1945 and 1970 must rank as one of the great success stories of American business and technology. During this period the number of miles of utility gas mains carrying natural gas increased from 218,000 to 906,925 miles, and a $17 billion high-pressure gas transmission pipeline network was extended into all of the lower 48 states. Natural gas consumption increased at an annual average rate of about 6.5% and moved from a position where it supplied 13% of the Nation's total energy consumption in 1945 to the point where it provided about 33% of the total energy consumed in 1970.

The Nation's gas reserves are distributed among 25,000-30,000 gas fields (shaded areas of Figure 1) which in many instances are geographically remote from the gas-consuming areas. The pipeline system which connects the consuming areas with their respective areas of supply can, in a general way, be characterized by a number of national pipeline corridors. For instance the interstate gas consumed in the New England, Great Lakes, Appalachian, and Southeastern regions (proportional to the width of the arrows in Figure 1) originates chiefly in the south Louisiana, Texas Gulf Coast, and Hugoton-Anadarko (Oklahoma Panhandle region) gas supply areas. In addition to these domestic supplies, the United States is also a net importer of gas from Canada and Mexico. Although net imports during 1970 amounted to only about 3.5% of national consumption, imports are an important contribution to the gas supply of some areas.

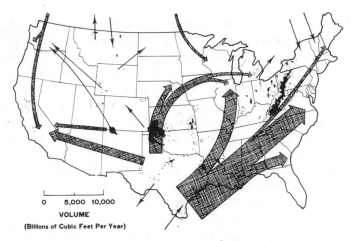

0   5,000 10,000
VOLUME
(Billions of Cubic Feet Per Year)

Figure 1. 1970 interstate natural gas movements

The requirements for gas are expected to increase significantly during the 1971-1990 period, not only because of the growth in total energy requirements but because of the clean nature of this fuel and its premium value from a pollution control standpoint. Unfortunately the deliverable supply of natural gas, which presents the fewest pollution problems of all the Nation's present primary energy sources, will be inadequate to meet all of the demand for it.

The American gas consumer has only recently begun to be affected by the developing imbalance between the supply of this environmentally superior fuel and the burgeoning demand for it. The emerging shortage of gas is evidenced by major pipeline companies and distributors in many parts of the country being forced to curtail service to some existing customers and to refuse requests for additional gas service from many new customers and from present large industrial customers. Present and projected trends in the supply and demand for gas in the United States indicate that the national supply deficit which has recently developed will continue throughout the 1972-1990 period.

Demand

Until recently gas requirements (demand) of the United States were equivalent to gas consumption because gas supplies were abundantly available as new markets for gas were developed. In retrospect then, demand for gas was approximately equal to domestic net production plus net pipeline imports. Prospectively, however, under conditions of insufficient gas supply, consumption will be less than demand.

While numerous projection of the future demand for gas have been made, the most recent projection of future gas requirements developed by the Future Requirements Committee (1) has been adapted in this analysis as the yardstick against which anticipated gas supply will be measured. On this basis the annual demand for gas in the lower 48 states is projected to grow from 22.6 trillion cubic feet (Tcf) in 1970 to 46.4 Tcf in 1990 (Figure 2). The growth of demand to this level reflects an anticipated average annual compound growth rate of about 3.7% during the 1970-1990 period compared with a historical average annual compound growth rate of over 6% for the 1950-1970 period.

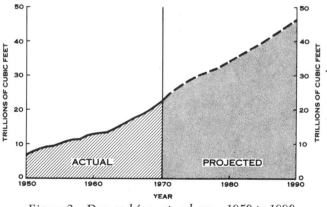

Figure 2.   Demand for natural gas—1950 to 1990

Historical Reserve and Production Trends

The historical domestic supply position of the United States, as reported by the American Gas Association (2, 3), is illustrated in Table I and Figure 3. These data exclude Alaskan resources because they are not presently available to the markets of the lower 48 states.

Prior to 1968 the annual net additions to reserves exceeded the annual production of gas, resulting in a surplus. In 1968, for the first time, production exceeded reserve additions by 7.3 Tcf. This historic reversal was followed by excesses of production over reserve addition of 12.3, 10.7, and 12.5 Tcf in 1969, 1970, and 1971, respectively. Because reserve additions during this 4 year period were considerably below the historical level and because production increased, the year-end inventory of proved reserves was reduced from its historical high of 289.3 Tcf in 1967 to a 1971 level of 247.4 Tcf.

A distinct change in the rate of production occurred during 1971 when production increased only 0.1 Tcf. Although this change results from many factors, including the fact that the 1971-1972 winter was unseasonably mild in many parts of the country, it may also indicate that the Nation's peak productive capacity is being approached. As will be discussed later, this peak has been projected to begin about 1973.

One commonly used indicator of the Nation's gas supply posture is the reserve-to-production (R/P) ratio. The R/P ratio is a measure of the remaining years of proved reserves at the current level of production. Although the R/P ratio does not consider many of the physical limita-

Table I. United States Natural Gas Supply
Excluding Alaska—1950-1971[a]

Year	Net Production (1)	Reserve Additions (2)	Year-End Reserves (3)	R/P Ratio (3/1) (4)	F/P Ratio (2/1) (5)
1950	6.9	12.0	184.6	26.8	1.7
1951	7.9	16.0	192.8	24.4	2.0
1952	8.6	14.3	198.6	23.1	1.7
1953	9.2	20.3	210.3	22.9	2.2
1954	9.4	9.6	210.6	22.4	1.0
1955	10.1	21.9	222.5	22.0	2.2
1956	10.9	24.7	236.7	21.7	2.3
1957	11.4	20.0	245.2	21.5	1.8
1958	11.4	18.9	252.8	22.2	1.7
1959	12.4	20.6	261.2	21.1	1.7
1960	13.0	13.8	262.2	20.2	1.1
1961	13.4	16.4	265.4	19.8	1.2
1962	13.6	18.8	270.6	19.9	1.4
1963	14.5	18.1	274.5	18.9	1.2
1964	15.3	20.1	279.4	18.3	1.3
1965	16.3	21.2	284.5	17.5	1.3
1966	17.5	19.2	286.4	16.4	1.1
1967	18.4	21.1	289.3	15.7	1.1
1968	19.3	12.0	282.1	14.6	0.6
1969	20.6	8.3	269.9	13.1	0.4
1970	21.8	11.1	259.6	11.9	0.5
1971	21.9	9.4	247.4	11.3	0.4

[a] Source: American Gas Association.

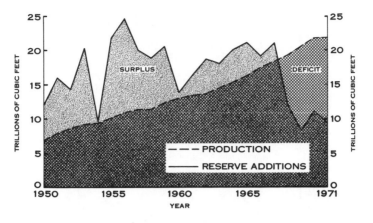

Figure 3. Natural gas production and reserve additions

tions which govern the rate of gas withdrawal, it is useful as an indicator of gas supply. The R/P ratio has declined steadily from 26.8 in 1950 to 11.3 in 1971. Considered by itself, the historical decline in the R/P ratio was not a major source of concern because it was believed by some that, ideally, the R/P ratio would stabilize at a point sufficient to enable the quantities of gas demanded to be met without the development of excessive reserves. A decline below the ideal level, however, results in deliverability problems, *i.e.*, reserves are insufficient to deliver the peak quantities of gas needed.

The findings (reserve additions)-to-production (F/P) ratio is another indicator which is sometimes useful when talking about gas supply. While reserve additions have fluctuated about an average value, production has been increasing, causing the F/P ratio to decline from about 2 in the early 1950's to 0.4 in 1971. This indicates that gas reserves are now being consumed faster than they are being renewed (Figure 4).

Future Domestic Gas Supply

Any analysis of future domestic supply necessarily involves an estimate of the level of future reserve additions. A recent analysis of natural gas supply and demand relationships by the Federal Power Commission (FPC) staff (4) reached several conclusions with respect to the future annual reserve additions depicted in Figure 5. First, an increase from the present level of annual reserve additions to the average national finding level of the past 10 years (17 Tcf annually) is consistent with estimates of the undiscovered potential gas remaining and recent regulatory actions which have increased the wellhead price of gas in several important supply areas. Second, it is unlikely that annual reserve addi-

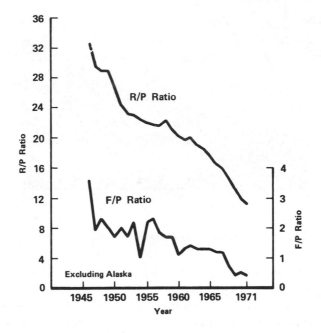

Figure 4.   National gas supply trends—R/P and
F/P ratios—1946 to 1971

tions will increase to a sustained level higher than the average of the
past 10 years. Finally, it is improbable that findings will increase immediately to the 17 Tcf level from the 1970 level of 11.1 Tcf. Accordingly,
for the purpose of projection, it is assumed that annual reserve additions
will increase by approximately 1 Tcf per year from the 1970 level of
about 11 Tcf until additions reach 17 Tcf per year in 1976. Reserve
additions are subsequently projected at 17 Tcf per year during the
period 1977 through 1990.

Cumulative reserve additions under this anticipated schedule would
amount to 325 Tcf from 1971 through 1990. This rate of reserve additions
is compatible with current independent estimates of potential gas supply
by the Potential Gas Committee (PGC) and the United States Geological
Survey (5, 6). Under this schedule of annual reserve additions, cumulative additions through 1990 would represent the development of about
38 and 21%, respectively, of gas supply in the lower 48 states as estimated
by PGC and the Geological Survey.

Average reserve additions for the 5 year period 1971 through 1975
would be 14 Tcf per year which was also the average experienced during
the period from 1966 through 1970. Reserve additions for 1971 were
projected by the Federal Power Commission staff to be about 12 Tcf.
In 1971, reported additions amounted to only 9.4 Tcf. Some reserves

resulting from drilling on acreage leased in the December 1970 Federal lease sale in offshore South Louisiana were not included, however, because data were insufficient to properly estimate the amount of proved reserves.

Estimates by the FPC staff have been made of the future annual production levels which could be supported by these projected additions to reserves. The period from 1971 through 1975 was focused on by projecting the national additions to reserves in an area-by-area analysis of the major producing areas of the country. Each area was examined by evaluating past drilling trends, reserve finding rates, and production history as well as the potential of the area for sustained contributions to national supply. Two things were established through this analysis: (1) a national reserve additions schedule through 1975 was reconciled with individual supply area considerations, and (2) the national production rate which could be anticipated by summing the area-by-area estimates of production capability was approximated.

The dynamics of the relationship between gas supply, demand, and production can result in changing inter-area relationships with the passage of time. For this reason production projections based on an area-by-area approach do not have much validity beyond 5 years. Beyond that time span, estimates of the production available from a given reserve base are probably best made on a national basis.

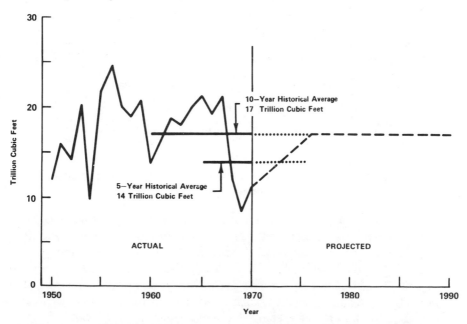

Figure 5. Actual and projected net reserve additions, contiguous 48 states

A commonly used method of approximating the productive capacity of a body of reserves is to assume that a minimum reserve-to-production ratio (usually 10) is required to provide for adequate delivery rates. This rule of thumb approach does not consider the sometimes rather wide variations experienced with actual gas reservoirs. In an attempt to make an improved approximation of future long-term gas deliverability, the FPC staff developed a method to estimate the national production capability for each year by the computerized application of a national availability curve. This curve was synthesized from FPC Form 15 deliverability data from more than 900 individual sources of supply which comprised more than 88% of the interstate and 62% of the national reserves in 1968. This method is superior to an R/P limit approach because it is derived from deliverability data which consider actual reservoir production characteristics.

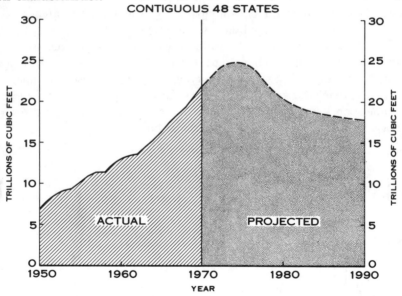

Figure 6. Actual and projected domestic production of natural gas, contiguous 48 states

The production projection for 1971 through 1990 (Figure 6) was derived from presently proved reserves plus anticipated reserve additions as scheduled by the methods described above and was computed by using the national availability curve. Annual gas production has increased exponentially in the past. In the 1971-1990 time interval, however, it is projected to peak at about 24.8 Tcf, around 1973-1974, and thereafter decline and stabilize at a somewhat lower level in the 1980's. Because demand is projected to grow while domestic supply is projected to stabilize within the time frame considered, a gas supply shortfall will develop. This supply deficit is projected to increase annually and reach 28.6 Tcf by 1990 (Table II).

Table II.   United States Domestic Supply and Demand—1972-1990 [a]

Year	Demand	Production	Domestic Supply Deficit
1972	26.1	23.8	2.3
1973	27.7	24.7	3.0
1974	28.8	24.8	4.0
1975	29.8	24.7	5.1
1980	34.5	20.4	14.1
1985	39.8	18.5	21.3
1990	46.4	17.8	28.6

[a] In Tcf.

Future supply and demand will not develop exactly as depicted in the above projections because precision is not possible in such a projection. Both demand and domestic production are susceptible to considerable deviation from the levels projected. In terms of sensitivity to error, it is obvious that the projection of domestic production is very susceptible because of its dependence upon the level of future reserve additions. Even if much more optimistic levels of reserve additions (and hence productive capacity) are assumed, however, increasing demand cannot be satisfied. Figure 7 illustrates a comparison of demand and three different levels of productive capacity should annual reserve additions exceed 17 Tcf per year. Reserve additions of 20, 25, and 30 Tcf are programed for every year beginning with 1971. Even under the best of these conditions, a substantial supply gap develops in the mid-1970's and worsens over the time span considered.

Supplemental Gas Supplies

When considered against the backdrop of a projected indigenous supply deficiency, the importance of the future role to be played by supplemental sources of gas is obvious. Pipeline imports of gas from Canada and Mexico constitute the only substantive source of supplemental gas presently available. However, significant supplemental supplies of gas are expected to become available from several other sources as development of the associated technologies and/or required systems proceeds. These major new supplemental sources are liquefied natural gas imports (LNG), gas from coal, and gas from Alaska (Table III). A positive contribution to gas supply will also be made by reformer gas derived from liquid hydrocarbons (SNG); however, the quantification of meaningful long-range projections with respect to this source is not practicable at this time.

Pipeline Imports. During 1970 net imports of natural gas to the United States from Canada and Mexico amounted to 794.5 billion cubic feet (Bcf). Of this amount, net imports from Mexico were only 26.7 Bcf. There appears to be little reason to expect any substantial increase in imports from Mexico chiefly because of Mexico's relatively small undiscovered gas potential. There are prospects for increased overland imports of gas from Canada, however, which depend in large measure upon the timely development of gas reserves in excess of those required to satisfy Canada's future internal requirements.

In April 1969 the Canadian Petroleum Association estimated the ultimate potential raw recoverable natural gas reserves of Canada to be 720.9 Tcf (at 14.73 psia and 60°F). If the total raw recoverable gas discovered through 1970 is subtracted from this value, a remaining undiscovered potential of 634.8 Tcf of raw gas is derived. Much of this undiscovered potential is attributed to Canada's frontier areas comprised of Northern Canada, Arctic Islands, Mackenzie Delta, Hudson Bay, and the continental shelf areas off the Atlantic, Pacific, and Arctic Coasts.

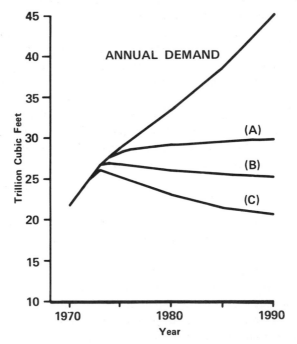

Figure 7. Levels of domestic productive capacity with annual reserve additions of: (A) 30 Tcf, (B) 25 Tcf, and (C) 20 Tcf

**Table III.   Supplemental Supplies of Natural Gas—
Projected 1971-1990** [a]

Year	Pipeline Imports	LNG Imports	Gas from Coal	Alaskan Gas	Annual Total
1970	0.8	SV [b]	—	—	0.8
1971	0.9	SV	—	—	0.9
1972	1.0	SV	—	—	1.0
1973	1.1	SV	—	—	1.1
1974	1.1	SV	—	—	1.1
1975	1.2	0.3	—	—	1.5
1980	1.6	2.0	0.3	0.7	4.6
1985	1.9	3.0	1.4	1.3	7.6
1990	1.9	4.0	3.3	2.3	11.5
Total	31.3	38.0	17.3	20.6	107.0

[a] In Tcf.
[b] Small volumes.

An important factor relative to Canada's natural gas potential is the inter-relationship between the possible development of the potential in the Mackenzie Delta and Arctic Islands areas and the effect that this would have in unlocking the proved and potential gas resources of Alaska. The successful development of Canada's Mackenzie Delta and Arctic Islands resources would greatly enhance current proposals to move gas from Alaska and Northern Canada to Canadian and United States markets.

Several significant gas discoveries have already been made in the frontier areas. Because of these discoveries, a future level of annual reserve additions greater than historical rates can reasonably be used to estimate the future gas surpluses which Canada may be able to make available for export. Annual reserve additions in Canada's traditional supply areas averaged 4 Tcf from 1966 to 1970. On the basis of the potential of the frontier areas, however, future annual average additions may be estimated at 6.5 Tcf. This finding level in conjunction with Canada's projected requirements and scheduled exports under existing licenses would result in an increase in the annually exportable volumes of 0.8 Tcf in 1970 to 1.9 Tcf by 1990 (Table III).

Liquefied Natural Gas. Many regions of the world have extensive volumes of developed natural gas reserves but have limited internal markets. These resources in conjunction with advancing technologies in the liquefaction, handling, and transportation of liquefied natural gas (LNG) have kindled an intense interest in the delivery of liquefied natural gas volumes to the energy hungry centers of the world.

By mid-1972 the Federal Power Commission had authorized only one long-term marine import of LNG into the United States. Several other proposals for the long-term import of base load LNG have been filed with the Federal Power Commission, however, and a number of other prospective projects have been widely discussed in the trade press. These

Table IV. **United States Gas Supply—Demand**
(All Volumes in Tcf at

Year	Annual Demand[a]	Net Pipeline Imports	LNG Imports	Gas from Coal	Gas from Alaska	Gas from Liquid Hydrocarbons
1966	17.9	0.4	—	—	—	—
1967	18.8	0.5	—	—	—	—
1968	19.9	0.6	SV[b]	—	—	—
1969	21.3	0.7	SV	—	—	—
1970	22.6	0.8	SV	—	—	—
1971	24.6	0.9	SV	—	—	—
1972	26.1	1.0	SV	—	—	ID[c]
1973	27.7	1.1	SV	—	—	ID
1974	28.8	1.1	SV	—	—	ID
1975	29.8	1.2	0.3	—	—	ID
1980	34.5	1.6	2.0	0.3	0.7	ID
1985	39.8	1.9	3.0	1.4	1.3	ID
1990	46.4	1.9	4.0	3.3	2.3	ID
1971–1990 Totals	707.6	31.1	38.0	17.3	20.6	ID

[a] Contiguous 48 states.
[b] Very small volumes.

filed and prospective LNG projects are an indication of the future availability of long-term LNG imports to the contiguous United States. While the estimated operational dates for these projects may be based on reasonable assumptions or on the most current expectations, other more difficult factors to evaluate such as the length of time required for the necessary governmental authorizations and the construction time necessary to build the extensive facilities required, make it unlikely that actual LNG imports will precisely follow current schedules and expectations. Current analyses of these projects indicate that the import of significant LNG volumes into the United States (0.3 Tcf) can first be expected in 1975 and that these imports will increase to about 2.0 Tcf annually by 1980 (Table III). In the longer term, the degree of precision in any forecast is even less clear, but numerous companies have indicated that certain additional projects are under active consideration or investigation. On this basis the growth rates expected in the 1975-1980 period should continue into the decade of the 1980's, thus yielding a projected LNG availability of about 4 Tcf annually by 1990.

Gas from Coal. Progress toward the development of improved processes to produce high-Btu, synthetic pipeline-quality gas from coal can currently be seen on several fronts. Two large-scale coal gasification pilot plants are currently in operation or under construction and plans to build two others are advancing. The pilot plant in operation is located

Balance—Actual 1966-1970; Projected 1971-1990
14.73 psia and 60°F)

Domestic Production	Annual Con-sumption	Un-satisfied Demand	Reserve Additions	Year-end Reserves	R/P Ratio
17.5	17.9	0.0	19.2	286.4	16.4
18.4	18.8	0.0	21.1	289.3	15.8
19.3	19.9	0.0	12.0	282.1	14.6
20.6	21.3	0.0	8.3	269.9	13.1
21.8	22.6	0.0	11.1	259.6	11.9
22.8	23.7	0.9	12.0	248.8	10.9
23.8	24.8	1.3	13.0	238.0	10.0
24.7	25.8	1.9	14.0	227.3	9.2
24.8	25.9	2.9	15.0	217.4	8.8
24.7	26.2	3.6	16.0	208.7	8.4
20.4	25.0	9.5	17.0	186.1	9.1
18.5	26.1	13.7	17.0	175.4	9.5
17.8	29.3	17.1	17.0	170.4	9.6
414.2	521.2	186.4	325.0	—	—

[c] Insufficient data for quantitative projection: unsatisfied demand will be reduced by the amount of SNG actually produced.

near Chicago, Ill., and employs the Hygas process developed by the Institute of Gas Technology. A plant using the Consolidation Coal Co.'s CO_2 Acceptor process is nearing completion at Rapid City, S. Dak. The Department of the Interior has awarded a contract to Bituminous Coal Research to build and operate a pilot plant based on their Bi-Gas process near Homer City, Pa., and construction on a fourth pilot plant, intended to study the Bureau of Mines Synthane process, was scheduled to begin in September 1972 in suburban Pittsburgh, Pa. The research and development work associated with these new coal gasification processes is not expected to be completed before the late 1970's.

In addition, two other major efforts have been announced to develop coal gasification facilities in northwestern New Mexico. These proposed plants would be based on an extension of the Lurgi technology which has been used in Europe for many years. The first is a project proposed by El Paso Natural Gas Co., and the second is a proposal by a consortium composed of Pacific Lighting Service Co., Texas Eastern Transmission Corp., and Utah International, Inc. Each of these projects calls for the construction of one or more gasification plants, each capable of producing about 250 million cubic feet per day, and would utilize some of the extensive coal reserves of the area.

The first few commercial coal gasification plants will probably be based on Lurgi technology, and the first of perhaps several Lurgi-type facilities could produce synthetic gas in commercial quantities by 1976. By 1980 the newer gasification processes is likely to have been fully demonstrated which will permit the significant expansion and development of a coal gasification industry in the period beyond 1980. Several factors will bear heavily on the rate of growth which can be attained by this new industry. Among these are the availability of substantial tonnages of coal for conversion, the tremendous capital expenditures which will be required for gasification plants and the supporting mining facilities, and the problems associated with locating the mine-plant complexes in areas able to provide the necessary uncommitted coal reserves as well as the required process water.

With these factors in mind, the availability of pipeline-quality gas from coal may be projected to rise from about 0.1 Tcf in 1976 to 0.3 Tcf annually by 1980, with these volumes most likely entirely attributable to Lurgi-type plants. Gas available from added facilities based on the newer process technologies currently under development is projected to bring the total annual volumes of gas available from coal gasification to about 1.4 and 3.3 Tcf, respectively, in 1985 and 1990.

Gas from Alaska. The year-end 1971 proved reserves of natural gas in Alaska were 31.4 Tcf. Of this amount about 26 Tcf are attributable to the Prudhoe Bay area of the North Slope. It is widely known, however, that because the North Slope gas reserves are chiefly associated– dissolved volumes related to the North Slope oil reserves, this gas can become available to market only as provision for the production of the oil is provided. Any projection of the availability of North Slope gas to the markets of the lower 48 states is therefore heavily dependent on the availability and timing of a transport capability for both the oil and the gas.

A geat deal of planning, research, engineering, and other preliminary work with respect to a trans-Alaska oil pipeline has already been completed. However, considerable delays in the initiation of construction of the proposed pipeline have been encountered, chiefly as a result of the environmental implications of the project. For the purpose of this projection, further delays were assumed to be minimal, and oil production from the North Slope was assumed to begin in 1976.

Three major proposals have been advanced which would provide large diameter pipeline transportation for North Slope gas as well as that gas which may become available in Canada's Northwest frontier areas. The Gas Arctic Systems group has proposed a 1550 mile system which would connect the Prudhoe Bay area with an extension of the existing Alberta Gas Trunk Line system in Alberta, Canada. This system could make gas available to U.S. West Coast and Midwest markets through pipeline interconnections with existing pipeline systems. Spon-

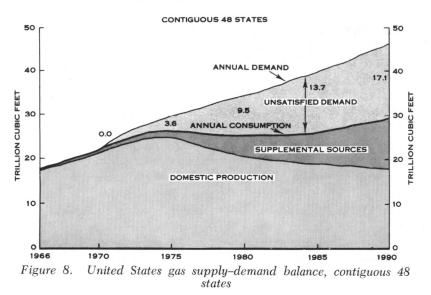

Figure 8.   *United States gas supply–demand balance, contiguous 48*
states

sors of the Mountain Pacific Project have proposed the construction of a system passing from the North Slope area through the Fort Liard region of the Northwest Territories and then southward through British Columbia to the international border where it would connect with a newly proposed U.S. carrier and serve Pacific Coast markets as far south as Los Angeles. A third proposal, advanced by the Northwest Project Study Group, would provide a 2,500 mile line extending from Prudhoe Bay to the Canadian-U.S. international boundary near Emerson, Manitoba. Whichever line is ultimately built will probably be capable of moving approximately 3 Bcf of gas daily when fully powered.

The projection of the availability of Alaskan gas (Table III) is based on the assumption that a gas pipeline system traversing Canada will be completed for initial service in late 1976 or in 1977. Although the timing of current plans to provide for the pipeline movement of North Slope oil and gas is subject to considerable conjecture, a projection of 0.7 Tcf of Alaskan gas in 1980 is reasonable. Alaskan natural gas production and transmission capability should expand to 1.3 and 2.3 Tcf annually by 1985 and 1990, respectively. These projections exclude those Canadian volumes which may be transported in the same pipeline system; all Canadian gas has been included with the projection of Canadian imports.

Conclusions

Projection of the United States gas supply-demand balance through 1990 is summarized in Table IV and Figure 8. The availability of gas from all sources is expected to fall increasingly behind demand. An annual unsatisfied demand for gas of about 9 Tcf by 1980 will increase to about 17 Tcf by 1990. Domestic production of natural gas is projected to peak in the mid-1970's and fall slowly thereafter, placing an increasingly heavy future reliance on imports and other supplemental gas supplies. While this outlook may appear to be pessimistic, it is not predicated on a pattern of failure. The future prospects for domestic reserve additions, pipeline and LNG imports, Alaskan gas, and synthetic gas from coal have been carefully analyzed and a reasonably successful program of development and implementation for each has been assumed. The purpose of these projections has been to approximate the likely national supply-demand balance over the period considered and to establish some idea of the probable supply-demand posture which the Nation can expect. If these projections portray the future with any degree of accuracy, it is obvious that solutions to the Nation's gas supply problem or a significant modification of the anticipated supply-demand balance will not be simple or swift.

Literature Cited

1. Future Requirements Committee, "Future Gas Requirements of the United States" (1971) **4** (4), 83.
2. American Gas Association, "Annual Report on Reserves of Crude Oil, Natural Gas Liquids, and Natural Gas in the United States and Canada, 1970" (1971) **25**, 256.
3. American Gas Association, *AGA News*, Mar. 29, 1972.
4. Federal Power Commission, "National Gas Supply and Demand, 1971-1990" (1972), Staff Report **No. 2**, 166.
5. Potential Gas Committee, "Potential Supply of Natural Gas in the United States (as of December 31, 1970)" (1971) 41.
6. Theobald, P. K., Schweinfurth, S. P., Duncan, D. C., "Energy Resources of the United States," U.S. Geological Survey (1972) **Circular 650**, 27.

RECEIVED February 15, 1973. The views expressed herein are those of the author and do not necessarily reflect the views of the Federal Power Commission or of individual Commissioners.

2

Low Sulfur Coal Supplies for Environmental Purposes

THOMAS W. HUNTER

Division of Fossil Fuels, Bureau of Mines, U.S. Department of the Interior, Washington, D. C.

Because of limited domestic supplies of other basic energy sources, coal production must be expanded. Reserves of low sulfur coal are large, even in the East, but many problems restrict their availability. The major problem is inadequate productive capacity in the East. Except for metallurgical coals, Eastern production historically has been principally of higher sulfur coals which now are environmentally restricted. Strong incentives must be provided for large capital investments to increase Eastern coal productive capacity. The quickest solutions would be increased low sulfur coal production in the East, supplemented by shipments of Western coals into the Midwest; the relaxation of environmental restrictions, where feasible; and acceleration in the development of technologies to permit the use of higher sulfur coals.

S̲ince this volume emphasizes national concern with adequate supplies of all forms of fuel consistent with environmental requirements, it is essential that coal be placed in perspective *vis-a-vis* other energy sources and the many problems associated with its availability both as a solid fuel and in converted form. If the nation's energy requirements are to be met and if a sound balance is to be achieved between indigenous and foreign sources of energy supply, the vital role that coal must play is underscored by the serious need for supplementary sources of natural gas, the decline in proved indigenous oil reserves, and the increased dependence on imported oil. Equally significant is that economic, technologic, and sociologic problems are delaying the availability of large-scale nuclear power availabilities.

Energy Needs

Concern for supplies of low sulfur coals, and other coals which can meet environmental requirements through chemical processing and other technologies, is compounded by enormously increasing needs for energy fuels by electric utilities, the extent to which low sulfur coals are held and used for coke production for steelmaking (both at home and abroad), and the relative availabilities of the other energy sources.

Electric power generation has become a basic must in our society, not only for our overall economic well-being but for such social goals as increased employment, better housing for an expanding population, and a better way of life for millions who do not yet enjoy our vaunted high standards of living. The demand for electricity approximately doubles every 10 years, so pending availabilities of nuclear power, the fossil fuels must expand their contribution to power generation. To the extent that domestic supplies of the other primary energy sources are limited, this means a much greater dependence on coal, either through increased availabilities of naturally low sulfur coal or through technological developments that will make coal environmentally acceptable. The major alternative for the short term is increased dependence on foreign sources of energy, with all the problems that this implies with respect to prices, reliabilities of supply, and changing international relationships.

Although the percentage contribution of coal to electric power generation has declined, 1955 to 1970 tonnages consumed increased from 141 million to 320 million tons. Notwithstanding power generation from other sources, including nuclear power, it is estimated that utilities will need between 750 million and 1 billion tons of coal by the end of the century if the nation's total energy demand is to be satisfied. Will low sulfur coal in this magnitude, or its equivalent through process technology, be available for power generation alone by the year 2000, and what will the availabilities be in the near-term and intermediate periods?

Coal Resources

Our coal resources are large, even our reserves of low sulfur coals, when compared with the relatively limited resources of our other indigenous energy fuels. There are many problems involved in the availability of low sulfur coals, however, including their extent and location; strong deterrents to, or lack of incentives for increased production; their need in relation to other energy supplies, including imports; the development of technologies to condition higher sulfur coals to meet environmental standards; and increasingly severe sulfur limitations which correspondingly narrow even our low sulfur coal resource base.

Among the major problems of low sulfur coal supply is the uneven distribution of reserves in relation to demand. Although major markets are in the East and Midwest, the largest reserves of low sulfur coals are in the West. Based on U.S. Geological Survey data, 57.5% of our identified coal resources (1024 billion tons) have a sulfur content of 1% or less, of which 928 billion tons are in the West and 95 billion tons in the East. In addition, however, there are approximately 141 billion tons of coal averaging between 1.1 and 2.0% sulfur content, of which 92 billion tons are in the East and 48 billion tons in the West.

Preliminary studies by the Bureau of Mines estimate that there are 251 billion tons of low sulfur coal reserves (mineable coal) at less than 1000 ft in depth, of which an estimated 198 billion tons are in the West and 53 billion tons east of the Mississippi River. Of these totals, 30 billion tons are considered to be low sulfur strippable reserves in the West at less than 100 ft deep and 2 billion tons in the East. Preponderantly, however, low sulfur reserves are at depths which would require underground mining. Approximately 50% of these quantities is recoverable in mining. Supplemental surveys and analyses are being made by the Bureau of Mines of low sulfur coal reserves and production, separately for both the Appalachian region and the rest of the country.

The low sulfur coals of the East are located primarily in the Southern Appalachian region (mostly in West Virginia, Virginia, and eastern Kentucky, with smaller amounts in Pennsylvania, Alabama, and Tennessee). There is very little low sulfur coal in the Midwest, which is a major area of electric power generation and other coal consumption. Even with washing, the high sulfur coals indigenous to the Midwest generally are above the sulfur limits of air pollution regulations in most states. Only the pyritic sulfur can be removed from the coal by conventional methods. Accordingly, to conform to regulations governing coal consumption, the huge markets of the Midwest will have to rely on the Southern Appalachian and Western areas for low sulfur coal supplies or on indigenous or other higher sulfur coals used with stack emission processes or other technological developments, including coal conversions to gaseous or liquid fuels.

In the East, most of the low sulfur coals produced customarily have been used for the production of coke for steelmaking both at home and abroad rather than for power generation. Heretofore these high quality coals have been too costly for utility use. Much of the coal used for power generation has been low-cost strip-mined coal. According to the Federal Power Commission (FPC), in the third quarter of 1972 approximately 46% of low sulfur coal delivered to utilities in the East and 92% delivered to utilities in the West were from surface mines. Correspondingly, 54% of the low sulfur coals delivered in the East and only 8% delivered in the West were from underground mines. The FPC now is studying, on the basis of a new canvass of the utility industry, the delivery of coal for power generation by sulfur content by states. This information will serve as an excellent guide to the problem of low sulfur coal availabilities for power generation. Because of other quality characteristics, however, such as differences in ash fusion temperatures, some low sulfur coals are not usable in some present combustion facilities.

The large low sulfur coal reserves of the West could become major suppliers to Midwestern markets as well as in their own areas. For example, using unit trains, Western coal now moves into Chicago and other Midwestern areas; these shipments were inconceivable only a few years ago. Although practically all Western coals shipped eastward are mined by low-cost stripping, deterrents to their immediate large-scale shipment to easterly markets are (1) their lower Btu content than Midwestern and Eastern coals because they are largely subbituminous and lignite coals; (2) their high transportation costs; and (3) some higher ash contents. In addition to unit trains there also are potentials for coal movements by pipeline and for the extra-high-voltage transmission of coal-produced energy. Coal slurry pipelines have proved their practicability. The best current example is the 175-mile line from the Black Mesa coalfield in Arizona to the Mohave Power Project in Nevada. Also there is the potential for the transmission of synthetic coal gas into markets far distant from coal and synthetic gas-producing areas.

Although there are significant low sulfur coal resources in the East (95 billion tons of 1% and less sulfur content) where the major coal markets are located, productive facilities have not been developed commensurately (beyond the production of metallurgical coals and supplies for more or less indigenous areas). Instead, most of the large additional reserves of high grade, high sulfur but lower cost bituminous coals have been developed, historically because of their close proximity to the principal energy-consuming areas. As a result, environmental requirements, rules, and regulations are of very serious concern to coal producers and consumers alike, as well as to those who are concerned with environmental standards. The magnitude and complexities involved in environmental regulations are compounded by the manner in which they have been promulgated, including some progressively more severe limitations. Relatively little time has been allowed for the coal-producing and control equipment industries to adjust to these restrictions. As a result, we are realizing that the large reserves of our great energy resources no longer are abundantly usable. Because of evolving social concepts, our energy resource output is being sharply reduced. The regulations have added significantly to the problem of our national energy self-sufficiency and to the need for increasing reliance on foreign energy supplies. The

Environmental Protection Agency (EPA) recently stated that about half of the new state standards limit the sulfur content of coal to less than 0.8%, even though it noted at the same time that not enough low sulfur coal supply is projected to meet these requirements. Accordingly, there will be limited supplies of low sulfur coal for power generation and other purposes unless it is determined that environmental standards need not be as stringent in some areas as initially considered.

Expectations

Because of the tremendous influence air pollution regulations will have on the future, socially as well as economically, it is reasonable to expect that the standards should be reassessed from time to time on the basis of pertinent new facts, particularly medical and other technical considerations. If the standards in some areas are even only modestly higher than what are really needed, enormous unnecessary costs will accrue, cumulatively, to all Americans, including unnecessary limitations to energy supplies, higher consumer utility rates than might otherwise be necessary, and social programs that are related both directly and indirectly to energy costs and availabilities. If the 92 billion tons of low sulfur coal resources between 1.1 and 2.0% sulfur content in the East, or even an appreciable fraction of them, were permissible, the seriousness of our energy supply situation would be relieved considerably. Regulations should be as strong as is proved necessary by factual appraisal and reappraisal of all elements involved, but not more so. The overall objective is to preserve, even improve, the environment while at the same time to attain other social goals without severe disruption to essential economic processes. This requires both judgment in the determination and application of controls and continued progress in the development of additional low sulfur coal-producing capacities and of new technologies to bring about a more favorable balance between our environmental and energy objectives.

It is essential that we have more detailed and accurate information on the extent, nature, and location of low sulfur coal reserves and some indications of their relative costs to consumers. Whatever the reserves, however, the availability of mining capacity will be the major factor in the availability of both low sulfur and other coals, including those needed for conversion into clean energy forms. In recent years practically all new deep-mine commercial capacity has been developed only under long-term contracts because large mines are developed for lengthy life spans. Contractual assurances of continuing markets and other strong incentives are necessary to encourage the large expenditures that will be required for the development of large-scale increases in capacity. Essentially this means long-term contracts with electric utilities.

Another important factor in the availability of coal is an adequate supply of transportation facilities, particularly railroad hopper cars. There is little or no storage at the mines except for unit train shipments, so mines generally cannot operate without an adequate supply of coal cars, which determines the number of days of active mine operation. Because of the close affinity of coal and rail transportation, the deterrents to expanded coal productive capacity also affect the development of new transportation facilities. Of considerable importance in the future will be an increase in the number of unit trains, which help to reduce transportation costs and the potentials for more coal slurry pipelines and for mine-mouth generating plants for the extra-high-voltage transmission of coal-produced electricity.

While substantially increased low sulfur coal availabilities would be the quickest solution for immediate coal needs, the development of new technologies to make the burning of high sulfur coal environmentally acceptable, and the production of clean coal-energy through conversion in large volumes as soon as possible are tremendously important. Perhaps of first importance, because of their near-term implications, are commercially acceptable processes for the removal of pollutants from stack gases. These devices should be developed as quickly as possible. Other technologies that need more immediate attention because of the lead times essential to their development to economic viability are the gasification of coal (both for high Btu pipeline-quality gas and low Btu gas for industrial uses), liquefaction processes, and, very importantly, methods for the solvent refining of coal to produce clean coal-energy for use as either a liquid or a solid.

Summary

In summary, although we have large reserves of low sulfur coal nationwide, their location and markets are largely in contraposition. The preponderance of reserves is in the Wst, with lesser, but still significant reserves in Southern Appalachia. Major markets, however, are in the industrial East and Midwest, at greater distances than for coal previously used for power generation and other purposes. Principal concerns regarding low sulfur coal supplies are in the East, where the problem is not one of reserves but of inadequate productive capacity. Mining capacity in the East, except for metallurgical coal, historically has been developed for high sulfur coals relatively near the nation's principal energy-consuming areas. Uncertainties in energy supplies and trends, to which environmental restrictions have contributed significantly, have deterred the large capital investments necessary to increase substantially low sulfur coal-producing capacity. Strong incentives are vitally needed to overcome deterrents and to encourage these investments, however, particularly in consideration of the limitations to domestic supplies of other basic energy sources. The quickest solution would be substantial increases in low-sulfur coal production, for which more long-term contracts with utilities would serve as a major catalyst. Increased easterly shipments of Western coals also would help considerably, subject to the constraints of long-distance transportation costs and lower heat content. Equally important would be some relaxation of environmental restrictions wherever environmentally feasible and acceleration in the development of technologies to permit the use of our huge resources of high sulfur coals.

RECEIVED February 15, 1973.

3

The Supply of Oil for Future U.S. Needs and the Subsequent Effects on the Environment

GENE P. MORRELL, DAVID R. OLIVER, and J. LISLE REED

Office of Oil and Gas, U.S. Department of the Interior,
18th & E Sts., N.W., Washington, D.C. 20240

Throughout the present decade the United States is going to become increasingly dependent on foreign oil supplies. Our requirements for imported oil will increase rapidly because of the lack of development of domestic natural gas production, the environmental constraints on the use of coal as an alternative source of energy, and a retardation in the development of Alaskan oil and offshore leases. Of primary importance is the form in which the oil will be imported. Import policy will dictate whether most of the additional imports will be crude oil or refined products such as residual fuel oil and will also have considerable bearing on the configuration of domestic refineries. Major modifications in refinery configuration resulting from changes in oil import policy could diminish the negative effects of future refinery capacity on the surrounding environment as well as increase the domestic production of clean fuels.

Throughout most of this century the United States has been self-sufficient in petroleum supply; however, since 1968 our rate of consumption of oil has been greater than our daily oil production capability. During the present decade, the gap between domestic petroleum demand and domestic production will increase. The gap is a result of three factors: first, a seriously insufficient exploration for, and development of natural gas and crude oil; second, the disqualification, for environmental reasons, of much of our high sulfur coal from its normal industrial and utility markets; and third, a lag in the construction and operation of nuclear electric power plants.

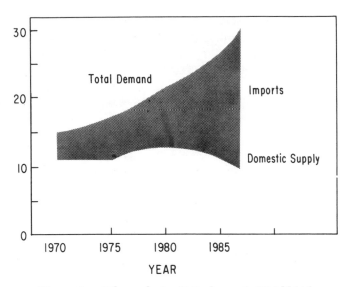

Figure 1.   Oil supply for U.S. demand, MM bbl/day

As shown in Figure 1, domestic production of crude oil and natural gas liquids appears to be leveling off in this country at slightly over 11 million barrels per day (MM bbl/day) and this may even be considered a slightly optimistic projection. Unless present finding and development rates are accelerated, production will soon begin to decline.

With U.S. petroleum demand constantly growing and domestic supply remaining relatively stable, it is proper to assume that this country will look increasingly to other countries for oil. Important questions are how much foreign oil will be needed and what area of the world will the oil come from? In the projection shown here, 6.5 MM bbl/day will be needed in 1975, and about 10 MM bbl/day in 1980.

Oil Supplies

There are four major exporting regions in the world: South America (Venezuela), Africa (Libya, Algeria, and Nigeria), Indonesia, and the Persian Gulf countries (Middle East). South American and Persian Gulf oil tends to be high sulfur oil whereas African and Indonesian oils tend to be low in sulfur. Environmental constraints in this country as well as other countries will probably require most fuel oil to be of low sulfur content. As a result, low sulfur crude oil probably will be sold at a premium price, compared with high sulfur oil, reflecting a cost savings on desulfurization equipment.

It would be difficult to predict exactly where all of our imported oil will come from, but as far as the environment is concerned, it should make little difference because most high sulfur crude oil used in the United States will be desulfurized. If European and Japanese environmental constraints lag behind U.S. criteria, domestic firms, anxious to save the cost of desulfurization, will outbid foreign firms for low sulfur crude. Of course this would accelerate environmental concerns in foreign developed areas because these countries would then be left with increasing quantities of high sulfur oil. Therefore, it seems logical that other developed nations will adopt environmental regulations similar to those that are forthcoming in the United States, and low sulfur crude oil will be distributed throughout the world by other considerations like transportation and product yield slates.

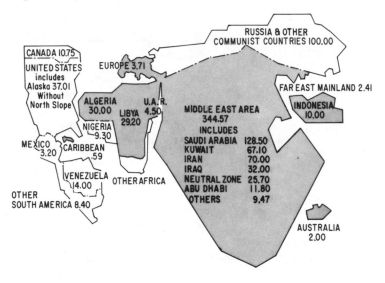

Figure 2.   Where the oil is

There is one other aspect that should be noted at this point. The United States is in a unique and slightly advantageous position compared with other large oil-consuming countries. Much of our domestic crude oil production in east Texas and Louisiana is low in sulfur. This will afford our domestic refineries some additional flexibility in optimizing the use of low sulfur oil, high sulfur oil, and desulfurization facilities.

Considerations for Different Oil Supplies

Crude oil producing areas of the world are depicted in Figure 2, and the areas are drawn in proportion to their known reserves. The crude oil production in all regions except the Persian Gulf is committed for consumption, a result of either proximity to a consuming area or quality of the oil. The crude oil production in these areas is insufficient to meet world consumption needs; because of this, most of our additional imports, as well as the oil of the rest of the importing countries, will come from the Persian Gulf.

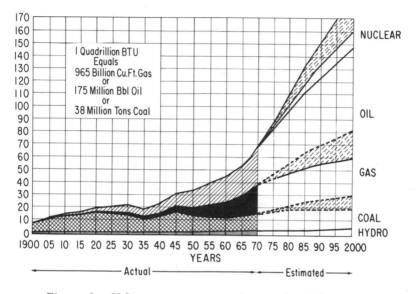

Figure 3.   U.S. energy consumption in the 20th century, quadrillion Btu

It is necessary to note some problems concerned with projecting the quality of oil that will be imported. An oil supply-demand balance was presented in Figure 1. The imports that are necessary for the country can be calculated by the difference in estimated oil demand and domestic oil supply, but other factors affect and complicate the issue. Figure 3 shows the total energy mix for the United States for the present century. As can be seen, oil is a large part of the total energy picture. More importantly, it is also the alternative or swing source of energy. If there are shortfalls in the development and use of nuclear, gas, or coal energy, oil will be required to fill the gap.

Projections of the timing and quantity of coal, gas, and nuclear development vary greatly. For instance, in Figure 4, projections by the Bureau of Mines, the Federal Power Commission, and the National Petroleum Council are given for domestic natural gas production. These gas projections appear to be quite different, but they are consistent with the bases and assumptions used by each group. There are many things that can happen which will affect the development of our various sources of energy; several assumptions can be made, and a lot of personal judgment is involved in anticipating fuel usage. This results in uncertainties

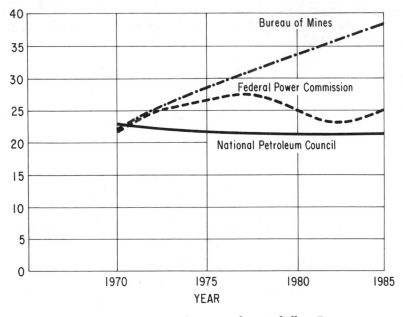

Figure 4.   Projected gas supply, quadrillion Btu

in the exact quantity of oil imports that will be needed for the future. Therefore, it is necessary to exercise caution when using this oil-import projection.

The form in which the oil will be imported, that is, crude oil or refined oil products, is an important consideration. Foreign residual fuel oil (a refined product) is, for all practical purposes, freely imported into District I (states on the Eastern Seaboard). However, the domestic refiner is not allowed freely imported foreign crude oil from which to manufacture residual fuel oil for District I. The domestic refiner must use higher cost domestic crude oil or foreign crude oil imported pursuant to an oil import quota to manufacture residual fuel oil; this has caused domestically produced residual fuel oil to be more costly and therefore noncompetitive. In Figure 5, the imports of foreign residual fuel oil over the past decade are shown in comparison with imports of foreign crude oil. Imports of residual fuel oil which were once about 50% of crude oil imports have now exceeded crude oil imports.

Residual fuel oil is a natural and significant product of crude oil. A yield of 50% residual fuel oil can be derived from typical or average crudes and a yield of 25% remains after mild or moderate petroleum refining. The average residual fuel oil yield in U.S. refineries is 5–6%. The lack of residual fuel oil production in the U.S. is a result of high conversion or severe refinery processing in a complex refinery configuration. The use of high severity processing in the domestic petroleum industry, which has resulted in the destruction and conversion of resid, was originally attributed to resid having to compete with low priced coal and natural gas as burner fuel. However, in the future, as a result of the inadequate development of natural gas and disqualification of certain coal uses, the lack of domestic residual fuel oil production must be attributed to the import situation.

The import situation is subject to change, and one possible change would be to allow domestic refiners to import foreign crude oil in proportion to the uncontrolled (freely imported) products that are manufactured in domestic facilities. This would have the beneficial effect of allowing refining facilities that may otherwise be built in foreign countries to be built domestically, and it would reduce the magnitude of high severity operations that are typical in the United States today. An important question at this point is what would be the effect on the environment from such an action?

There would be two significant results of such an action, and they would have either no effect or possibly a beneficial effect on the environment. First, there would be more crude oil imported and less products (resid); however, the total level of oil imported would be unchanged. Oil that is imported and processed is handled and transferred a little more than oil that is imported and distributed directly to consumers, but this aspect probably has a negligible effect on the environment. Second, there

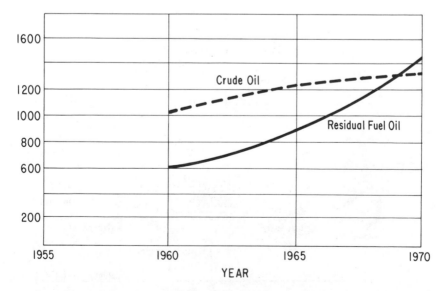

Figure 5. Crude oil imports compared with residual fuel oil imports, MM bbl/day

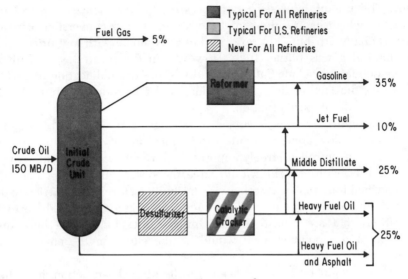

Figure 6.   Foreign refinery

would probably be more crude oil refined in this country than would otherwise be. This additional processing may possibly have a slight beneficial effect on the environment because it would reduce the need for high severity processing.

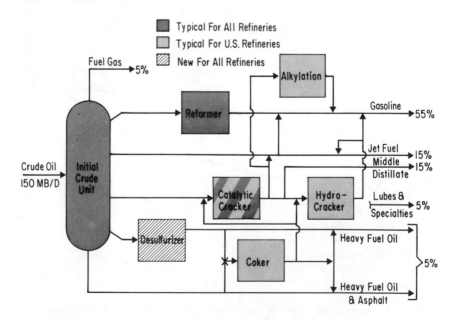

Figure 7.   U.S. refinery

Modifications to Meet New Supplies

The last point is most significant and can best be illustrated by Figures 6–8. Figure 6 is a schematic of a foreign refinery configuration. The process equipment is straightforward: a crude fractionation tower to separate the crude components and a reformer to upgrade the naphtha cut into gasoline. A catalytic cracker is shown, but it is only partially shaded in order to illustrate that it is not really typical for foreign refineries although there are some in existence. The desulfurizer depicts new equipment that will be added to many refineries.

Figure 7 illustrates a schematic for a U.S. refinery configuration. The contrast of the U.S. refinery to the foreign refinery is apparent; there is a great amount of equipment (hydrocracker, coker, alkylation unit, and cat cracker) that is dedicated to converting the residual fuel oil portion of the crude oil to light products. If, however, the increasing demand for residual fuel oil is considered, and the domestically produced resid is made competitive with foreign resid by a change in the oil import program, the yield of resid will be greater.

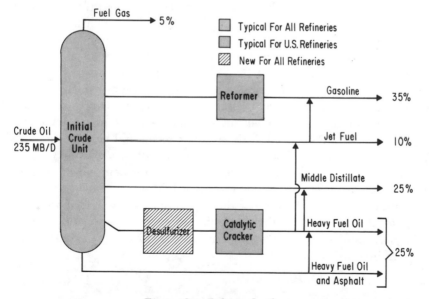

Figure 8. Balanced refinery

Figure 8 illustrates the change in refinery configuration which would result from increased resid production. There would be a larger crude oil feed rate, thus, a larger crude fractionating tower. However, many of the light products that were made in Figure 7 by severe cracking would be derived from distillation of crude oil. Furthermore, much of the resid produced by distillation would not be converted but would be sold as a product. The net result is that more crude oil would be processed, but there would be much less processing of product streams. The type of processing that is reduced is the type that directionally has the most adverse effect on the environment. The high conversion operations generally operate at high temperatures which require significant quantities of fuel and cooling water. Also the processes produce unsaturated hydrocarbons (naphthalenes) and other organic compounds (phenols) that are resistant to biodegradation.

The ultimate refinery configuration would approach that of the foreign refinery. Existing refineries would probably find it advantageous to expand the crude fractionation sections and redistribute product streams to conversion units. The expected result would be a decreased per cent conversion for the total crude oil feedstock.

In summary, imports of foreign oil should increase rapidly in this decade. Much of the oil will probably be high sulfur crude oil from the Persian Gulf. Expected modifications of the oil import program will enable the refinery equipment that will process the oil to be located domestically. This would be beneficial to national security, trade balance, and the domestic economy. The ultimate effect such modifications in the oil import program would have on domestic refinery configurations would probably be slightly beneficial to the environment.

Earlier, we referred to the interrelationships of oil, gas, coal, and nuclear energy. All these energy sources and the exotics, which are being developed, will be needed, yet the federal government, as it is structured, does not encourage development of a unified energy policy. About 61 federal agencies are involved in some aspect of oil and gas decisions, and this fragmentation of responsibility can only result in inefficiency.

As a first step in overcoming this problem, President Nixon proposed to centralize major energy resource responsibilities in a new Department of Natural Resources. Passage of this legislation is essential if we are to integrate energy conservation and development efforts and alleviate what more and more people are coming to realize is a serious energy supply problem.

RECEIVED February 15, 1973.

The Demand for Sulfur Control Methods in Electric Power Generation

ROBERT M. JIMESON

Office of the Advisor on Environmental Quality, Federal Power Commission, Washington, D. C. 20426

Projections are developed for the supply and demand of various quality fuels and control devices necessary to meet requirements for electric power generation constrained by federal and state sulfur oxide regulations. By 1975 a demand for 425 million tons of coal and 565 million bbl of oil is forecast for electric generation. About 94 million tons of naturally occurring low sulfur coal and 359 million bbl of low sulfur oil can be seen as a possible supply that meets air quality regulations. Thus, about 331 tons of coal and 206 barrels of oil of high sulfur content will be burned in approximately 1350 units, each requiring control devices. To the extent that the supply of control equipment is deficient, there will be an equivalent demand for processing high sulfur fuels.

This paper examines the features of air quality legislation that have an impact on the demand for sulfur oxide control measures for the power industry, the limitations on sulfur imposed by emission regulations, and the electric power supply situation. Estimates of probable demand are derived for various quality fuels and for sulfur oxide control equipment in the electric power industry in the next several years.

Air Quality Regulations

The Clean Air Act of 1967 called for the designation of air quality control regions by the Federal Government with the consent of the state and local governments. Furthermore, the Federal Government had to issue for each pollutant, air quality criteria from which standards could be established. It had to issue companion reports on control technology

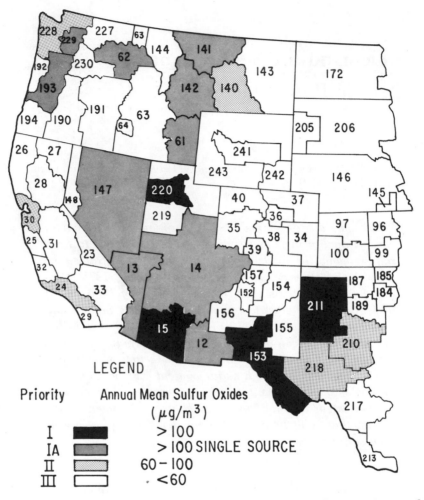

Figure 1. Priority of air quality

for the reduction of emissions from various sources. Then state governments were to establish air quality standards for their designated regions
and adopt plans for implementation of control programs that would
achieve constituted standards.

Under the provisions of the 1967 Act, areas were designated as
control regions in a sequence according to their severity of pollution,
proceeding from the worst to the least polluted. This approach appeared
to have a built-in mechanism for accelerated and achievable control
activity while simultaneously permitting the primary energy supply and
control equipment industries to adjust in an orderly and timely manner
to a gradual but intensified demand for high quality fuels and emission

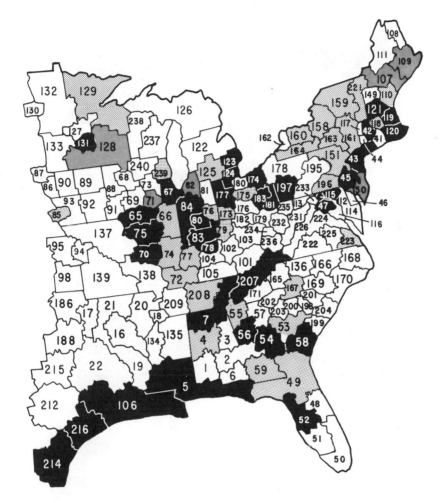

control regions—sulfur oxides

control equipment. However, to some the procedures appeared too tedious and slow. Consequently the Clean Air Act as amended in 1970 was designed to shorten the procedures and hasten the day in which all areas of the nation would be brought under control, regardless of the current air quality of a particular region. The provisions of this recent legislation accentuate the demand for control equipment and all forms of clean energy.

The Clean Air Act as amended in 1970 required that all areas of the nation be designated very quickly as air quality control regions. Every part of the United States has now become part of an intrastate or interstate air quality control region. There are 237 control regions in the lower

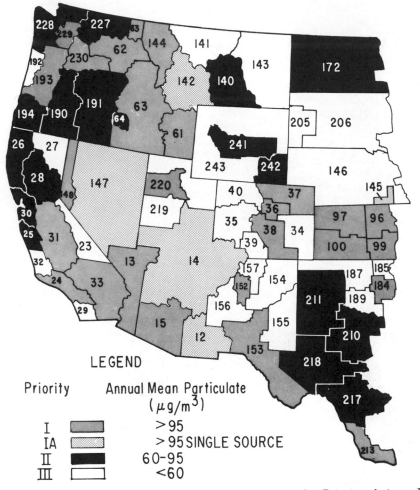

LEGEND

Priority	Annual Mean Particulate ($\mu g/m^3$)
I	>95
IA	>95 SINGLE SOURCE
II	60-95
III	<60

Figure 2.   Priority of air quality

48 states. All sources of pollution anywhere in the nation are now subject to regulation; thus the demand for various control measures is immediately intensified nationwide. The location of the regions and the magnitude of their current pollution problem is shown in Figures 1 and 2.

The legislation also required the Environmental Protection Agency (EPA) to establish national primary ambient air quality standards to protect health and secondary standards to protect the public welfare. Ambient standards were greatly needed as a guide to the degree of emission controls required in various regions. National standards for particulates, sulfur oxides, nitrogen oxides, carbon monoxide and hydro-

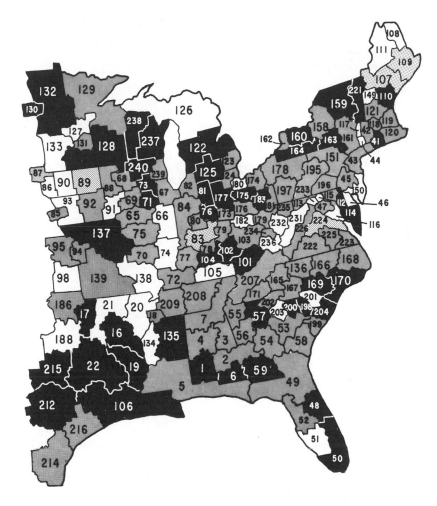

control regions—particulates

carbons, and photochemical oxidants were issued in April 1971. The states could set standards within their own boundaries more stringent than those of the Federal Government. However, by July 1975 the states had to achieve air quality equal to or better than the national standards.

The principal pollutants of concern to fossil fuel-fired electric power plants are sulfur oxides, particulates, and nitrogen oxides. The national ambient air quality standards for these three pollutants are shown in Table I.

By January 30, 1972, each state was required to adopt and to submit to EPA a plan providing for the implementation, maintenance, and

Table I. National Ambient Air Quality Standards

Pollutant	Averaging Time	Primary Std		Secondary Std	
		$\mu g/m^3$	ppm	$\mu g/m^3$	ppm
Sulfur oxides	annual	80	0.03	60	0.02
	24 hr[a]	365	0.14	260	0.1
	3 hr[a]	—	—	1300	0.5
Particulate	annual	75	—	60	—
	24 hr[a]	260	—	150	—
Nitrogen oxides	annual	100	0.05	100	0.05
	24 hr[a]	250	0.13	250	0.13

[a] Not to be exceeded more than once per year.

enforcement of a program which would enable it to meet the national primary ambient air quality standards within its regions by mid-1975. EPA approved or rejected these plans or portions of them by May 30, 1972.

Because of the short time, the states had a tendency to determine the degree of reduction in emissions needed to meet the national or their own more stringent ambient air quality standards for their worst polluted region, and then to apply the same degree of reduction to all other regions in the state. Lack of individual regional analyses which tailor regulations to the specific needs of each region intensifies the demand for clean fuels and control equipment because of excessive requirements. Noncritical regions are thus put in competition with the critically polluted regions for the limited clean fuels and control devices.

EPA also had to establish national emission standards for certain categories of new sources. Table II shows the Federally mandated emission standards for new and modified fossil-fired steam generators. They apply to units with a capacity of 250 MMBtu/hr (i.e., about 25 MW) or larger for which major construction or modification contracts are signed after August 17, 1971.

Outlook for Electric Power Generation

Having examined the air pollution regulations influencing the demand for various quality fuels and for control devices, consider next the nation's need for electric generation as a factor in the magnitude of the demand for controls. Many of the projections used in this section were taken from the Federal Power Commission's 1970 National Power Survey (1). More than 100 experts representing all segments of the electric power industry and branches of government contributed to its contents.

As illustrated in Figure 3 the electric power industry of the United States in 1970 generated nearly 82% of the electricity in fossil-fueled

Table II. Standards of Performance for New Fossil-Fired Steam Generators (Construction Commenced after August 17, 1971)

| | Standards, $lb/MMBtu$ | | |
Fuel Type	Particulate	Sulfur Oxides	Nitrogen Oxides
Solid	0.10	1.2	0.70
Liquid	0.10	0.80	0.30
Gaseous	—	—	0.20

plants. Almost all of the remainder, except for 1.4% produced by nuclear plants, was generated by hydro-power. Nuclear generation is expected to increase significantly in the next two decades and, consequently, the relative position of fossil-fueled generation will decrease from about 82% in 1970 to about 44% in 1990.

Figure 4 shows that the electric power industry generated 1.541 billion MW-hrs in 1970. In the process it consumed approximately one-quarter of all the primary energy used during that year by all segments of the American economy. During the next two decades total electric power generation by electric utilities is expected to about double every 10 years. Total generation is estimated to reach 3.11 billion MW-hrs in 1980 and close to 6 billion MW-hrs in 1990. In the same period fossil-fueled generation will increase to about 1.9 billion MW-hrs in 1980 and about 2.6 billion MW-hrs in 1990. While fossil-fueled steam plants will supply a decreasing portion of the total as shown in Figure 3, the fossil-

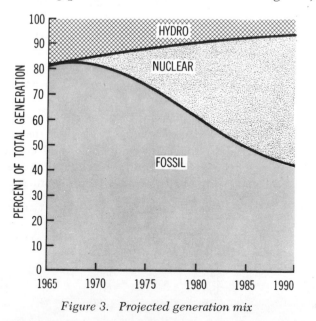

Figure 3. Projected generation mix

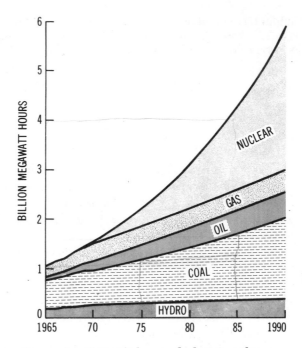

Figure 4. Estimated annual electric utility generation by primary energy sources

fueled units will supply twice as much electric energy in 1990 as in 1970. This is further reflected in projected fossil-fueled capacity additions from 1970 to 1990, shown in Table III.

The fossil-fueled energy was generated at plants having 3298 boiler-generator units with a total steam-electric generating capacity of 259 thousand MW. The capacity will increase to 558 thousand MW by 1990. Average size of the units will increase from 80 to 370 MW and the number of units will decrease to 1520 in 1990.

During the same period, 1970 to 1990, total generating capacity, including nuclear and hydroelectric plants, is expected nearly to quadruple from 340 thousand to 1260 thousand MW—an increment of 920 thousand MW. Some of the 920 thousand MW of generating capacity will be required by the clean primary energy and control process industries,

Table III.   U.S. Fossil-Fueled Steam-Electric Capacity

Year	Capacity, MW (Thous.)	No. of Units	Avg. Size, MW (Thous.)
1970	259	3298	80
1975	320	2900	110
1980	380	2389	160
1990	558	1520	370

sewage treatment plants, incinerators, and others to accomplish the environmental goals of air and water pollution control and solid waste management. Electricity is very necessary for the achievement of this nation's environmental goals, and serious thought must be given to the trade-off of the environmental benefit of the use of electricity relative to the environmental impacts of its generation.

In the shorter range projection to the year 1975, when the state air pollution control programs are to be implemented, Table III shows that there will be about 2900 fossil-fueled units with a total estimated capacity of 320 thousand MW. The average size of the fossil-fueled units in operation during that year will be about 110 MW.

The Federal Power Commission, with the cooperation of the EPA, collects air and water quality control data for each fossil fuel-fired electric generating plant of 25 MW and greater. Under this program the FPC collected information for the year 1969 (2) from 655 fossil-fueled plants with 2995 boiler-generator units having a total capacity of 244 thousand MW, compared with the 3298 units with a total capacity of 259 thousand MW reported in Table III for the year 1970.

The data show that of the 2995 units surveyed for the year 1969, 1150 units were primarily coal-fired, 945 units were primarily oil-fired, and about 900 units were primarily gas-fired. If we assume that the 303 small units not covered by this program divide in the same proportions, then the distribution of number of units in operation in 1970 by type of fuel fire is shown in line 1 of Table IV.

From information reported on April 1, 1971, by the nine Regional Electric Reliability Councils in response to the Commission's Statement of Policy on Adequacy and Reliability of Electric Service, Order No. 383-2, the author estimates that about 116 additional units with 70 thousand MW of capacity might be in operation by the end of 1975. As shown in the second line of the table, 66 are expected to be coal-fired, 26 oil-fired, and 24 gas-fired.

Table IV. Projected Mix of Fossil-Fueled Generating Units

	Coal	*Oil*	*Gas*
Projection	Type of Fuel		
Number of units, 1970	1265	1045	990
Additions	+66	+26	+24
Subtotal	1331	1071	1014
Retirements	−281	−141	−80
Subtotal	1050	930	934
Conversions	−90	+120	−30
Number of units, 1975	960	1050	904

There were 1004 fossil-fueled units with a total capacity of about 18 thousand MW which were installed in 1940 or earlier but were still in operation in 1970. Some of these units were installed in the first two decades of this century. These units were estimated to be 56% coal-fired, 28% oil-fired, and 16% gas-fired. Assuming that one-half of each of the types of older units will be retired by 1975, then 281 coal-fired, 141 oil-fired, and 80 gas-fired units will be retired. In addition 90 coal-fired and 30 gas-fired units are expected to be converted to oil-fired units. Consequently, by 1975 there will be 960 coal-fired and 1050 oil-fired for a total of 2010 units which will require some form of sulfur emission control either through stack devices to remove sulfur dioxide from flue gases or through low sulfur fuels.

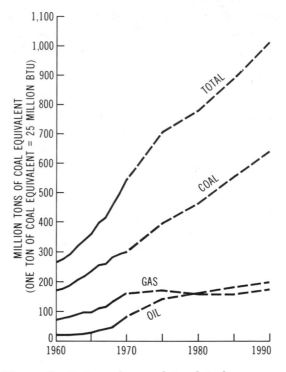

Figure 5.   Estimated annual fossil fuel require-
ments for electric utility generation

Fossil Fuel Demand for Electric Power Generation

The National Power Survey projections of electric power generation, when translated into primary energy demand based on energy conversion efficiencies now demonstrated and anticipated during the next several years, indicate a continuing growth in fuel consumption in the form of coal, oil, and gas. Projected requirements of these fuels for electric power generation in terms of coal equivalent quantities are shown in Figure 5. The most remarkable element of this projection is the very rapid decline in the growth rate of natural gas usage for electric power generation. This projection is supported by a variety of gas curtailment cases currently before the Commission. It means that we may not depend on gas, the only clean fossil fuel, to make a significant contribution to the reduction of undesirable emissions from electric power plants. The use in 1969 of the various fossil fuels for electric power generation, expressed in their customary units of measure, was 310 million tons of coal, 251 million bbl of oil, and 3486 billion ft^3 of gas.

Current Quality of Fuels

Figure 6 was prepared from information collected by the FPC and shows the quantities of coal at the various sulfur levels consumed by electric utilities in 1969. The 303 million tons of coal burned by electric utilities reporting in 1969 ranged in sulfur content from 0.4 to as much as 6 wt %. The bulk of the coal, however, was in the 2-4% sulfur range; the weighted average was 2.58%. The distribution curve is bimodal, with one peak below 1% sulfur. This, most likely, reflects an early response by several utilities to local air pollution control regulations requiring fuels with less than 1% sulfur.

The quality of coal burned by electric utilities in 1969 was compared plant-by-plant and state-by-state with regulations in state implementation programs. About 44 million tons of coal consumed by electric utilities in 1969 in 255 units could meet the standard, whereas 259 million tons with an average sulfur content of 2.81% was burned in 1010 units that could not meet standards and would require control measures.

Likewise, Figure 7 shows the quantities of oil at various sulfur levels consumed by electric utilities. Similarly, the sulfur content of the oil used in 1969 ranged from a fraction of a per cent to nearly 3%, with a major portion of the oil in the 1.4-2.6% sulfur range. The weighted average was 1.66%. Three peaks were observed in the oil distribution curve: one peak at 0.3%, another at slightly below the 1% sulfur level, and the largest peak at an average sulfur content of 1.9%. Both peaks under 1% sulfur undoubtedly reflect response to local sulfur-emission control regulations.

The quality of the oil burned by electric utilities in 1969, compared plant-by-plant and state-by-state with the preliminary state implementation programs, shows that 59 million bbl of oil burned in about 310 units could meet the standards and that 199 million bbl of oil burned in 735 units would require some type of control measures to meet the proposed sulfur limitations.

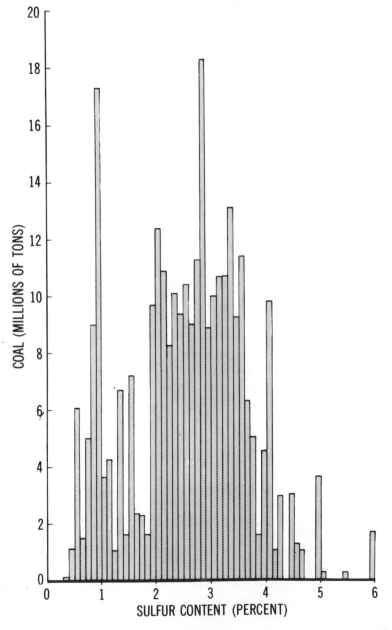

Figure 6.   Distribution of sulfur content of coal burned by electric utilities, 1969

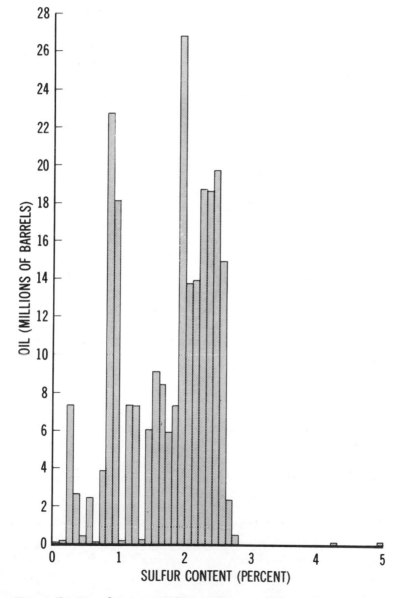

Figure 7.   *Distribution of sulfur content of oil burned by electric utilities, 1969*

Table V shows fuel requirements projected in the National Power Survey. In 1975 when state plans are to be fully implemented, except where a two-year extension is granted, 425 million tons of coal will be required and 565 million bbl of oil will be needed.

Next consider company plans for supplies of low sulfur fuels to estimate the order of magnitude of added supplies of low sulfur fuels that would be required in 1975 if control devices were not in operation at the electric generating units. The National Coal Policy Conference in 1971 estimated that there would be 300 million tons of new mine capacity by 1975, of which 75 million tons would be in low sulfur coal. Assume two-thirds or 50 million tons could be dedicated to the electric utilities. This quantity added to the 45 million tons of low sulfur coal, which already meets the standards, yields 94 million tons of naturally occurring low sulfur coal that could be available in 1975. Subtracting 94 million tons from the total requirement of 425 million tons leaves 331 million tons of high sulfur coal which will be burned in utilities with devices. Or in the absence of devices, this quantity of coal must be processed to low sulfur standards.

The Bureau of Mines in August 1971 (3) in its study on Oil Availability by Sulfur Levels estimated the additional U. S. and Caribbean residual desulfurization capability would be about 300 million bbl. When this is added to the 59 million bbl of low sulfur oil which already meets the standards, a total of 359 million bbl of low sulfur oil will be available in 1975. If this quantity is deducted from the total utility requirement of 565 million bbl, then about 206 million bbl will be burned in utilities with control devices, or must be processed to low sulfur content in the absence of devices.

Summary

The Clean Air Amendments of 1970 and the accompanying regulation have intensified the demand for clean fuels and control devices on a nationwide basis. These control measures must be in operation by 1975, or in some instances, 1977.

In general there will be a demand for 425 million tons of low sulfur coal and 565 million bbl of low sulfur oil. The majority of this fuel will

Table V.   Fossil Fuel Requirements for Electric Power Generation

Year	Coal, million tons	Oil, million bbl	Gas, billion ft³
1969	310	251	3486
1970	322	332	3894
1975	425	565	4110
1980	500	640	3800

require some type of processing. Clean fuels are a preferred pollution control for electric generation because they are fail-safe and compatible with load-changing characteristics of power plant operations. About 94 million tons of naturally occurring low sulfur coal and 359 million bbl of low sulfur oil can be foreseen as a possible supply that meets air quality regulations. About 331 tons of coal and 206 bbl of oil will be burned in 1300-1400 units, each requiring control devices in operation in 1975. To the extent that control equipment is deficient in these numbers of units operating in 1975, there will be an equivalent demand for processing portions of each of the high sulfur quantities of coal and oil.

The challenge is great, the time is short. Achievement of the ambient air quality objectives by the electric power industry in that short a period of time will require the utmost effort on the part of suppliers of low sulfur fuels and manufacturers of sulfur-emission control equipment, dedication on the part of the electric power industry, a great deal of investment capital, and the cooperative spirit of environmental groups and the public.

Literature Cited

1. Federal Power Commission, "The 1970 National Power Survey," 4 vols., U.S. Government Printing Office, Washington, D. C., Dec. 1971.
2. Federal Power Commission, "Steam-Electric Plant Air and Water Quality Control Data for Year Ended December 31, 1969" (FPC Form No. 67), U. S. Government Printing Office, Washington, D. C., Jan. 1973.
3. U. S. Bureau of Mines, "Oil Availability by Sulfur Levels," Environmental Protection Agency, Office of Air Programs, 209 pp., Aug. 1971.

RECEIVED February 15, 1973.

5

The Effect of Desulfurization Methods on Ambient Air Quality

KURT E. YEAGER

Environmental Protection Agency, Washington, D. C. 20460

The State Implementation Plans for achieving national sulfur dioxide ambient air quality standards have generally assumed that the degree of improvement in air quality is equivalent to emission reduction irrespective of emission source. If these proposed plans were implemented, they would produce a sumulative low sulfur coal and oil supply deficit in 1975 of 8×10^{15} Btu. However, selective source control strategies based on established diffusion modeling techniques can effectively eliminate this forecast supply deficit without sacrifice in the achievement of ambient air quality standards. These potential strategies are supported by actual sulfur dioxide emission and ambient concentration data collected in the Metropolitan Chicago Air Quality Control Region.

The introduction of ambient air quality standards effectively restricting the pollutant content of fossil fuels consumed in stationary sources has a fundamental impact on fuel supplies. Prior to these regulations, utility and industrial consumers selected fuel based primarily on the lowest cost per unit of heat. As a result, lower-cost, high pollutant-containing coal and residual oil have supplied over 75% of the stationary power sources of the eastern United States.

It has become clear that the achievement of ambient air quality standards will increase the cost of stationary combustion and industrial process operations. For example, the cumulative capital and operating expenditures for air pollution control on stationary sources to achieve these standards is estimated at $37.6 billion during this decade (*1*). This however, is only one of two basic concerns. The second difficulty is the identification and development of sufficient low pollution fuel sources or alternative control technologies which can satisfy national energy demands. The implementation of ambient air quality standards without a foundation of developed and coordinated pollution control technology has forced the nation into an apparent dilemma known as the energy crisis. In its simplest terms this crisis would seem to reduce to a choice between the near-term protection of the environment and continued domestic self-sufficiency in meeting all energy demands. This paper will examine and attempt to put in perspective the available near-term (1975–1985) options which can reduce, if not eliminate, this apparent energy/environmental conflict.

Ambient Air Quality Standards

The Clean Air Act of 1967, amended in 1970, called upon the Administrator of the Environmental Protection Agency (EPA) to promulgate national primary and secondary ambient air quality standards for each air pollutant for which air quality criteria have been issued (2). A national primary ambient air quality standard is the maximum ground level pollutant concentration which in the judgment of the Administrator of EPA can be tolerated to protect the public health, based on the published air quality criteria. A national secondary ambient air quality standard is a more stringent concentration level which in the judgment of the Administrator is required to protect the public welfare from any known or anticipated adverse effect associated with the presence of the air pollutant in the ambient air. The criteria for an air pollutant, to the extent that is practical, shall include those variable factors which may alter the effects on public health or welfare by the air pollutant and any known or anticipated adverse effects on welfare.

In response to these requirements national ambient air quality standards were promulgated in April 1971 for sulfur dioxide, particulate matter, photochemical oxidants, hydrocarbons, and nitrogen oxides. The standards for sulfur dioxide are summarized in Table I (3). The implementation, maintenance, and enforcement of a program to meet the national ambient air quality standards is the responsiblity of each state. In satisfaction of this responsibility, each state submitted to EPA an imple-

Table I.   National Ambient Air Quality Standards
for Sulfur Dioxide (3)

Averaging	Primary Standard, $\mu g/m^3$	Secondary Standard, $\mu g/m^3$
Annual	80	60
24 hr[a]	365	260
3 hr[a]	—	1300

[a] Not to be exceeded more than once per year.

mentation plan describing how it would meet the air quality standards by mid-1975 (4).

The Problem

. Two hundred thirty-eight Air Quality Control Regions (AQCR's) encompassing the entire continental United States have been established by the federal government with state and local approval. These regions range in size from a single metropolitan area to an entire state and are established according to meteorological, technical, socio-economic, political, and other similarities which would be essential to a unified and

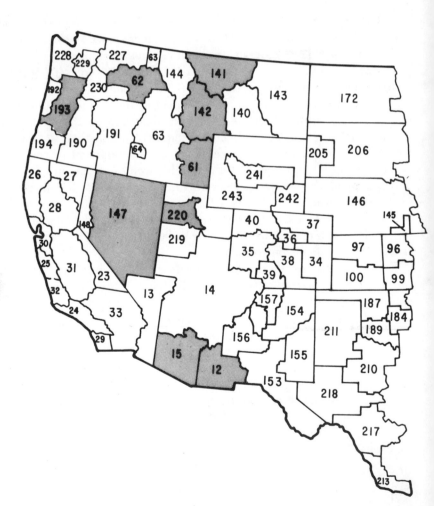

Figure 1. AQCR's exceeding the national

coordinated solution to the air pollution problem peculiar to a geographic area of the nation. Figure 1 identifies both the geographical extent of AQCR's and those in which the measured average annual ground level sulfur dioxide ambient air concentration exceeded the primary air quality standard in 1970. The portion of the population residing within these 54 AQCR's which are subject to excessive sulfur dioxide concentration is estimated at about 70 million. Eighty percent of this population group resides in 41 AQCR's located in the eastern portion (including Iowa and Missouri) of the United States. The sulfur dioxide problem in this eastern region is caused primarily by the heavy dependence on coal,

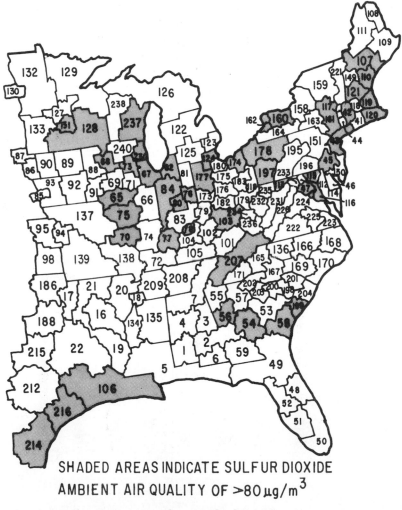

SHADED AREAS INDICATE SULFUR DIOXIDE
AMBIENT AIR QUALITY OF >80 $\mu g/m^3$

primary annual ambient air quality standard for SO$_x$

residual oil, and, in some high density urban areas, distillate oil for combustion. In the western portion of the country the excessive sulfur oxide
concentrations are generally a result of industrial process emissions, particularly non-ferrous metallurgy and petroleum refining. The seriousness
of the problem was typified by the fact that the maximum measured average annual sulfur dioxide concentrations found in several eastern urban
centers were as much as 300 $\mu g/m^3$ prior to 1970.

Two basic methods, the proportional model and the diffusion model,
are available to the states in determining the level of emission control
required in their implementation plans to achieve the air quality standards.
The proportional roll-back model assumes that the degree of improvement in air quality is equivalent to emission reduction, irrespective of the
type of emission source. Although used in the majority of state implementation plans because of its simplicity and ease of operation, the model does
not account for topography, spatial distribution of emissions, or stack
height. Therefore gross results are obtained which are not capable of
differentiating individual sources or even source categories.

The diffusion model approach uses the Air Quality Data Model
(AQDM) of the EPA Implementation Planning Program (IPP) (5).
This model is designed to simulate the spatial distribution of sulfur
dioxide concentrations throughout an AQCR. The pollutant concentration
output from this program is derived from an atmospheric diffusion model
which transforms the regional source emissions and meteorological data
for a given long-term period into estimated ground level arithmetic

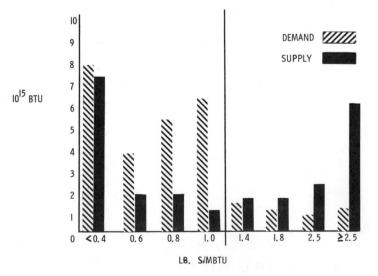

Figure 2.   1975 Coal/oil supply demand relationship for stationary sources

average pollutant concentration values. Aside from the cost and complexity involved in computer simulation, the successful use of this technique obviously requires an accurate, source-by-source emission inventory and meteorological data base.

Figure 2 summarizes the basic difference between the 1975 national stationary source demand for low sulfur coal and oil, based on State Implementation Plan (SIP) estimates of that necessary to achieve primary ambient air quality standards and the projected 1975 supply of these fuels (*6, 7, 8, 9, 10, 11*). The net result is a forecast coal/oil supply deficit on the basis of sulfur content and including foreign imports, of approximately 8×10^{15} Btu. This is equivalent to a combined annual shortage of about 230 million tons of coal and 300 million barrels of primarily residual oil. Table II shows the regional distribution of these shortages. In the judgment of the author, uncertainties in factors such as sulfur content analyses, production potentials, and the commercial impact of environmental standards by 1975 limit the accuracy of these supply deficit forecasts to about ±20%.

Table II. Potential Stationary Source Fuel Shortages—1975—Based on Sulfur Content Regulations

Source	*East*	*Central*	*West*	*Nation*
Coal (tons $\times 10^6$)	56	162	13	231
	Pad I, II, III	*Pad IV*	*Pad V*	*Nation*
Residual fuel oil (bbl $\times 10^6$)	270	3	29	302

Figure 3 indicates that a supply/demand deficit for essentially sulfur- and particulate-free natural gas is also forecast by 1975 (*12*). Thus, not only will natural gas fail to reduce the problem, but it can be expected to actually increase the supply/demand deficit for oil and coal because gas supplies going to utility and industrial sources will probably be cut back in favor of residential applications.

The fundamental problem in increasing the supply of low sulfur domestic fossil fuels to meet demand is indicated in Table III. The cumulative consumption of fossil fuels, both in direct use (*e.g.*, transportation and space heating) and for the generation of electricity during the period 1960–2000, is compared with known recoverable and total estimated domestic reserves. Only for coal are we safely within our known recoverable reserves. On the other hand, for natural gas essentially the total estimated reserves in the ground, irrespective of the economics of recovery, will be depleted.

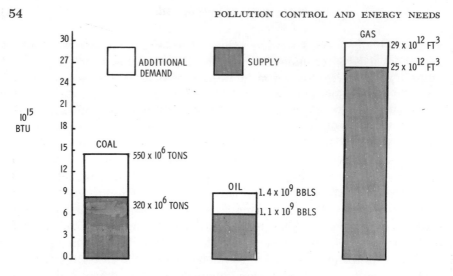

500 MILLION TONS COAL EQUIVALENT DEFICIT IN 1975

Figure 3.   1975 low sulfur fossil fuel supply/demand

Table III.   Comparison of Consumption with Resources (1960-2000)
(10^{15} Btu)

	Cumulative Consumption	*Known Recoverable Reserves*	*Total Estimated Reserves*
Petroleum			
Direct use	1,300		
Electricity	75		
	1,375	280	2,000(37,500) shale oil
Natural gas			
Direct use	800		
Electricity	200		
	1,000	280	1,180
Coal			
Direct use	300		
Electricity	600		
	900	4,500	89,000

Although nearly 40% of the known recoverable coal reserves of the United States are low in sulfur content (less than 1 lb sulfur/MM Btu), these reserves are concentrated in the Rocky Mountain Region, remote from the eastern industrial demand centers. At current unit train costs of about 4¢/MM Btu per 100 miles, an incremental transportation cost of 40¢ to 80¢/MM Btu would be incurred.

Figure 4 estimates the percentage, as a function of delivered cost of the total industrial coal and oil demand, which can be met by fuels of these types meeting the sulfur constraints indicated in Figure 2. Level 1 is indicative of the baseline situation existing prior to the establishment of local and national air pollution control standards beginning in 1968–1970. At that time delivered industrial fuel costs could be maintained at or about 30¢/MM Btu. Level 2 is indicative of costs associated with achieving the supply levels indicated in Figure 3. This is about the practical maximum supply of natural low sulfur fuel which can be developed in the near term without major disruption of industrial fuel consumption patterns and the redesign of fuel distribution and utilization systems. Level 2 is also indicative of the stationary fuel costs which can be expected by 1975. When costs rise above level 2, a number of fossil fuel processing and conversion options currently being developed to produce synthetic non-polluting fuel begin to become commercially viable. Level 3 is indicative of the low pollution fuel supply growth rate which appears to be possible by these methods within a cost upper bound by about $1.25/MM Btu.

Beginning in 1966, both industry and government started working seriously to develop processes capable of removing sulfur dioxides from

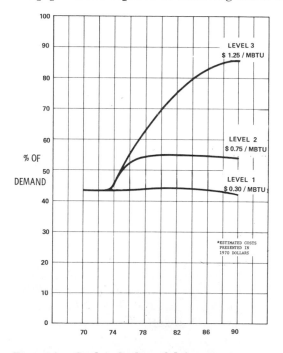

*Figure 4.   Coal and oil availability as a function
of delivered cost*

fossil fuel combustion flue gases. Because of the operating complexity and cost associated with these essentially chemical processing facilities, their practical application at the present state-of-the-art is limited to large industrial and utility steam generators (> 100,000 lbs steam/hr—equivalent to about 10 MW). Table IV indicates the portion of the total stationary source fossil fuel demand included in this class. As a result of this activity about a dozen processes have been developed to the point where they are being studied on full-scale industrial facilities. Nine of these processes are variations of the slurry scrubbing concept using ash, lime, limestone, or magnesium oxide as the reactant. Development results to date generally indicate a sulfur dioxides removal capability of 80–90%. As of April 1972, 23 commercial and demonstration slurry scrubbing installations were under construction or on order for use on existing and new electric utility steam generators. These installations encompass 6600 MW of generating capacity at an average contract cost of $40 per kW of controlled capacity. The continuous successful operation of these prototype installations for the extended period of time (6 months to one year) considered necessary to define their commercial-scale emission control capability, operating reliability, and economics, is expected to be completed in 1974–1975.

The most serious inherent limitation in the broad commercial applica-

Table IV.   Fossil Fuel

	Total Capacity, 10^6PPS	No. of Boilers, $\times 10^3$
< 100,000 lb steam/hr (PPS)		
Residential/commercial	3,500	33,000
Industrial	400	100
Total	3,900	33,100
> 100,000 lb steam/hr (PPS)		
Industrial	1,700	40.0
Utility	2,100	3.3
Total	3,800	43.3

tion of these processes is disposal of the unmarketable waste gypsum by-product. Aside from the immediate spatial problem associated with the shortage and handling of this waste product, disposal must be performed in a manner which does not cause a water pollution.

Further flue gas desulfurization development efforts are currently directed toward solving this constraint through the ultimate production of elemental sulfur. It should be noted, however, that even recovery of 40% of the total sulfur emitted from industrial and electric utility emitters would exceed the projected 8 million ton total domestic market for sulfur in 1975.

The immediate question is the extent of commercial application which can be achieved by effluent treatment technology and the rate at which this application can be achieved. The extent of application is essentially a question of economics. Based on field surveys it is theoretically possible to retrofit as much as 80% of all existing utility and large industrial coal and residual oil-fired combustion sources with effluent treatment processes for the removal of sulfur dioxides. In reality, however, considerations such as process packaging within available space, by-product transport and disposal, reactant availability, plant capacity use factor, age, and size will limit the degree of application. For example, the range of annualized SO_x control process capital and operating costs (incremental costs of control) required to satisfy 80% of existing utility and industrial combustion facilities extends from 10¢/MM Btu of fuel consumed to over $1.00/MM Btu. A practical upper bound on the ultimate extent of flue gas control application would be about 40% of large utility and industrial coal and residual oil capacity. This level of application would imply an incremental effluent control cost on the order of 40¢/MM Btu. When combined with a no-sulfur-guarantee fuel cost of 40¢/MM Btu, a good comparison with level 2 of Figure 4 is achieved.

Combustion—1969

		Fuel Usage, 10^{12} BTU		
Coal, 10^{12} Btu	Resid, 10^{12} Btu	Distillate, 10^{12} Btu	Gas, 10^{12} Btu	SO_x Emissions, 10^6 tons
300	750	3,800	6,500	2.1
110	275	300	500	0.4
410	1,025	4,100	7,000	2.5
1,900	1,400	320	7,000	4.2
7,500	1,900	100	3,500	17.7
9,400	3,300	420	10,500	21.9

Several additional factors must, however, be examined before we can reach a final conclusion. The first is the rate at which control technology can be commercially installed. Forty per cent of the coal- and oil-fired utility and industrial capacity indicated in Table IV, extrapolated to 1975, implies that nearly 20,000 coal- and oil-fired steam generating units consuming about 7.0×10^{15} Btu annually (approximately equivalent to 150,000 MW capacity) could conceivably require effluent control. At an average incremental control cost of 30¢/MM Btu, a yearly national cost of control of $2.1 billion is indicated. Based on the rate-determining factors of competition for skilled construction labor and the fabrication of major process components, it is the consensus of the industry supplying control equipment that a minimum of five years would be required to retrofit the combustion capacity demand indicated above. This situation is summarized in Figure 5.

It is clear from Figure 5 that the combination of natural low sulfur fuels and flue gas desulfurization technology will not control the quantity and size range of combustion capacity required to achieve national ambient air quality standards. Thus, a third category of control technology, fuel desulfurization, is also included in Figure 5. These processes for not only desulfurization but total pollutant cleanup of coal and residual oil are required to achieve ambient air quality standards. Their basic role is two fold:

(1) provide control technology for combustion sources to which other alternatives are not technically or economically applicable;

(2) provide synthetic, low pollution fuel augmenting the limited domestic supply of natural gas.

These approaches range from the application of currently commercialized mechanical coal cleaning technology, through chemical coal and oil desulfurization technology which maintains the clean fuels in its original physical state, to coal conversion technology for the synthesis of high-Btu pipeline-quality gas. The development cycle for these latter efforts, however, restricts commercial application until 1978–1985.

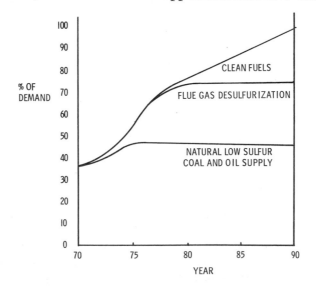

Figure 5.   Control supply/demand relationship for achieving primary ambient air standards

The Potential Solution

A serious government/industry program to abate air pollution from stationary sources has been underway for about five years. Until recently this program has concentrated on the development of effluent treatment technology directed to the electric utility industry. This prioriy was based primarily on mass emission, *i.e.*, that 70% of total U.S. SO_x emissions as indicated in Table IV come from electric utilities.

The recent development of valid diffusion-model computer programs for sulfur dioxide in the form of the AQDM provides the ability to relate the emissions of any source to an annual average (or other long-term) ambient air concentration at any receptor location. The model is based on a Gaussian diffusion equation which describes the diffusion of a plume as it is transported from a continuously emitting source. This model computes estimates of concentration of air pollutants as a function of spatial coordinates from a continuous source with a given effective height, using a binomial continuous plume diffusion equation. The model uses climatic wind velocity data, the amount of pollutant emitted at each source, the exit velocity and stack height, and a basic grid system of receptor areas for the APCR. The concentrations are computed from both point and area sources. The contribution of each source to the ambient air concentration is calculated for each receptor.

This model has been exercised on a variety of AQCR's for which an accurate emission inventory, meteorological data base, and measured ground level pollutant concentrations are available. The results discussed in this paper represent analyses of the New York, Philadelphia, Niagara Frontier, St. Louis, and Milwaukee AQCR's (*13, 14*). These AQCR's represent a reasonable cross-section of the eastern urban AQCR's where the primary sulfur dioxide ambient air quality problem exists. The results of these analyses indicate that the level of control required by emission source to achieve ambient air quality standards can be forecast with greatly increased assurance. The following conclusions from this exercise should be considered in the near-term achievement of ambient air quality standards.

Conclusion 1. The impact by source on ground level ambient air SO_x concentration is not directly related to its mass emission. Figure 6 summarizes this conclusion, in terms of the average emission/ambient-air-quality relationship trends for four emitter categories: (*a*) utility combustion, (*b*) industrial combustion, (*c*) industrial process, and (*d*) area sources (residential and commercial and industrial sources emitting less than 100 tons of SO_x per year). For example, although electric utilities typically contribute over 50% of all SO_x emissions in an eastern urban AQCR, well known factors such as stack height limit the corresponding

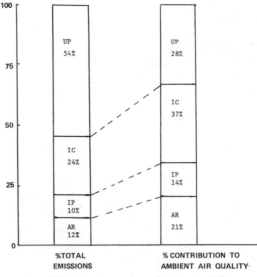

Figure 6. Relationship between SO_x *source contribution and impact on* SO_x *ambient air quality: UP = power plants; IC = industrial combustion; IP = industrial processes; AR = area sources*

impact on the ground level ambient SO_x concentration to only about 20% of the total. Conversely, area and industrial combustion sources typically contribute only 35% of the emission inventory but over 60% of the ground level ambient sulfur dioxide concentration.

The relationship between emissions and ambient air quality, shown in Figure 6, is developed from the term A/E, where A is the per cent contribution of an emitter (or in composite, an emitter category) to the total ambient air quality of a receptor (or, in composite, to an AQCR) and E is the per cent contribution of an emitter (or in composite, an emitter category) to the total emission within an AQCR. Table V indicates the average value and standard deviation of A/E values by emitter category. These averages are developed from individual source/receptor AQDM analysis of all receptors having ambient sulfur dioxide concentrations greater than 80 $\mu g/m^3$ in the five AQCR's listed above. Based on the

Table V.   A/E Values by Emitter Category

Category	Average	Standard Deviation
Utility combustion	0.44	0.08
Industrial combustion	1.31	0.25
Area combustion	1.48	0.15
Industrial process	1.22	0.32

narrow data spread indicated in Table V, these A/E values suggest trends which may be generally applicable to at least the eastern AQCR's where combustion sources predominate.

Application of these A/E values to the 41 eastern AQCR's exceeding the primary standard indicates several important factors. First, although electric utilities consume about 80% of the coal and 60% of the residual oil, even complete desulfurization of this consumption without attention to the other source categories would only bring 21 of these problem AQCR's within the primary air quality standard in 1975.

On the other hand, complete desulfurization of industrial combustion and area sources consuming 20% of the coal and 40% of residual oil without attention to the utility sector would bring 31 AQCR's within the primary air quality standard by 1975. The significance of these extremes is that, if a near-term limited supply of both fuel and control technology exists to achieve air pollution standards, this limitation can be greatly reduced by directing these resources to the sources having the greatest impact. Table VI summarizes the impact of the prioritization of the 1975 available coal and oil supplies indicated in Figure 2. Two con-

Table VI.   Impact of Fuel and Combustion Control Primary Prioritization on Achieving National Ambient Air Quality Standard in Eastern Problem AQCR's

Priority	Source Category	Additional AQCR's	Coal Capacity Controlled, 10^{12} Btu	Oil Capacity Controlled, 10^{12} Btu
I	area and industrial combustion	12	1300	4400
II	utility combustion	6	5000	1800
III (Effluent treatment)	utility combustion	14	3300	100
Totals		32	9600	6300

straints are applied to the approach in Table VI: (a) The approach does not consider changing the basic coal and oil consumption patterns, *i.e.*, oil is not substituted for coal, or *vice versa*, and (b) current regional fuel transportation constraints are not modified in a manner which changes current fuel distribution systems or introduces new cost differentials. First priority was given to area and industrial combustion sources and second priority to utility combustion. Third, in those AQCR's not achieving the primary standard by fuels alone, effluent-desulfurization processes having 80% sulfur removal efficiency were applied to utility combustion sources.

Of the remaining nine problem AQCR's in the eastern United States, seven could achieve the primary standard by the additional control of industrial process sources, particularly oil refineries. Only in two AQCR's does elimination of coal and oil combustion in favor of natural gas or synthetic sulfur-free fuel appear necessary to achieve the primary standard.

This strategy not only uses the limited low sulfur fuels available to better advantage in achieving ambient air quality, but it also reduces the demand for effluent desulfurization technology from the 20,000 units and 150,000 MW indicated by the roll-back strategy to about 200 utility steam generators with a total capacity of 45,000 MW. This capacity is essentially all coal fired.

Conclusion 2. The ability to meet ambient air quality standards depends on the ability to control individual emission sources adequately. This conclusion results from taking one step further the source category analysis discussed in conclusion 1 above. It frequently occurs that a limited number of major contributing sources create the primary impact on ambient air quality in a region. If these major contributors are collectively combined into an average of total sources, the significance of their impact is lost. On the other hand, an understanding of the source-by-source impact on ambient air quality can significantly reduce the number of sources requiring control. The effect of this consideration has been examined in three separate AQCR's in which Air Quality Data Model results are available.

Analysis of the 10 worst receptors in the Philadelphia AQCR indicated an average annual ambient SO_x concentration ranging from 166 to 255 $\mu g/m^3$. Here the emission sources which must be controlled to achieve the SO_x ambient air quality standard at these receptors include the industrial combustion and industrial process categories, particularly sulfuric acid plant and petroleum refining combustion operations. As shown in Table VII, the level of control required on these selected sources is considerably above the average indicated for the total Philadelphia AQCR. If selective controls could be applied to the Philadelphia AQCR, it would be necessary to control, at a 75% effectiveness level, only 53 of the emitters or 19% of the total emissions to achieve the primary standard.

The second example is the Niagara Frontier AQCR (Buffalo, N.Y.). The highest annual average ambient SO_x concentration recorded at any receptor in this AQCR is 197 $\mu g/m^3$. The ambient SO_x concentration at this receptor could be reduced below the primary ambient air quality standard of 80 $\mu g/m^3$ by the control of one source only to a level of at least 95%. The importance of this single industrial combustion source can further be shown by the fact that, if all other sources impacting on this worst receptor had 100% control, this single combustion source would

Table VII. **Selective Reduction of SO$_x$ Emission to Achieve 80 μg/m^3—Philadelphia**

| Emitter Category | Present Emissions Sources, tons/day | | Number of Sources Requiring Control at efficiency of: | | | |
| | | | 100% | | 75% | |
	Sources	tons/day	Sources	tons/day	Sources	tons/day
Industrial combustion	238	555	3	172	10	293
Industrial processes	165	300	5	41	13	124
Utility power	21	1345	6	519	9	578
Area sources	276	4378	11	148	21	222
Totals	700	6578	25	880	53	1216

still require at least a 70% control level to achieve the primary ambient air quality standard.

The calculated values for SO$_x$ ambient air quality in the Niagara Frontier AQCR for the top 10 receptors ranged from 114 to 197 μg/m^3. Table VIII provides the results of the analysis of source impacting those receptors. The application of selective controls in the Niagara Frontier AQCR would provide for reduction of ground level SO$_x$ concentration to the national primary standard through application of 75% effective means to 17 of their 541 emitters or 27% of the emissions.

The highest calculated SO$_x$ ambient air quality in the New York AQCR was 308 μg/m^3. The lower value for the top 10 sets was 244 μg/m^3. Results of the New York analysis are given in Table IX. As would generally be expected a large degree of control will be required in

Table VIII. **Selective Reduction of SO$_x$ Emissions to Achieve 80 μg/m^3—Niagara Frontier**

| Emitter Category | Present Emissions | | Number of Sources Requiring Control at efficiency of: | | | |
| | | | 100% | | 75% | |
	Sources	tons/day	Sources	tons/day	Sources	tons/day
Industrial combustion	199	280	12	134	14	148
Industrial processes	117	81	1	8	3	31
Utility power	1	260	0	0	0	0
Area sources	304	45	0	0	0	0
Totals	541	666	13	142	17	179

Table IX.   Selective Reduction of SO_x Emissions to Achieve 80 $\mu g/m^3$—New York

| | Present Emissions | | Number of Sources Requiring Control at efficiency of: | | | |
| | | | 100% | | 75% | |
Emitter Category	Sources	tons/day	Sources	tons/day	Sources	tons/day
Industrial combustion	106	238	0	0	14	111
Industrial processes	42	79	0	0	0	0
Utility power	31	1,389	1	590	21	10,389
Area sources	1,106	2,020	132	650	265	1,248
Total	1,285	3,726	143	1,240	300	2,398

the New York AQCR, e.g., 64% of the emissions, all combustion in origin, require control at a 75% effective level to achieve the primary ambient air quality standard. Considering that New York is projected to consume some 5 million tons of coal and 215 million barrels of residual fuel oil, relaxed controls on 36% of that fuel would be a major contribution toward achieving a supply/demand balance.

These points are clearly not isolated instances. The AQCR's examined, particularly Philadelphia and Niagara Frontier, are typical of the eastern urban AQCR's where the primary SO_x problem exists. Extrapolation of the trends indicated by these three AQCR's as well as similar analyses of the St. Louis and Milwaukee AQCR's suggests that, with the exception of New York, the primary SO_x ambient air quality standard could probably be achieved in each eastern AQCR by the selective control of a set of sources using 30% or less of all coal and oil consumed in the AQCR.

At a 30% selective control level it is estimated that the annual national coal deficit associated with the universal achievement of the primary SO_x ambient air quality standard could be reduced from 230 million tons under SIP regulations to less than 20 million tons. Similarly the 300 million barrel annual residual oil deficit would be reduced to about 125 million barrels.

As noted earlier, an accurate selection of sources requiring control can best be achieved through the application of the Air Quality Display Model for each AQCR of interest. It is estimated that the total one-time cost of such an exercise at a level of accuracy necessary to predict source sulfur dioxide control requirements for each of the 245 AQCR's would be about $10 million with an additional annual maintenance cost of $500 thousand to allow for emission inventory changes. For comparison, this investment would save approximately $2 billion annually in additional national fuel costs created by current SIP regulations.

Measurement data supporting the concept of selective control and re-evaluation of SIP requirements are becoming available from the National Aeromatic Data Base (NADB) compiled as a public service by EPA. The NADB consists of ambient air quality monitoring data collected by EPA as well as state and local agencies throughout the nation and permits a time-correlated indication of changes in ambient pollutant concentrations. Generally, most AQCR's are represented by only a few sensors. In the Metropolitan Chicago AQCR, however, data are available from 79 monitoring sites. Nineteen sites in Chicago alone provide a history of continuous 24 hr and annual average sulfur dioxide ambient concentration data over the period 1967 through 1972. Figure 7 indicates that a marked down trend in ambient SO_x concentration, particularly since 1970, has occurred. As a result, by mid-1972 no site in Chicago reported values above the national secondary SO_x ambient air quality standard. Although less complete data are available for the remaining 59 monitoring sites, similar trends are apparent with no sites in the Illinois portion of the AQCR currently exceeding the 24 hr ambient standard.

Only 3 of 15 sites in the heavily industrialized Gary, and Hammond, Ind. portion of the AQCR currently indicate sulfur dioxide concentrations

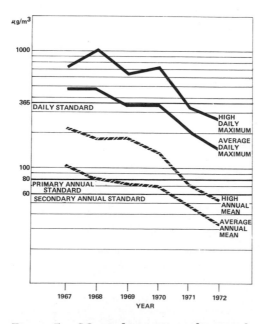

Figure 7.   SO₂ ambient air quality trend,
city of Chicago

exceeding the maximum 24 hr ambient standard. It should be noted however that SO_x standards in Indiana during this period were both less stringent than in Illinois and without record of enforcement.

Enforced local regulations causing this ambient air quality improvement during the period 1970 through mid-1972 have been limited to the City of Chicago and the remainder of Cook County which comprise only 16% of the total area of the AQCR. In July 1970 Cook County limited the sulfur control of all fuel consumed to 2.0 wt % or less regardless of source category. This was subsequently reduced to 1.25 wt % sulfur in September 1971. In July 1970 the City of Chicago developed a set of selective fuel sulfur regulations ranging from 2.0 wt % sulfur for industrial combustion and existing area sources to 1.0 wt % sulfur for new area sources. These were later modified in the following manner: (a) In November 1970 maximum fuel sulfur content for industrial combustion was reduced to 1.5 wt %. (b) In September 1971 maximum fuel sulfur content for existing area sources was reduced to 1.25 wt %. (c) In January 1972 maximum fuel sulfur content for electric utility sources was reduced to

Table X.   Summary of Emission

1970

	Emis-tons (SOx)	Coal, tons × 10³ (%S)	Oil, bbl × 10³ (%S)	Gas, Mcf
Area (NEDS)				
Chicago	109,044	1,367 (2.8)	19,308 (0.57)	182,989
Cook Co. xcpt				
Chicago	69,716	874 (2.8)	12,345 (0.57)	88,347
Aqcr xcpt Cook	40,670	399 (3.14)	9,828 (0.52)	111,450
Industrial (NEDS)				
Chicago	17,867	623 (1.4)	319 (1.23)	93,160
Cook Co. xcpt				
Chicago	11,790	267 (1.4)	1,155 (1.23)	104,235
Aqcr xcpt Cook	244,475	2,407 (2.82)	20,350 (1.72)	112,490
Utility (FPC)				
Chicago	100,924	2,043 (2.6)	0	39,951
Cook Co. xcpt				
Chicago	57,323	930 (2.9)	2,303 (0.8)	1,775
Aqcr xcpt Cook	723,685	11,542 (3.3)	0	56,090

[a] *Sources of data for table.*

1970. Area source and industrial fuels were drawn from the National Emission Data Survey (NEDS) except gas consumption in the City of Chicago which was taken from Peoples Gas Co. sales data. because the NEDS area source data only refer to Cook Co. as a whole, it was necessary to distribute the fuels. This was done on the basis of population percentages. Utility data were taken from FPC Form 67 and National Coal

1.0 wt %. Table X indicates the change in sulfur dioxide emissions and fuels consumed in the Metropolitan Chicago AQCR as a result of these regulations.

In summary, national secondary ambient air quality standards for sulfur dioxide appear to have been achieved throughout the Illinois portion of the Metropolitan Chicago AQCR. This achievement, involving an average 50% reduction in ambient sulfur dioxide concentration within the City of Chicago over the period January 1970 through June 1972, has been caused by only a 15% reduction in sulfur dioxide emissions within the total AQCR. On a source category basis within the total AQCR, area source sulfur dioxide emissions were reduced 34%, industrial combustion emissions were reduced 4%, and electric utility combustion emissions were reduced 13%.

Although monitoring data in the NADB from other eastern urban AQCR's are less complete on either a geographic or chronological basis, indications are that at least the primary national ambient air quality standard for sulfur dioxide has generally been achieved.

Reductions—Chicago AQCR

1972 Est.

Emis-sions, tons (SOx)	Fuel Consumption		
	Coal, tons × 10³ (%S)	Oil, bbl × 10³ (%S)	Gas, Mcf
57,950	1,000 (1.0)	20,706 (5.7)	208,419
45,680	682 (1.25)	15,675 (0.57)	88,347
40,670	399 (3.14)	9,828 (0.52)	111,450
10,231	224 (1.0)	1,838 (1.0)	81,145
9,610	96 (1.25)	1,805 (1.23)	104,235
244,475	2,407 (2.82)	20,350 (1.72)	112,490
27,075	1,425 (1.0)	0	36,732
16,257	0	6,153 (0.8)	1,775
723,695	11,542 (3.3)	1	56,090

Association (NCA) data. Emissions data were calculated based on the above fuel data and EPA emission factors, 1972. Gas data were taken from Peoples Gas Co. data. Area and industrial coal consumption was estimated using the rate of decreasing end use exhibited between 1970 and 1971 and the Btu demand converted to coal demand. Utility demand was based on extrapolation of 1971 NCA data. Emissions were then calculated as for 1970.

It is hoped that future environmental policy at all levels will recognize these encouraging circumstances and re-examine additional planned regulations affecting fuel consumption by using the analytical tools available. Energy and air quality need not be in conflict if even modest thought is given to resource allocation.

Literature Cited

1. "Environmental Quality," 3rd Annual Report of the Council on Environmental Quality, pp. 272–275, August 1972.
2. "The Clean Air Act," Environmental Protection Agency, Washington, D.C., December 1970.
3. "Environmental Protection Agency—National Primary and Secondary Ambient Air Quality Standards for Air Pollution and Control," *Federal Register* **36**, No. 21, Part II, Jan. 30, 1971.
4. "Environmental Protection Agency—Requirements for the Preparation, Adoption, and Submittal of Implementation Plans," *Federal Register* **36**, No. 158, Part II, Aug. 14, 1971.
5. "Air Quality Implementation Planning Program," **I**, Operators Manual, Environmental Protection Agency, Washington, D.C., Nov. 1970.
6. "U.S. Energy Demand Forecast by AQCR, 1970–1985," Battelle Columbus Laboratories, 1971.
8. Hoffman, L., Yeager, K. E., MTR–6086, The Mitre Corp. EPA, Contract No. F19628–71–C–0002, May 1972.
9. "Reserves of Crude Oil, Natural Gas Liquids, and Natural Gas in the United States and Canada; and United States Productive Capacity as of December 31, 1970," American Petroleum Institute, 1971.
10. "U.S. Energy Outlook, An Initial Appraisal, 1971–1985; An Interim Report of the National Petroleum Council," **1**, July 1971.
11. "United States Energy: A Summary Review," U.S. Department of the Interior, January 1972.
12. "Natural Gas Supply and Demand 1971–1990," Bureau of Natural Gas, Staff Report No. 2, U.S. Government Printing Office, Washington, D.C., February 1972.
13. Krajeski, E. P., *et al.*, MTR–6158, The Mitre Corp. EPA Contract No. F19628–71–C–0002, May 1972.
14. Yeager, K. E., Abstracts, 71st National Meeting of AICHE, Feb. 1972, No. 27d.

Received February 15, 1973.

6

Chemical Removal of Pyritic Sulfur from Coal

J. W. HAMERSMA, M. L. KRAFT, E. P. KOUTSOUKAS, and R. A. MEYERS

TRW Systems Group, One Space Park, Redondo Beach, Calif. 90278

A new approach for the chemical removal of pyritic sulfur from coal is described. The process is based on the discovery that aqueous ferric salts selectively oxidize the pyritic sulfur in coal to chemical forms which can be removed by vaporization, steam, or solvent extraction. Data for removal of the pyritic sulfur from four major coals (Lower Kittanning, Illinois No. 5, Herrin No. 6 and Pittsburgh) are presented together with a discussion of the process chemistry. The effect of variables, such as coal particle size, acid and iron concentration, reaction time, and temperature are discussed. The results show that near complete removal of pyritic sulfur can be obtained under mild conditions, resulting in a reduction of the total sulfur content of the coals from 40 to 80%, depending on the original pyritic sulfur content.

The Meyers process for the chemical removal of pyritic sulfur from coal is a TRW proprietary process currently being developed under the Demonstration Projects Branch of the Environmental Protection Agency. Laboratory results which preceded the current activities are presented here. These results show that 40–75% of the total sulfur content, corresponding to near 100% of the pyritic sulfur, can be removed from all coals tested by a mild aqueous extraction. This process does not affect the coal matrix in any way that would hinder its use as a steam coal.

Background

The concept of chemically removing pyrites from coal has not previously been advanced as a solution to the sulfur oxide air pollution problem because iron pyrites are not soluble in any known liquids. For example, the acids hydrochloric, hydrofluoric, sulfuric, or combinations of these which dissolve many inorganic salts have little or no effect on iron pyrites. However, pyrites may be oxidatively converted to sulfates (soluble in strong acid) by strong oxidizing agents such as nitric acid or hydrogen peroxide, and in fact, this process is used for the analysis of the pyritic sulfur content of coal. However, these reagents have never seriously been advanced as a method for lowering the sulfur content of coal because even though they are strong enough to dissolve pyrite, they also oxidize (in the case of nitric acid, nitrate) the coal matrix.

An economically viable process for the chemical removal of pyrites from coal would require an oxidizing agent (most likely aqueous) which is (a) selective to pyrite, (b) regenerable, and (c) highly soluble in both oxidizing and reduced forms. Ferric sulfate and ferric chloride meet the above combination of requirements, and these reagents form the basis of the process chemistry described here.

Chemistry

In the Meyers process, aqueous ferric sulfate or -chloride (mild but effective oxidizing agents) selectively oxidizes (without affecting the coal matrix) the pyritic sulfur content (1) of coal to form free sulfur and sulfate. Iron sulfate dissolves in the aqueous solution. The free sulfur may then be removed from the coal matrix by steam or vacuum vaporization or solvent extraction and the oxidizing agent may be regenerated and recycled. See Reactions below:

$$2Fe^{+3} + FeS_2 \rightarrow 3Fe^{+2} + 2S \tag{1}$$

$$14Fe^{+3} + 8H_2O + FeS_2 \rightarrow 15Fe^{+2} + 2SO_4^{-2} + 16H^+ \tag{2}$$

$$S \cdot Coal \longrightarrow S + Coal \tag{3}$$

$$3Fe^{+2} + 3/2[0] \rightarrow 3Fe^{+3} + 3/2[0^{-2}] \tag{4}$$

The aqueous extract solution which contains iron in both the ferrous and ferric state may be regenerated in several ways including air oxidation of the ferrous ion to ferric (Reaction 4) (2, 3, 4). An advantage of this process is that iron is used to remove iron; on regeneration it is not necessary to separate the iron which is extracted from the coal from the metal oxidizing agent. Eventually accumulated iron can be removed by diverting a part of the solution.

In the process, the coal is treated with aqueous ferric chloride or -sulfate solution at approximately 100°C to convert the pyritic sulfur to elemental sulfur and iron sulfate. The aqueous solution is separated from the coal, and the coal is washed to remove residual ferric salt. The elemental sulfur which is dispersed in the coal matrix is then removed by vacuum distillation or by extraction with a solvent like toluene or kerosene. The resulting coal is basically pyrite free and may be used as low sulfur fuel.

Experimental

Sampling. A determined effort was made to obtain samples with uniform composition. The cleaned coal samples were taken by the U.S. Bureau of Mines (Lower Kittanning and Pittsburgh) and the Illinois Geological Survey (Illinois No. 5 and Herrin No. 6). Each gross sample ($\frac{1}{4}$ $\times$ 0 mesh) was coned and quartered or riffled to smaller samples and ground to the desired mesh sizes by the appropriate ASTM method. The analyses in Table I are an average of determinations on five or more samples representing both -14 and -100-mesh samples taken or ground on several different occasions.

Standard Runs. Coal, 100 grams of the desired mesh (14×0 or 100×0), was added to a 1-liter resin kettle equipped with a stirrer and reflux condenser together with 600 ml ferric chloride or ferric sulfate, $1M$ in ferric ion. The solution was brought to reflux ($102°C$) for the desired time (usually 2 hrs), filtered, and washed thoroughly on the filter funnel. This washing procedure was sufficient for runs using ferric sulfate, but a much more thorough washing procedure is necessary in the ferric chloride runs to reduce the chloride content to usable levels. After removal of the iron salts, the coal was refluxed with 400 ml toluene for 1 hr to remove the sulfur from the coal, and then the coal was dried at $150°C$ under vacuum. All calcuations are based on the dry weight of the coal.

Multiple-Pass Runs. These were performed in the same way except that the ferric chloride was changed every hour for a total reaction time of 6 hrs, and the ferric sulfate was changed at 1, 2.5, and 4.5 hrs with a total reaction time of 8.5 hrs. After the final filtration and wash, the sulfur was removed by toluene extraction and the coal was dried in the normal manner.

Coal analyses were performed by Commercial Testing and Engineering Co., Chicago, Ill. Data handling and curve fitting were done on the TRW Timeshare/CDC 6500 computer system.

Results

Four coals were selected for process evaluation whose sulfur form distribution is typical of coals east of the Mississippi River and which represent major U.S. coal beds: Pittsburgh, Lower Kittanning, Illinois No. 5, and Herrin No. 6. The Pittsburgh bed has been described as the most valuable individual mineral deposit in the United States and perhaps in the world. Its production accounts for approximately 35%. of the total cumulative production of the Appalachian bituminous coal basin to January 1, 1965 and 21% of the total cumulative production of the United States to that date (5). The Lower Kittanning bed together with its correlative beds contains even larger reserves than the Pittsburgh seam. The No. 5 bed is the most widespread and commercially valuable coal bed in the eastern interior coal basin. The Herrin No. 6 bed is second in commercial importance only to the No. 5 bed.

Analysis of the four coal samples that were used for this study are shown in Table I. The indicated tolerances are the standard deviations. Five or more coal samples were used for sulfur, ash, and heat content analyses while three or more samples were used for sulfur forms analyses (6).

Table I. Dry Analyses of Coals

Analysis	Lower Kittanning	Illinois No. 5	Pittsburgh	Herrin No. 6
Pyritic sulfur	3.58 ± 0.08	1.57 ± 0.03	1.20 ± 0.07	1.65 ± 0.04
Sulfate sulfur	0.04 ± 0.01	0.05 ± 0.01	0.01 ± 0.01	0.05 ± 0.01
Organic sulfur	0.67 ± 0.10	1.86 ± 0.04	0.68 ± 0.16	2.10 ± 0.06
Total sulfur	4.29 ± 0.06	3.48 ± 0.03	1.88 ± 0.07	3.80 ± 0.04
Ash	20.77 ± 0.59	10.96 ± 0.26	22.73 ± 0.48	10.31 ± 0.28
Btu	12,140 ± 55	12,801 ± 58	11,493 ± 60	12,684 ± 55
Rank	medium volatile bituminous	high volatile B bituminous	high volatile A bituminous	high volatile B bituminous

Both ferric chloride and ferric sulfate have been used in this study with good results. However, ferric sulfate has the following advantages: (a) it is less corrosive, (b) regeneration is less complicated and expensive because the iron sulfate formed (Reaction 2) does not have to be separated from iron chloride, and (c) the removal of residual leach solution is easier and therefore more economical. Thus, it is planned that ferric sulfate will be used exclusively in all studies.

The extent of the reactions indicated by Equations 1 and 2 or the molar sulfate-to-sulfur ratio is 2.4 ± 0.2 when rock pyrite is used and 1.4 ± 0.4 for sedimentary pyrite found in the coals used in this work. Although both materials are FeS_2 of the same crystal structure, differences in reacivity have been documented which are attributed to impurities and crystal defects peculiar to the various possible modes of formation (7). For coal, no significant variation in this ratio was found with ferric ion concentration, acid concentration, coal, or reaction time. The results for each coal are found in Table II.

We studied the effect of acid concentration, coal particle size, ferrous and sulfate ion concentrations, and reaction time on pyrite removal. These parameters were studied under conditions (see Experimental) that give 40–70% pyritic sulfur removal, rather than 85–90%, so that the effects of parameter variations are clear and not so small as to be masked by experimental error. In addition, studies were performed to demonstrate

Table II. Sulfate-to-Sulfur Ratio for Extraction of Coal and Mineral Pyrite with Ferric Chloride Solution

Substrate	Sulfate-to-Sulfur Ratio[a]
Mineral Pyrite	2.4 ± 0.2
Lower Kittanning	1.4 ± 0.3
Illinois No. 5	1.6 ± 0.4
Pittsburgh	1.3 ± 0.3
Herrin No. 6	1.4 ± 0.3

[a] Average of all runs ± standard deviation.

90–100% pyritic sulfur removal using both ferric chloride and -sulfate, and a set of experiments were designed to illustrate the differences between ferric sulfate and ferric chloride.

The effect of added hydrochloric acid concentration was studied in order to determine whether or not the acid had any effect on pyrite and ash removal, sulfate-to-sulfur ratio, final heat content, and possible chlorination of the coal. Coal has many basic ash constituents, so increased ash removal was expected, as well as some suppression of the sulfate-to-sulfur ratio because the reaction that results in sulfate formation also yields eight moles of hydrogen ion per mole of sulfate (common ion effect). Added acid was studied in the range of 0.0 to 1.2M (0.0, 0.1, 0.3, and 1.2M) hydrochloric acid in 0.9M ferric chloride. Duplicate runs were made at each concentration with all four coals for a total of 32 runs. The results showed no definite trends (except one-*vide infra*) even when the data were smoothed *via* computer regression analysis. Apparently the concentration range was not broad enough to have any substantial effect on the production of sulfate or to cause the removal of additional ash over that which is removed at the pH of 1M ferric chloride (≈pH 2).

An important consideration in any chemical process is the selectivity of the desired reaction. In the oxidative leaching of pyrite by ferric ion, the extent of the reaction of the reagent with the coal matrix can have an effect on the process economics. The extent of this reaction varies from small to substantial depending on the acid concentration, coal, and ferric anion. In order to define this effect quantitatively, the ratio of actual mmoles of ferrous ion produced to the mmoles of ferrous ion necessary to produce the sulfate and elemental sulfur that was recovered was calculated for each run (*see* Reactions 1 and 2). This ratio, Fe(II) (experimental)/Fe(II)(calculated), has a value of one for 100% selectivity and a higher value for less than 100% selectivity. The data for ferric chloride in Table III were smoothed by linear regression analysis using the values generated in the acid matrix; the ferric sulfate values are the average of triplicate runs.

Table III. Variation of Ferric Ion Consumption with Acid Concentration and Ferric Anion

| Coal | $Fe(II)(Exptl)/Fe(II)(Calcd)$ | | 0.4N $Fe_2(SO_4)_3$ |
| | 0.9N $FeCl_3$ | | 0.0M H_2SO_4 |
	0.0M HCl	1.2M HCl	
Lower Kittanning	1.2	1.4	1.2
Illinois No. 5	3.8	6.6	1.6
Pittsburgh	2.2	3.4	1.5
Herrin No. 6	3.7	6.4	2.4

The higher ranked Appalachian coals (Lower Kittanning and Pittsburgh) react to a lesser extent with ferric ion under all experimental conditions than do the lower ranked eastern interior coals (Illinois No. 5 and Herrin No. 6). In addition, the ferric chloride runs show that a very substantial acid-catalyzed reaction occurs in this system which is most evident for the Illinois No. 5 and Herrin No. 6 coals. In these coals, a reduction of about 42% in ferric ion consumption is observed when the starting HCl concentration is reduced from 1.2M to 0.0M. The corresponding reductions for Pittsburgh and Lower Kittanning coals are 35 and 14%, respectively. When ferric sulfate is used, further reductions in ferric ion consumption ranging from 3% for Lower Kittanning coal to 63% for Illinois No. 5 coal are observed. From these early data, ferric sulfate is the preferred form of ferric ion for increased selectivity.

The data in Table IV indicate the relationships of excess ferric ion consumption and dry mineral matter- and pyrite-free Btu. Note that the Btu losses are small, and even a 6.6-fold excess ferric ion consumption

Table IV. Variation of Final Heat Content with Reaction Conditions Dry Mineral Matter- and Pyrite-Free Heat Content [a]

Coal	Heat Content, Btu/lb			
		Final		
	Initial	0.9N $FeCl_3$		0.4N $Fe_2(SO_4)_3$ 0.0M H_2SO_4
		0.0M HCl	1.2M HCl	
Lower Kittanning	15,069	14,963	14,876	15,192
Illinois No. 5	14,278	13,981	13,672	14,020
Pittsburgh	14,787	14,648	14,466	14,742
Herrin No. 6	14,039	13,805	13,506	14,038

[a] Values are corrected for both ash and heat content associated with the exact amount of pyrite present.

(Table III) results in only a 4–5% loss in the heating value. Thus for a 14,000 Btu/lb, dry mineral matter-free coal and 2–3% pyritic sulfur, each 100% excess ferric ion consumption results in a 60–100 Btu/lb reduction in the heating value of the coal. In certain coals with relatively high sulfur levels and little or no reaction with the coal matrix, there is an increase in heat content of 1–5% when it is calculated on a dry basis, only because of ash reduction caused by pyrite removal.

The data listed in Table V illustrate the effect of top mesh size on pyritic sulfur removal. The coal samples were prepared by the same comminution techniques, and consequently the size distribution of the samples should be similar for each case (*8, 9, 10, 11, 12*). The ¼-inch mesh was "as received" coal, while the 14 × 0 and 100 × 0 mesh samples were obtained by grinding a representative sample in a ball mill until it

Table V.   Effect of Top Mesh Size on Pyritic Sulfur Removal

Coal	Sulfur Removed[a], %		
	−1/4[b]	−14	−100
Lower Kittanning	35	60	65
Illinois No. 5	45	35	50
Pittsburgh	—	45	60
Herrin No. 6	—	70	50

[a] Values rounded to nearest 5%.
[b] Representative sample ground to ¼ inch × 0, etc.

was 100% the desired mesh. In general, pyrite removal increases for smaller top sizes as expected because of exposure of pyrite encapsulated within the coal matrix. The Illinois No. 5 and Herrin No. 6 coals deserve special comment because reaction of the ferric ion with the coal matrix resulted in greater than 75% depletion of the reagent. For the No. 5 coal, this effect was approximately the same for all three sizes and the resulting depletion of the reagent may have had a leveling effect on the results. For No. 6 coal, substantially less ferric ion was consumed by the −14-mesh coal (68 *vs.* >95%) which is probably the reason for the increased removal. Thus, while pyrite removal is decreased with a larger coal top size, it does not appear to be a strong function of mesh size. It is expected that the internal surface and permeability of the coal to aqueous media are important factors along with the surface exposure of pyrite caused by grinding. In addition, the top mesh size may have an effect on the ultimate amount of pyrite removal, and further research is necessary to clarify the exact nature of these effects.

An examination of Reactions 1 and 2 shows that both ferrous ion and sulfate ion could have a retarding effect on pyrite extraction. It could also be expected that the rate is dependent on the ferric ion concentration. Because a commercial process may require various ferric-ferrous ion concentration mixtures, these are important parameters. Work with mineral pyrite has indicated that there is no significant rate difference with ferric ion concentration between 0.5 and 3.0M as long as enough ferric ion is present to dissolve all the material. Results with −100 and −14-mesh Lower Kittanning coal, using both ferric sulfate and ferric chloride, indicate virtually (±2%) the same removal when the leach is 1.0, 2.0, or 2.5M in ferric ion. The 0.4M ferric chloride instead of 0.4M ferric sulfate seems to increase pyrite removal by more than 10% in Pittsburgh coal. In addition, a series of experiments were performed with a starting ferrous ion concentration of 0.5M and a ferric ion concentration of 1.0M. Under the conditions used, the pyrite removal was reduced 7–8% from a baseline of 62%. Thus, the effect of ferrous ion, when present, is small.

Ferric sulfate has several advantages over ferric chloride in a process, so a test matrix was performed (summarized in Table VI) to compare the abilities of ferric sulfate and -chloride to remove pyritic sulfur from all four coals. Slightly less sulfur was removed by 0.4N ferric sulfate than was indicated with 0.4N ferric chloride. However, 0.9N ferric sulfate removed an equal or greater amount of sulfur than 0.9N ferric chloride.

Table VI.   Comparison of Ferric Sulfate and Chloride for Pyrite Removal [a]

| Coal | Pyritic Sulfur Removed, wt % | | | |
| | 0.4N Fe^{+3} | | 0.9N Fe^{+3} | |
	Cl	SO₄	Cl	SO₄
Lower Kittanning	43	38	43	54
Illinois No. 5	48	43	50	50
Pittsburgh	50	33	58	—
Herrin No. 6	35	33	52	64

[a] Conditions: 600 ml 0.4 and 0.9N Fe^{+3} solution, 100 grams −100-mesh top size coal, refluxed at 100°C for 2 hrs.

| Ferric Sulfate-Treated Coal (0.4N Fe^{+3}), wt % Sulfate | | Removal Correction |
Initial	Final	Abs. %[b]
0.07	0.17	+3
0.05	0.17	+8
0.01	0.08	+7
0.05	0.20	+9

[b] Increase ferric sulfate extraction values by this per cent to correct for retained sulfate.

Analysis of the coals also showed that a small amount of sulfate remains with the coal after a simple washing procedure. Preliminary results show that this can be reduced to starting values by using more rigorous washing procedures. If all the sulfate can be removed, the values for sulfur removal by ferric sulfate extraction can be increased 3–9%, depending on the coal.

Table VII. Pyrite Extraction as a Function of Successive Leaches

	Leach Content, mmole sulfate			
Leach	Lower Kittanning	Pittsburgh	Illinois No. 5	Herrin No. 6
Initial pyritic sulfur	102	37.5	43.4	49.7
Extd pyritic sulfur as sulfate[a]				
1	31.2	13.5	11.4	12.5
2	12.4	6.0	5.5	6.3
3	9.2	4.6	3.6	5.0
4	4.8	2.1	1.8	2.1
5	0.4	0.6	0.7	1.0
6	0.3	0.3	0.5	0.6

[a] A nominal 40% of the pyritic sulfur remains with the coal as elemental sulfur. All indications are that the sulfur-to-sulfate ratio is constant.

Attempts to increase pyrite removal by increasing the reaction time met with limited success under our standard conditions because reaction of the ferric ion with the coal matrix depleted the ferric ion that was needed for extraction of the pyrite. Thus, for example, increasing the coal reaction time from 2 to 12 hrs only increased pyritic sulfur removal from 60 to 80% for Pittsburgh coal. Similar results were obtained for the other three coals. The only alternatives were to increase the amount of leach solution or to use a continuous or semi-continuous (multiple-batch) reactor. A multiple-batch mode was chosen because it was a simple laboratory procedure and at the same time it could approximate conditions encountered in a commercial plant. A 1-hr-per-batch leach time was used because our 2 hr results indicated that in the early stages of removal the rate begins to decrease after 1 hr, and six leaches (or batches) per run were used to assure that any pyrite that could be removed in a reasonable amount of time was removed. The progress of removal was monitored by analyzing the sulfate content in each spent leach solution; elemental sulfur was not removed until all the leaches were completed. Table VII shows pyrite extraction as a function of successive leaches as followed by sulfate analysis of the leach solution. Note that the major portion of pyritic sulfur is removed in the first two leaches or 2 hrs, followed by lesser amounts in

Table VIII.   Pyritic Sulfur Removal Data[a]

| Coal | Total Sulfur Analysis | | | |
	Start, %	Finish, %	Total S[b] Removed, %	Pyritic S Removed, %
Lower Kittanning	4.32	0.93	78	95
Pittsburgh	1.88	0.75	60	95
Illinois No. 5	3.48	1.88	46	102
Herring No. 6	3.80	2.04	46	107

| Pyritic Sulfur Analysis[c] | | |
Start, %	Finish, %	Pyritic S[b] Removal, %
3.58	0.06	98
1.20	0.09	93
1.57	0.10	94
1.65	0.05	97

[a] Six 1 hr leaches with fresh $1M$ $FeCl_3$ ($0.1M$ HCl).

[b] Assuming total sulfur removal $= \dfrac{S_o - S_f}{S_o} \times 100$,

where $S_o = \%$ sulfur content at start and
$S_f = \%$ sulfur content after extraction.

[c] Based on sulfur forms analysis.

the third and fourth leaches, and only small amounts in the final two leaches.

The results in terms of final sulfur values and pyrite removal are given in Table VIII. Note that pyritic removal computed from either sulfur forms analyses or the difference in total sulfur between processed and untreated coal (Eschka analysis) resulted in essentially identical values of 93–100%. This corresponds to total sulfur removal of 40–70%, depending on the organic sulfur content of the coal. The observation of greater than 100% removal is a result of cumulative error in analysis and the removal of small amounts of sulfate (0.02–0.04%). Presently, these experiments are being duplicated using ferric sulfate, and preliminary analysis indicates the same results.

Acknowledgment

The authors acknowledge the technical assistance of J. M. Hom, D. R. Moore, and D. B. Kilday.

Literature Cited

1. Meyers, R. A., U.S. Patent 3,768,988.
2. Sercombe, E. J., Gary, J. K., Brit. Patent 1,143,139 (1969).

3. Emilov, V. V., Romanteev, Y. P., Shchurouskii, Y. A., *Tr. Inst. Met. Obogashch., Akad. Nauk Kaz. SSR* (1969) **30**, 55–64.
4. Liepna, L., Macejevskis, B., *Dokl. Akad, Nauk SSR* (1967) **173**, 1336–1338.
5. Averitt, P., *U.S. Geol. Sur. Bull.* **1257**, Jan. 1, 1967.
6. "Annual Book of ASTM Standards," Philadelphia, 1971, Part 19, Gaseous Fuels; Coal and Coke.
7. Mellors, J. W., "A Comprehensive Treatise on Inorganic and Theoretical Chemistry," vol. XIV, pp. 221–232, John Wiley and Sons, New York, 1961.
8. Rosin, P., Rammler, E., *J. Inst. Fuel* (1933) **7**, 29–36.
9. Bennett, J. G., *J. Inst. Fuel* (1936) **10**, 22–39.
10. Geer, M. R., Yancy, H. F., *Trans. Met. Soc. AIME* (1938) **130**, 250–269.
11. Scott, A. S., *Bureau Mines Rept. Investigations* **3732**, 1943, 9 pp.
12. Landry, B. A., *Bureau Mines Bull.* **454**, 1944, 127 pp.

RECEIVED February 15, 1973. Work supported under Contract EHSD 71-7, Environmental Protection Agency.

7

A Solvent-Refined Coal Process for Clean Utility Fuel

ROBERT G. SHAVER

General Technologies Corp., 6621 Electronic Dr., Springfield, Va. 22151

Solvent-refined coal (SRC) as a de-ashed, low sulfur fuel for electric utilities is discussed from the standpoint of economics. The overall lowest delivered cost of SRC results from processing at minehead sites because of minimized transportation costs of the ash and sulfur fractions that are eventually removed by the processing. A potential market of 300–800 million tons per year of SRC by 1990 is projected on the basis of the competitive price of delivered Btu's from low sulfur fossil fuels and synthetic fuels at the various power-generating sites in the U. S. SRC can be supplied in either a liquid or solid form; therefore it is a potentially versatile competitor for the low sulfur, fossil-fuel power generation market.

Several processes for conversion of coal to clean fuels are undergoing development. The solvent refining of coal, a non-catalytic process under development by the Pittsburgh and Midway Coal Mining Co. for the U. S. Bureau of Mines, Office of Coal Research, is an outstandingly advantageous conversion process from the standpoint of economics. Compared with other coal conversion processes it requires less costly equipment and less severe operating conditions. It consumes less hydrogen and has no need for a catalyst (1). The earlier work in hydrogenation of coal was directed toward production of distillate fuels, and catalysts were necessary for reasonable yields. Despite improvements in catalysts and in process technology this route of coal conversion is still not economically attractive. In solvent refining the coal is not converted to distillate fuel, but rather to a de-ashed, low sulfur semisolid fuel resembling pitch.

The fuel product of this process has a very consistent heating value of 16,000 Btu per pound regardless of the coal feedstock to the process. This uniformity has been demonstrated in pilot productions from both lignite and bituminous coal (*1*). The principal variation in the product is the sulfur content, a result of the variation in feedstock sulfur content. This variation arises from the characteristic of the process to remove all of the mineral sulfur (pyrites) and a part of the organic sulfur above 60%. High ash, high sulfur coals can as readily be brought to a processed fuel of less than 1% sulfur as a lower ash content coal having appreciable organic sulfur content. Typically, it can be expected that 85% of the sulfur content of the coal can be removed in the process; a 4% sulfur coal, for example, results in a solvent-refined coal product at a heating value of 16,000 Btu per pound and a sulfur content well below 1%.

The process, in brief, is as follows: pulverized coal feedstock is mixed with a coal-derived solvent oil with a 550°–800°F boiling range; the mixture is passed with hydrogen through a preheat and reactor; excess hydrogen plus the hydrogen sulfide and light hydrocarbons formed are separated; the solution is filtered; the solvent is flash-evaporated; and the bottoms are recovered as either a hot liquid fuel or a cooled solid product. During the reaction phase, the hydrogen reacts with organic sulfur compounds to form hydrogen sulfide. The hydrogen also stabilizes the solubilized coal products. The pyritic sulfur leaves the process in the filtration step, as does the ash component.

In this discussion, the sole market considered for solvent-refined coal is that of fuel for power-generating utilities because this market is the overwhelmingly large one for this product (*2*). The legislation regarding atmospheric pollution will eventually restrict the sulfur dioxide emissions for the entire nation, and it appears that fuels will be limited to sulfur content less than 1% in general and to less than 0.5% in several highly populated regions. The impact of these restrictions on the direct use of coal as a power-generation fuel will be great because the supplies of coal of such low sulfur content are quite small compared to the total U.S. coal reserves, and they are inconveniently located relative to the power needs. The solvent-refining process allows the coal supply to be used, regardless of its sulfur content. When considered as a clean fuel for power generation, then solvent-refined coal not only comes into competition with coal itself in conjunction with stack gas treatments but also with natural gas, fuel oil, and nuclear power.

Discussion of Technology

The schematic of the recent process technology for the Pittsburgh and Midway Solvent Refined Coal process is shown in Figure 1. The salient aspects of the process technology as they affect economics are: (a) delivery of the product as a solid fuel product or as a hot liquid; (b) by-products—light liquid hydrocarbon, sulfur, and electrical power; (c) fly ash or mineral residue waste; (d) hydrogen or process fuel feeds to the process. The distinction between the solid and liquid forms of solvent-refined product is principally one of whether or not the distillation bottoms are cooled below the 300°F solidification point prior to disposition. Probably this issue will depend on whether the product is used in an on-site or nearby power plant or shipped to a distant location. It has been estimated that the additional processing cost to solidify for shipping is 2¢/MM Btu (1).

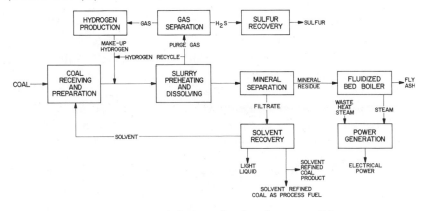

Figure 1. Solvent-refined coal process (1)

The liquid hydrocarbon by-product has a high cyclic content and so is useful as a petroleum refinery feedstock or as a source of aromatic organic chemicals. This material has a relatively high nitrogen content compared with the corresponding petroleum fraction. Its use as a refinery feedstock would require additional nitrogen removal processing by the refinery.

If the solids from the filtration operation are burned to obtain the heating value, the sulfur dioxide produced can be combined with the hydrogen sulfide from the process to produce elemental sulfur by a Claus-type procedure. This appears to be practical in this case because of the concentrated gas streams encountered. As much as 1–2% of the coal feed weight is the hydrogen requirement for the process. The by-product gas can be used to form all of the required hydrogen by steam reforming. This would eliminate the need for a hydrogen raw material input. The use of a part of the fuel product as process fuel would also eliminate the need for natural gas feed to the process. Whether or not these steps are taken in a given solvent-refining plant depends on local availability of low cost by-product streams of hydrogen and low cost availability of natural gas. It is important to bear in mind that the efficient operation of this process does not require their availability.

Catalytic Conversion of Coal. The most recent catalytic method for converting coal to low sulfur fuel is called the H-coal process, originally developed under sponsorship of the Office of Coal Research. This process uses a desulfurization catalyst and is very effective in reducing the organic sulfur content to levels of 0.1–0.2%. The process, however, is more costly than solvent refining because of the catalyst and the internal recycle required for its use. The coordinated use of the solvent refining and H-coal processes for their peculiar individual advantages has been suggested (*1*), and this may be the most economical way to achieve very low (less than 0.5%) sulfur contents in the fuel.

Coal Gasification. Although the costs for producing synthetic gas from coal would be higher than those for producing heavy fuel from coal by solvent refining, several such coal gasification processes are now being developed. The hydrogen requirements are greater and the processing conditions are more severe. The gas fuel product from such a process will very likely compete as a premium fuel with natural gas and will not be in primary contention for the bulk of the power-generation fuel needs. The combustion characteristics of semisolid and liquid SRC have not been fully characterized by large-scale boiler operation; this step is required for full qualification of the fuel but is not required for synthetic gas, whose combustion characteristics are fully developed.

Degree of Sulfur Reduction. The present development of the solvent-refining process allows for about 85% of the sulfur in the feed coal to be removed. All of the pyritic sulfur and about 60–70% of the organic sulfur is removed. For the most common type of coal, in which the sulfur is roughly 50–50 in these two forms, the final product sulfur content is well below 1%, of the order of 0.8%. It may be possible to reduce the organic sulfur content further by utilizing greater quantities of hydrogen than in the present design (*3*), although in the extreme this merges with the catalytic processes such as the H-coal.

Projected Economics

Solvent-refined coal as a low sulfur fuel for power generation would compete primarily with other energy sources such as fuel oil, gas, and nuclear power, as well as with coal itself fired in boilers served by stack gas treatment processes. The latter, a much studied method of combating pollution from combustion of coal, is an awkward expedient to permit the extended use of high sulfur coals. Electric power companies should not be nor do they desire to be in the chemical production and marketing business, which is the natural outcome of using a stack gas treatment process on a coal-fired boiler and having to dispose of the wastes and by-products. It is more sensible for the chemical processing industry to provide low sulfur fuel from efficient, optimally located and optimally sized coal conversion plants. This comparison of costs of operating utilities for SRC vs. stack gas treatment has been shown in detail (3).

There are two strategies for carrying out this processing-distribution sequence. One is the location of solvent-refining plants at minehead sites centrally located to the principal marketing areas, to which the product is shipped as a solid fuel. The other is to have consolidated minehead processing plants and power-generating facilities in regions where both the coal supplies and the power requirements are in reasonable conjunction. The latter type of facility could, of course, also furnish solid fuel for shipment.

Projection of Demand for Fossil Fuel for Power Generation. Projections of electric power generation expect growth in fossil fuel consumption through the next two decades (3). As shown in Table I, the total expected use of fossil fuels should grow from 13.6 $\times$ 10^{15} Btu in 1970 to 19.5 $\times$ 10^{15} Btu in 1980 and 25 $\times$ 10^{15} Btu in 1990, nearly doubling in two decades.

Table I.   Fossil Fuel Projection for Electric Power Generation

	10^{15} Btu		
Fuel	1970	1980	1990
Coal	8.1	12.5	16
Oil	2.1	4.0	5
Gas	3.4	3.0	4
Total	13.6	19.5	25

Growth is expected in both coal and oil but not in gas. In fact an actual decline in gas use is projected between 1975 and 1980, and the whole growth rate of gas use will decline dramatically after its vigorous growth prior to 1970.

The federally mandated emission standard for new and modified fossil, solid fuelfired steam generators with capacity exceeding about 25 MW (equivalent) for construction commenced after August 17, 1971 is 1.2 lbs sulfur per MM Btu. This corresponds to roughly 0.8% sulfur in a high heat content coal and about 0.4% for lignite. Even the vast resources of Western coals of markedly low sulfur content are unsuitable without further control efforts. Thus essentially all of the coal market for power generation is potentially available to a sulfur-reduced coal product such as solvent-refined coal in the near future. Looking at the fossil fuel market for its potential in regard to solvent-refined coal production leads to the possibilities shown in Figure 2. In view of the recent cost studies of solvent-refined coal (2, 4), a sales price range of 50 to 100¢/MM Btu seems to be within reason. The projections of market potential through 1990 at prices in this range are made with two assumptions: the limiting one in which all the fossil fuel market for power generation is captured and the more reasonable one which sizes the market at that estimated for coal. A vast sales market ranging between about $4 and 25 billion is potentially available to the investors in such a process.

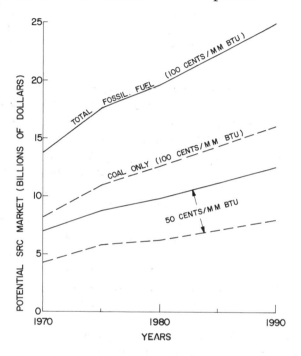

Figure 2.   Potential of fossil fuel market to SRC production

Oil Prices for Power Generation. A feasible price range for solvent-refined coal can be inferred by examining the price range of competitive low sulfur fuels for power generation. Low sulfur fuel oils are currently in great demand for power generation in highly populated areas, and the demand should, if anything, intensify in coming years. Recent quotations of oil prices in several locations (5) have been put on a consistent fuel basis of cents per MM Btu in Table II.

It is well to note the effect of supply and demand in the prices in Table II. In Oklahoma, the demands for oil for power generation is nil because gas is used for all power plants. Residual oil from substitute natural gas plants has been valued at 57–60¢/MM Btu at the plant. Based on these facts, very low sulfur residual oil can be valued at 66–69¢/ MM Btu currently at the ports. Delivery costs are superimposed on these.

Table II.   Current Price Variation in Oil for Power Generation

Location	Sulfur, %	Price, ¢/MMBtu
New York	0.3 max.	73
	0.5 max.	69
	1.0 max.	61
	Bunker C	53
Chicago	1.0 max.	75
	1.25 max.	73
	1.5 max.	71
Oklahoma	>1, <2	40-42

The effect on future prices of processing to desulfurize residual oils can be estimated by using processing data for the hydrodesulfurization process (6). Operating cost data to reduce to the 1% sulfur level vary between 7 and 19¢/MM Btu and depend on the type of residual oil feedstock, with vacuum residual oils consuming the most hydrogen and hence having the highest operating costs. The above figures do not include a return on investment. Nevertheless we could expect a desulfurized residual oil product at about the 1% sulfur level to be no less than 50¢/MM Btu at a low demand location like Oklahoma and to be at least 65¢/MM Btu at a high demand seacoast location like New York. With increased legislative pressure for the use of low sulfur fuels, the price at the power plant that most of the major utilities burning fuel oil will face seems to certainly be in the 70-100¢/MM Btu range at current dollar values. This helps to define a competitive price range for solvent-refined coal product for such use.

Impact of the Sulfur By-Product from Processing of Coal. The supplies of natural low sulfur fuel will clearly not be equal to the demands upon them in the upcoming decades. The desulfurization of oil and coal by one or another means must make up the deficit. If we look at the recent experience in coal use with regard to sulfur content as shown in Figure 3, we see that the amounts of sulfur to be removed will be considerable. The weight-average sulfur content of all the coal fired at power generation in 1969 was 2.6% (3), and we can assume that the coal mined in the future, if an economically feasible desulfurization process is being used, will not be lower than this experience. If the overall sulfur content allowed in solid fuels is reduced to an average of 0.6 wt % of coal used in 1990, the sulfur by-product generated by desulfurization of coal will increase to about 12–13 million tons in 1990. This figure is sufficiently high to make the recovery of significant economic value by sale of sulfur improbable on the whole. The sulfuric acid market, the principal user of sulfur, recently consumed about 9 million tons of sulfur, so the existence of by-product sulfur in the quantities possible is certain to cause it to be stockpiled and not sold in any significant quantities at current price levels. It would seem that no credits for sale of sulfur by-product should be taken in realistic projection.

Elements of Cost Pertaining to Solvent-Refined Coal Price. Estimation of the selling price of the solvent-refined coal product has been undertaken for a minehead plant in the Ohio-Illinois-Kentucky area on a 10,000 ton per day basis (*1, 4*). The most recent price estimates range

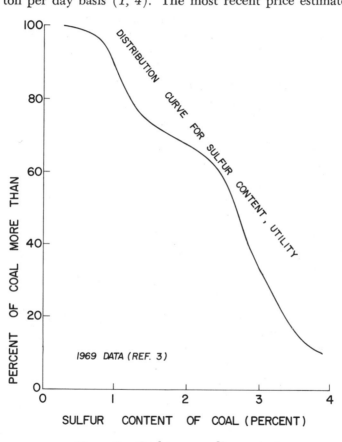

Figure 3.   Coal use vs. *sulfur content*

from 41¢/MM Btu where all by-products are sold, to 47¢/MM Btu where none is sold. In the latter case the light liquid by-product is combined with the solvent-refined coal for sale in the power plant product. These prices do include a return on investment but no transportation charges. The annual sulfur by-product sale at $10 per ton we believe to be unrealistic for the long run in which the sulfur market is glutted with pollution control induced sulfur. Reducing the credit for by-products by this amount increases the necessary FOB plant selling price for the optimistic case to 42¢/MM Btu. The elements of cost that these estimates cover are mining, solvent refining, and return on investment.

The transportation of product to the user is a widely variable cost element. A power plant located at the minehead-processing plant site would have effectively no transportation cost. Rail transport of solid product would probably experience the same costs as coal itself (2). This can be estimated in lieu of specific foreknowledge of rail rate schedules through 1990 as 1¢ per ton-mile. As an example of current costs to ship coal, low sulfur Western coal was shipped recently to New Jersey for utility use at a cost of $22 per ton, which corresponds closely to 1¢ per ton-mile.

In a system of well located processing plants, shipping in excess of 500 miles probably would not be necessary in most cases. The users remotely located from the processing plant would then pay an additional 3–17¢/MM Btu for the solid product delivered to the power plant, which includes a cost to solidify the product for shipment. This raises the total estimated price for solid product from 44¢/MM Btu at the plant to 45–64¢/MM Btu delivered.

When solvent-refined coal is compared with low sulfur oil as a competitive fuel, the local delivered price situation would determine the competitive balance. For example, in the Chicago area where low sulfur fuel oils are selling for 71-75¢/MM Btu, the solvent-refined coal could be furnished from the aforementioned hypothetical plant for 53–75¢/MM Btu. However, on seacoast locations such as New York, the Gulf Coast, and the West Coast, low sulfur fuel oil could be currently obtained for 61–73¢/MM Btu. For the East Coast, a mine-processing plant complex in West Virginia could deliver solvent-refined coal for 53–65¢/MM Btu at most population and industrial centers, which is certainly competitive. However the longer transportation distances between a plant in the Wyoming area and the West Coast areas would probably be less attractive in comparison with delivered fuel oil.

Coal Costs. One cost element in the production of solvent-refined coal that is likely to increase noticeably in the future is the cost of mined coal. This is the result of several factors including increased labor cost and increased investment for mine safety. A minehead selling price for coal of $6 per ton seems realistic for the near future, which is about 24¢/MM Btu for a good quality coal. Adjusting the estimated solvent-refined coal prices for this raw material cost would raise the price about 15¢/MM Btu. Adjustment for this higher coal cost would bring the estimated selling price of a solvent-refined coal utility fuel to 56–63¢/MM Btu at the plant location, and to 59–94¢/MM Btu delivered; however, this is still well within a competitive range for low sulfur fuels even under present-day price experience.

When selling in competition with coal itself in conjunction with stack gas treatment, the cost of the raw material coal in solvent-refined coal is irrelevant (2). The principal considerations are the lower transportation cost per MM Btu and the reduced investment and maintenance at the power plant with the SRC. In a similar way, the relative position between SRC and other coal-derived fuels would not shift greatly because of coal cost.

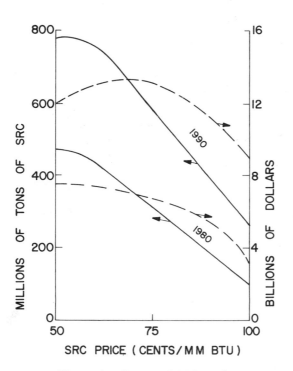

Figure 4.   Projected SRC market

Projected Market for Solvent-Refined Coal. By considering efficient solvent-refined coal plants at four U.S. locations, West Virginia, southern Illinois, Wyoming, and New Mexico, and by examining the projected competitive price per MM Btu for the several fossil fuels and derivative fuels in low sulfur-emission power plant use, we projected the fractions of the potential market shown in Figure 2 that could be obtained by SRC by virtue of price. These market projections are given in Figure 4 over a range of SRC selling prices at the processing plants from 50 to 100¢/MM Btu. The mid-range selling price of 75¢/MM Btu should yield a market of about 300 million tons in 1980 and 550 million tons in 1990. This selling price also seems to be the optimum in 1990 for sales dollar volume.

Conclusion

The continued wide use of coal in the United States as a fossil fuel source of energy for power generation is inescapable in the upcoming decade and beyond. Of the several developing processes for producing clean fuels from coal, solvent refining is the most simple and economical. SRC can be used as either a solid or a liquid fuel and has been estimated to capture a very large market in direct competition with other low sulfur forms of fossil fuels in power generation.

Literature Cited

1. Schmidt, B. K., Bull, W. C., "Production of Ashless, Low-Sulfur Boiler Fuels from Coal," *Amer. Chem. Soc. Div. Fuel Chem. Prepr.*, (1971) **15** (2), 38–49.
2. Shaver, R. G., "Study of Cost of Sulfur Oxide and Particulate Control Using Solvent Refined Coal," Final Report Contract No. CPA 22-69-82, National Air Pollution Control Administration, Washington, D. C., April 1970.
3. Jimeson, R. M., Grant, J. M., *Ann. Meetg., Amer. Inst. Mining, Met. Petrol. Eng.*, Washington, D. C., 1969.
4. R&D Report No. 53, Interim Report No. 1, Contract No. 14-01-0001-496, U. S. Bureau of Mines Office of Coal Research, June 1970.
5. Platt's Oil-Gram, June 1972.
6. Gregoli, A. A., Hartos, G. R., ADVAN. CHEM. SER. (1973) **127**, 98.

RECEIVED February 15, 1973.

Production of Low Sulfur Fuel Oils from Utah Coals

S. A. QADER and G. R. HILL

Department of Mining, Metallurgical and Fuels Engineering, University of Utah, Salt Lake City, Utah 84112

Low sulfur fuel oils were prepared from a high volatile bituminous coal by hydrogenation under high temperatures and pressures. At a coal conversion of 80%, the ratio of oil-to-gas yields was about three, and 23% of the coal sulfur was contained in the oil. Sulfur content of the oil, however, remained the same at different coal conversion levels. The data obtained in the semi-continuous, dilute phase hydrogenation system showed that the whole oil can be directly used as a fuel oil where 1% sulfur is tolerated. Fuel oils containing 0.5 and 0.25% sulfur were produced by desulfurization of the whole oil. A preliminary economic evaluation indicated that low sulfur fuel oils can be produced from coal by hydrogenation at a manufacturing cost of about $5–6 per barrel.

Coal can be converted to a synthetic crude oil by hydrogenation under high temperatures and pressures. The synthetic crude can be subsequently converted to a low sulfur fuel oil by desulfurization. Four different approaches may be used in the hydrogenation of coal to liquid fuels. In the German process (*1*), a paste of coal, oil, and catalyst is hydrogenated under high pressures of 5000–10,000 psi. The H-coal process (*2*) uses an ebullating bed of catalyst to hydrogenate a mixture of coal and oil under medium pressure conditions of 2000–4000 psi. Fixed beds (*3*) of catalyst are used by the Bureau of Mines for the hydrogenation of coal and oil mixtures under conditions of high turbulence and high hydrogen flow. Coals impregnated with catalysts are hydrogenated in dilute phase, free fall reactors under medium pressures of 2000–3000 psi to produce synthetic oil at the University of Utah (*4*). In the present investigation, coal was hydrogenated in batch and dilute phase systems to produce crude oil. The crude oil was then desulfurized in fixed and ebullating bed reactor systems to produce low sulfur fuel oils. The economics of producing fuel oils containing 0.5 and 0.25% sulfur are presented

Experimental

High volatile sub-bituminous coals from Utah were used in this work. The coal was ground to less than 200 mesh and impregnated with 10 wt % of zinc chloride. The hydrogenation experiments were performed

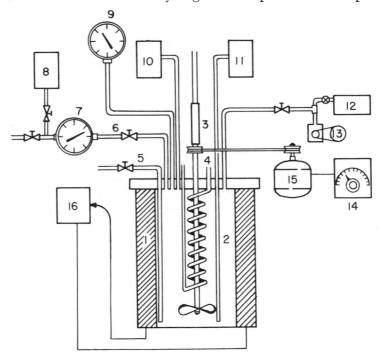

1. Heating jacket	9. Pressure gage
2. Thermowell	10. Pressure recorder
3. Magnetic drive assembly	11. Temperature recorder
4. Cooling coil	12. Hydrogen tank
5. Liquid sampling line	13. Vacuum pump
6. Gas sampling line	14. Stirrer controller
7. Flow meter	15. Moter
8. Gas chromatograph	16. Temperature controller

Figure 1.   Batch stirred tank reactor

in batch (Figure 1) and semi-continuous (Figure 2) reactor systems. The coal oil produced in the semi-continuous system was desulfurized in fixed and ebullating bed reactor systems using a commercial desulfurization catalyst containing sulfides of nickel and tungsten supported on alumina. Product evaluations were done by standard methods.

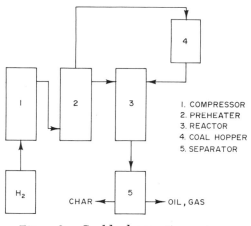

Figure 2.   Coal hydrogenation system
(bench scale)

Table I.   Sulfur Distribution in Products
(Sulfur Content of Coal = 1.31%)

Reaction Time, min	Coal Conversion wt %	Product Yield, wt %			Sulfur Distribution, wt %		
		Oil	Gas	Char	Oil	Gas	Char
20	41	36	5	59	16	9	75
30	52	43	9	48	18	10	72
40	61	51	10	39	20	13	67
50	73	57	16	27	22	16	62
60	81	61	20	19	23	17	60

Results and Discussion

The product distributions obtained in the batch work are given in Table I. Hydrogenation was performed at 500°C and initial hydrogen pressure of 2000 psi. The results show that, at a coal conversion of about 80%, the ratio of oil-to-gas yields will be about three, and 23% of the coal sulfur will be contained in the oil. The data given in Table II indicate that the sulfur content of the oil remains almost the same at different coal conversion levels and probably depends upon the organic

Table II. Sulfur Distribution in Oil

Coal Conversion, wt. %	Sulfur Content of Oil, wt. %
41	0.53
52	0.54
61	0.52
73	0.51
81	0.52

Table III. Analysis of Coal Oil and Its Fractions

(Sulfur Content of Coal = 2.5%)

Property	Whole Oil	−300°C Fraction	+300°C Fraction
Distribution, vol. %	100.0	42.0	58.0
Sulfur, wt %	1.01	0.49	1.53
Nitrogen, wt %	1.22	0.65	1.31
Oxygen, wt %	5.65	4.54	6.57
H/C (atomic)	1.09	1.25	0.96
Asphaltene, vol %	26.5	10.5	39.6

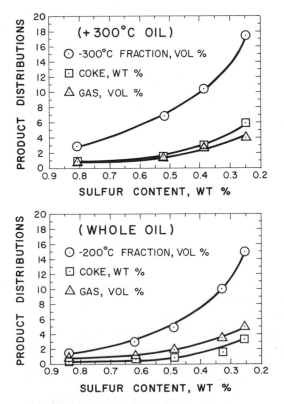

Figure 3. Influence of desulfurization on product distribution (fixed bed)

sulfur content of the coal. The data given in Tables I and II were obtained from a coal containing about 0.6–0.7% organic sulfur.

The properties of the oil obtained in the semi-continuous, dilute phase hydrogenation system (4) are given in Table III. These oils were prepared from a coal containing about 2.5% total sulfur. The data show that the whole oil can be directly used as a fuel oil where 1% sulfur is tolerated. A 0.5% sulfur oil can be produced by desulfurization of either whole oil or the +300°C fraction. If a fuel oil of less than 0.5% sulfur is desired, it may be necessary to desulfurize the whole oil.

The whole oil and +300°C fraction were desulfurized in bench-scale, fixed and ebullating bed reactor systems, and the product distributions obtained are shown in Figures 3 and 4. The data show that fuel oils

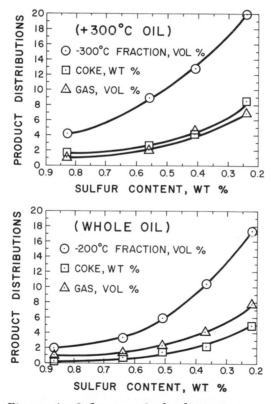

Figure 4. Influence of desulfurization on product distribution (ebulating bed)

containing about 0.2% sulfur can be obtained by desulfurization of either the whole oil or the +300°C fraction. As the sulfur content of the product oil decreases, there will be an increase in the yields of low boiling oil, gas, and coke. A comparison of the data indicates that the fixed bed system produces more gas and coke than the ebullating bed system, irrespective of the type of feed oil used.

A conceptual material balance of a refinery producing 100,000 bbl/day of fuel oil from coal was calculated (Table IV) based on the bench-scale data obtained by the authors and the published data available. In this projection, a coal containing 7.5% moisture, 10% ash, and 2.5% total sulfur is used as the feed. The hydrogenation can be performed in any type of reactor system in the ranges of 500°–550°C and 2000–3000 psi. The process conditions will be optimized for a coal conversion of about 80%. The hydrocarbon gases produced in the process will be used

Table IV.　Material Balance
(Capacity: 100,000 bbl/day of Fuel Oil)

| | Sulfur Content of Fuel Oil, wt % | |
Materials	0.50	0.25
Raw Materials		
Coal, tons	39,500	43,500
Hydrogen, MM SCF	1,073	1,275
Catalyst, tons	732	800
Products		
C_1-C_4 gases, MM SCF	271	317
Naphtha, bbl	36.280	49,000
Fuel oil, bbl	100,000	100,000
Char, tons	8,052	8,800
Sulfur, tons	175	175
Ammonia, tons	350	350
Water, MM gal.	1.1	1.1

Table V.　Economic Summary
(Capacity: 100,000 bbl/day of Fuel Oil)

| | Sulfur content, wt % | |
Parameter	0.50	0.25
Fixed capital, $MM	312	344
Working capital, $MM	31	34
Total Revenue, $MM		
Fuel oil price:		
$5/bbl	238	261
$6/bbl	271	294
$7/bbl	304	327
Total operating cost, $MM	194	327
Rate of Return, %		
Fuel Oil Price:		
$5/bbl	6.9	5.4
$6/bbl	12.2	10.2
$7/bbl	17.5	15.0

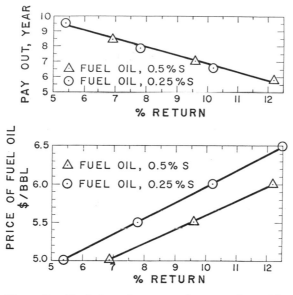

Figure 5.   Variation of return and payout time with fuel oil price

for making process hydrogen. The residual char will be used as a fuel. Based on the conceptual data, we made a preliminary economic evaluation of the process for making fuel oils of 0.50 and 0.25% sulfur (Table V). The calculations were based on approximate energy and material balances and estimated equipment costs. The data indicate that fuel oils can be produced from coal by hydrogenation at a manufacturing cost of about $5–6 per barrel. The data (Figure 5) also show that the cost of reducing the sulfur content of fuel oil from 0.5 to 0.25% will be about 30–40¢ per barrel.

Literature Cited

1. Gordonk, K., "Report on the Petroleum and Synthetic Fuel Oil Industry of Germany," Ministry of Fuel and Power, Her Majesty's Stationary Office, London, 1947.
2. Alpert, S. B., Johanson, E. S., Schuman, S. C., *Chem. Eng. Prog.* (1964) **60**, 35.
3. Aktar, S., Friedman, S., Yavorsky, P. M., Bureau of Mines Technical Progress Report **35**, July 1971.
4. Qader, S. A., Haddadin, R. A., Anderson, L. L., Hill, G. R., *Hydrocarbon Process.* (1969) **48**, 147.
5. Qader, S. A., Hill, G. R., *Hydrocarbon Process.* (1969) **48**, 141.
6. Qader, S. A., Wiser, W. H., Hill, G. R., *Erdoel und Kohle, Erdgas, Petrochem.* (1970) **12**, 801.

RECEIVED February 15, 1973. Work supported by Office of Coal Research and University of Utah.

9

Hydrodesulfurization of Residuals

A. A. GREGOLI

Cities Service Co., Chemicals and Metals Group, Drawer 8,
Cranbury, N.J. 08512

G. R. HARTOS

Cities Service Co., Planning and Economics Division, 60 Wall St.,
New York, N.Y. 10005

*Commercial H-Oil experiences using 1/32 inch extrudate
and fine catalysts were equally successful. Important design
parameters considered in residual desulfurization include
the feed characteristics, catalyst characteristics, and operating severity. The range of operating conditions employed
for residual desulfurization and process design considerations using the fine or extrudate catalyst are discussed. The
most attractive system will depend on each application.
The costs of desulfurizing Middle East and Venezuelan
feedstocks are presented.*

Since the first commercial H-Oil unit came on-stream at Lake Charles
in 1963, a variety of feedstocks have been processed, including heavy
cycle oils, atmospheric bottoms, vacuum bottoms, and cutback propane
deasphalter bottoms. The unit has operated successfully with both
microspheroidal and extrudate catalysts and has been expanded to 6000
bbl/day.

In addition to the Lake Charles H-Oil unit, three other commercial
units were designed for hydrocracking. The units, although designed for
hydrocracking, can be used for desulfurization. That is now the primary
objective for the Cities Service Lake Charles Unit.

Lake Charles H-Oil Experience

The H-Oil unit was designed to convert 2500 bbl/day of West Texas
sour vacuum bottoms into lighter products (*1*). Later it was found possible to process a heavier, lower value feedstock, cutback propane

deasphalter bottoms (2). In late 1966 and early 1967 a commercial demonstration of residual desulfurization, feeding West Texas atmospheric residuum, was quite successful. Sulfur was reduced from 2.5–3.0 wt % in the feed to 0.3–0.5 wt % in the product. Catalyst usage was approximately 0.05 lb/bbl.

From 1963 to 1967 a 1/32 inch extrudate catalyst was used. In 1967 relatively minor modifications were made to accommodate a microspheroidal fine catalyst. This eliminated the need for the internal recycle pump previously required to supply the liquid velocity necessary for bed expansion. Operating and performance data have been described previously (3, 4).

From 1967 through 1971 the unit operated with the fine catalyst. During this period the feed was West Texas sour vacuum bottoms cutback with 20% heavy cycle oil. In the last few months of operation with the fine catalyst, conversion of vacuum bottoms to distillate ranged from 55 to 75%, with 75–80% sulfur removal. The performance of the microspheroidal or fine catalyst was equivalent to the performance of the 1/32 inch extrudate. The unit capacity was expanded from 2500 to 6000 bbl/day. It was necessary to return to the extrudate catalyst at the higher feed rate to avoid excessive expansion of the catalyst bed.

Factors Affecting Design

A number of design factors must be considered when desulfurizing resids because of: (1) the complex feedstock characteristics, (2) the tendency to deposit metallic impurities and coke on the catalyst, (3) the required operating severity, (4) the extent and desirability of concurrent reactions, such as hydrocracking, and (5) the relatively high hydrogen consumption and design considerations given to the heat released.

Feedstock Characteristics. Several important feed characteristics considered in H-Oil desulfurization are: (1) the character of the residuum, *i.e.*, whether vacuum, atmospheric, deasphalter bottoms, cracked tars, or blends; (2) the asphaltene and metal content; (3) the sulfur level and degree of desulfurization required. These feed characteristics ultimately influence the selection of operating temperature, hydrogen partial pressure, space velocity, and catalyst type and usage.

Catalyst. Microspheroidal and extrudate catalysts have been used commercially. These catalysts consist of a combination of metals such as cobalt and molybdenum or nickel and molybdenum on an alumina support. An earlier publication reported that a 1/32 inch extrudate performs (3) better than a 1/16 inch extrudate (5). The most active catalyst is the one with the greatest surface area (6, 7).

Table I. Feed-

Feedstock Data	Atmospheric Residuals			
	West Texas	Kuwait	Khafji	Venezuelan
Gravity, °API	17.9	16.5	15.1	15.3
Sulfur, wt %	2.5	3.9	4.1	2.1
Carbon residue, wt %	8.4	9.5	11.0	10.4
Vanadium and nickel, ppm	40	60	95	370
975°F+, vol %	45	43	43	52
Sulfur, wt %	3.2	5.1	5.4	2.5

Organometallic compounds in the feed are the primary cause of catalyst deactivation. The deactivation rate is influenced by feedstock characteristics, catalyst characteristics, and operating severity.

Operating Conditions for Residuum Desulfurization. Temperature, space velocity, hydrogen partial pressure, and catalyst consumption (or cycle life for fixed beds) are the essential operating conditions considered in residual desulfurization. These normally range from 700 to 800°F (6), 0.3 to 3.0 V/hr/V (8), and 0.02 to 1.0 lb/bbl, respectively. The ranges do not necessarily represent technical limits but are based on judgment and economic considerations.

Design Considerations. The reaction in residuum desulfurization is exothermic. In the ebullated bed the reactor is isothermal. The temperature is controlled by charging the feed below the reactor temperature. Solids entering with the feed pass through the expanded catalyst bed without causing a pressure buildup. Catalyst activity and product quality are maintained by adding and withdrawing catalyst while on-stream. Cor.stant catalyst replacement gives the refiner flexibility when changing feedstock.

With the fine catalyst, the velocity required to expand the catalyst is achieved by the flow of the liquid-gas feed mixture passing upward through the reactor (4). Catalyst inventory and bed expansion are essentially a function of the catalyst particle size and density, liquid viscosity, and liquid and gas velocities. Catalyst is added with the feed and leaves with the product.

The extrudate catalyst requires higher liquid velocities than the fine catalyst to maintain the desired bed expansion. The liquid velocity is provided by recycling a portion of the effluent back to the inlet. The recycle or ebullating pump can be located internal or external to the reactor.

stock Properties

	Vacuum Residuals		
West Texas Sour	Kuwait	Khafji	Venezuelan
11.6	7.7	5.0	7.5
3.1	5.1	5.4	3.2
14.8	16.0	21.0	21.4
65	124	252	760
80	100	100	100
3.7	5.1	5.4	3.2

H-Oil Desulfurization Costs

A variety of atmospheric and vacuum residuals can be desulfurized using the H-Oil process. Costs for desulfurizing Kuwait atmospheric, Kuwait vacuum, Khafji atmospheric, Khafji vacuum, Venezuelan atmospheric, and Venezuelan vacuum residuals are presented. These feedstocks were selected because they are representative of different types of crudes. The Kuwait atmospheric and vacuum residuals are representative of a high sulfur and low metals crude with moderate gravity and asphaltene content. The Khafji atmospheric and vacuum residuals reflect a high sulfur and moderate metals crude with moderate gravity and high asphaltene content. The Venezuelan atmospheric and vacuum residuals are representative of a low sulfur and high metals crude with moderate gravity and high ashpaltene content. The important feedstock properties are shown in Table I.

Figure 1 shows 975°F+ conversion and chemical hydrogen consumption varying with sulfur content in the 400°F+ fuel oil product. It is apparent that the relationship is an inverse one. In addition, the high metals (or Venezuelan feedstocks) experience the highest increase in conversion and hydrogen consumption when going to lower sulfur levels —followed by the Khafji and then the Kuwait, respectively. As expected the vacuum residual feeds consume the most hydrogen and represent the highest conversion operations.

Figure 2 is a graphical presentation of the processing costs for the feedstocks considered. The costs represent 1971 dollars and include fuel, power, labor, supervision, overhead, water, catalyst, and hydrogen. Figure 2 is intended to show the relative costs for desulfurizing the residual feedstocks considered. The economics, although accurate for this purpose, may not be specific enough for a given company because the costs do not reflect a return on investment. As is well known an acceptable rate

of return on investment differs among companies. Figures 1 and 2 are
based on pilot plant and commercial experience with some feedstocks.

The Kuwait atmospheric residual is the least expensive to process of
the six stocks. The Venezuelan vacuum bottoms are the most expensive,

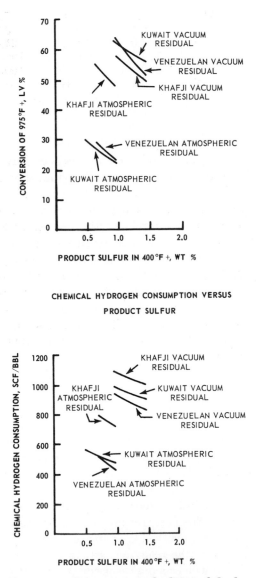

Figure 1. Conversion and chemical hydrogen consumption for hydrodesulfurization of
residuals with H-Oil

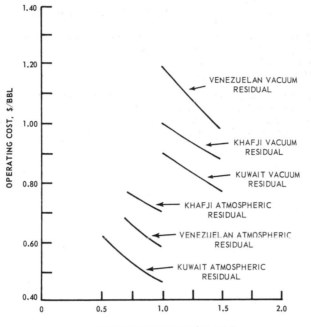

Figure 2.   *Processing costs for hydrodesulfurization of residuals with H-Oil*

Top: conversion vs. product sulfur. Bottom: chemical hydrogen consumption vs. product sulfur.

Note: Costs represent 1971 dollars and are for Gulf Coast Construction. Fuel @ 25¢/MM Btu, power @ 1¢/kW hr, water @ 1¢/M gal, labor @ $5.00/hr, supervision and overhead @ 50% of labor, catalyst @ 95¢/lb, hydrogen @ 35¢/MSCF, and depreciation @ 10% of investment. On-stream factor is 0.9.

followed by Khafji vacuum, Kuwait vacuum, Khafji atmospheric, and Venezuelan atmospheric, respectively. In addition, the Venezuelan stocks show the highest rate of increase in operating costs when going to lower sulfur levels.

Literature Cited

1. Stewart, N. C., Van Driesen, R. P., *Amer. Petrol. Inst., Div. Refining, Midyear Meetg., 29th,* May 12, 1964.
2. Griswold, C. R., Van Driesen, R. P., *Amer. Petrol. Inst., Div. Refining, Midyear Meetg., 21st,* May 11, 1966.
3. McFatter, W., Meaux, E., Mounce, W., Van Driesen, R. P., *Amer. Petrol. Inst., Div. Refining, Midyear Meetg., 34th,* May 13, 1969.
4. Mounce, W., Rubin, R. S., *AIChE, Nat. Meetg., 68th,* Feb. 28, 1971.
5. Galbreath, R. B., Van Driesen, R. P., Johnson, A. R., Alpert, S. B., *Jap. Petrol. Cong., Tokyo, Japan,* March 10, 1970.

6. Galbreath, R. B., Van Driesen, R. P., *World Petrol. Cong., Proc., 8th,*
   Moscow, June 13, 1971.
7. Alpert, S. B., Chervenak, M. C., Shuman, S. C., Wolk, R. H., *AIChE, Nat.*
   Meetg., 64th, March 16, 1967.
8. McKinnery, J. D., Stipanovich, J., *Amer. Petrol. Inst., Div. Refining, Mid-*
   year Meetg., 36th, May 13, 1971.

RECEIVED February 15, 1973. The H-Oil process was developed by Cities
Service Research and Development Co. and Hydrocarbon Research Inc. Units
have been licensed to the Kuwait National Petroleum Co., Humble Oil and
Refining Co., Petroleos Mexicanos, and Cities Service Oil Co.

H-Oil Desulfurization of Heavy Fuels

AXEL R. JOHNSON, RONALD H. WOLK, RAYMOND F. HIPPELI, and GOVANON NONGBRI

Hydrocarbon Research, Inc., 115 Broadway, New York, N.Y. 10006

Desulfurization of residual oils is of increasing importance because of the growing market for low sulfur fuels and the large share of the fuels market now being supplied by heavy oils. The following basic characteristics should be considered in the fuels-processing facility: the ability to process fuel oil at low unit cost, the ability to handle a range of residual fuels as feedstock, the capability of meeting changing fuel oil specification requirements, and the possibility of converting to an economical alternative process if there is a decreased demand for low sulfur fuel oils. The H-Oil process has the flexibility required to accomplish extremely low sulfur fuel oils even from difficult-to-process residues. Desulfurization is represented by a pseudo second-order kinetic model. The problems of low level sulfur content and catalyst aging can be successfully handled by the H-Oil process by using a multi-stage reactor approach with backstaging of the catalyst on a daily addition basis.

In many areas of the world residual fuel oil has become the principal source of industrial, commercial, and utility fuel. In these services it has historically been the marginal energy source with locally produced coal or natural gas being the fuel of choice for economic reasons. However air pollution control regulations relating to fuel sulfur content have limited many sources of coal, and in many important areas low cost natural gas is becoming critically short in supply. Because of these factors, fuel oil consumption is growing rapidly, and in many instances at a rate substantially above the normal growth in energy demand. This growth in demand, coupled with increasingly stringent sulfur-content specifications, is leading in the direction of a shortage in residual fuels, particularly those of lower sulfur contents.

These factors have already led to a substantial investment in fuel oil-desulfurization facilities in several parts of the world, notably Japan, the Middle East, and the Caribbean. With few exceptions these facilities have been based on indirect desulfurization, *i.e.*, vacuum distillation, desulfurization of the vacuum gas oil, and reblending. This technique has limits in a market for fuels below the 1% sulfur level because none of the heavy, high sulfur vacuum residue is processed. To some extent this can be mitigated by preferentially blending this material to bunkers and by using naturally occurring low sulfur residues as blending stocks.

In many supply and consumption areas we are now nearing or have passed the limits of these approaches, and the industry is giving serious consideration to facilities that will process the entire residue to achieve the desired end-product. This paper considers some of the problems associated with processing residual oils and presents some new developments in the H-Oil process. Because of these new developments it is now possible to design a processing facility which can economically produce fuel oils of 0.3% sulfur content interchangeably from a range of feedstocks encompassing most of the commercially important residues. One of the most significant aspects of these new developments involves the ability to economically desulfurize the high metals-content residues from Venezuela.

Factors Affecting a Fuels-Processing Facility

In this paper we will concentrate on the problems associated with a market-related fuels-processing facility—specifically one which would serve the U.S. East Coast. Planning such a facility involves the several fundamental questions considered below:

Source of Supply. The traditional source of fuel oil for the U.S. East Coast has been Venezuelan imports. Under the impact of the newer sulfur-content specifications, an increasing portion of this fuel is being taken from African crudes, and it is possible that the Middle East may also become an important supplier in this market. For these reasons, as well as from a national security standpoint—particularly as we become more dependent on fuel oil for basic energy—the refiner will be faced with the problem of handling a range of feedstocks.

Market Requirements. The requirements for low sulfur fuel oil have become increasingly stringent, and the market requirements for this product are subject to the vagaries of local and national regulations. Consequently market requirements cannot be forecast with a high degree of accuracy, and the facility must be flexible in terms of the quality of product produced.

Adaptability. In the future the market for low sulfur fuel oil may become less attractive for several reasons. Among these are: increasing use of nuclear energy, installation of stack gas-desulfurization processes, and increased availability of low sulfur fuels. Should this occur it would be desirable to put to alternative use any facility installed today to desulfurize fuel oil. At such a time, the market could revert to the traditional U.S. pattern in which high sulfur residual oil is a low value material, and there would be a consequent economic incentive to convert it to lighter products.

Considering these factors an optimum fuels-processing facility should possess the following basic characteristics: the ability to process fuel oil at low unit cost, the ability to handle a range of residual fuels as feedstock, the capability of meeting changing fuel oil specification requirements, and the possibility of converting to an economical alternative process if the demand for low sulfur fuel oils decreases. In a later section of this paper we describe a facility which meets these requirements. First, however, we consider some of the technical problems associated with residual oil processing, and how the solutions to these problems are approached in the H-Oil process.

Technical Aspects of Residue Desulfurization

Reaction Mechanism. Various investigators have shown that a first-order kinetic model adequately describes the desulfurization of the individual sulfur compounds contained in petroleum fractions. However we are not dealing with individual compounds or with a few similar species in residual oils but rather with a complex mixture of compounds having widely differing reaction rates. The compounds which react most easily will tend to disappear first and those having a lower reaction rate constant will desulfurize last, so desulfurization of these materials overall does not follow a first-order kinetic model. Beuther and Schmid (1) found that desulfurization of residues can be represented adequately by a second-order model. We recognized that the individual reactions were probably first order but that a second-order model would best represent the overall data. In a pseudo second-order approach, the increasing difficulty of desulfurization is reflected in the concentration term of the rate equation, enabling one to use a fixed-reaction rate constant.

Our work in this area has confirmed the observations of Beuther and Schmid, and in Figure 1 we show, for the desulfurization of Kuwait atmospheric residue, a comparison of the fit of the data to first- and second-order models. In developing this plot, average first- and second-order K values were calculated from data taken under various operating conditions over fresh catalyst. The curves shown were then prepared and compared with the data. The second-order relationship more accurately represents the situation. It must be remembered, however, that this is an empiricism and data extrapolations must be treated with caution.

A practical consequence of the pseudo second-order model is that, as market requirements dictate a lower sulfur content product, the reaction rate in the final stages of a process will be quite low. With a second-order model the reaction rate in the final incremental portion of a reactor system will be only one-tenth at the 0.3% sulfur level what it would be at the 1% sulfur level.

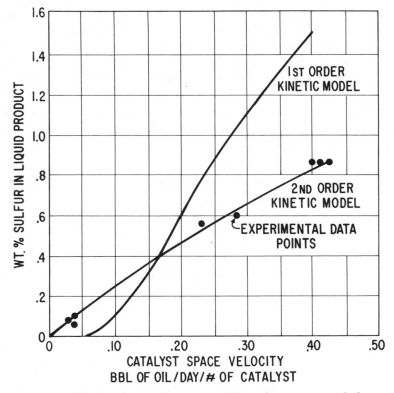

Figure 1. Comparison of kinetic models with experimental data, Kuwait atmospheric residual

Catalyst Aging. In hydroprocessing of residual oils, catalysts lose activity at a much higher rate than in gas-oil processing. This is a result of the organometallic compounds, asphaltenes, and the higher molecular weight of the material being processed. Further, there is a considerable range in the metals contents of the various stocks available for processing, and residues from different crudes will deactivate catalysts at different rates. Figure 2 illustrates this point in a comparison of the aging charac-

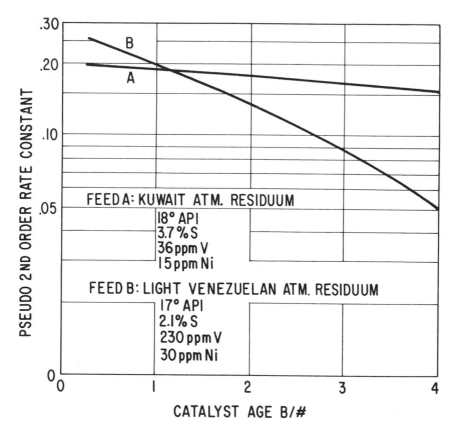

Figure 2. Variation of rate constant with catalyst age

teristics of Kuwait and Venezuelan atmospheric residues. Pseudo second-order reaction rate constant *vs.* catalyst age is plotted for these two stocks processed under the same conditions. Although both stocks exhibit a rate of activity decline considerably above that which would be experienced in processing gas oils, the effect of the higher metals content in the Venezuelan oil is readily apparent from the higher rate of activity decline.

Effect of H_2S on Reaction Rate. As the desulfurization reaction proceeds, H_2S is produced. This material, although mainly in the vapor phase, is in equilibrium with a concentration of dissolved H_2S in the liquid. Under certain conditions the mass action effect of this material can strongly influence the overall rate of the desulfurization reaction. Figure 3 shows the effect for one set of circumstances of H_2S partial pressure on the pseudo second-order reaction rate constant. Again the constant shown is not a true reaction rate constant—which would be independent of such parameters—but is an overall representation of several simultaneously occurring forward and reverse desulfurization reac-

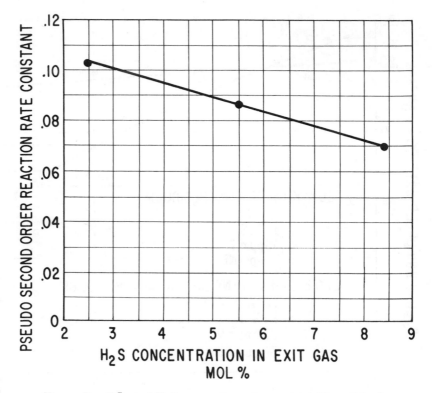

Figure 3.   Effect of H$_2$S on reaction rate constant, Kuwait feed

tions. When operations are directed to achieving very low levels of sulfur in the product, this effect—coupled with the other difficulties of such an operation—can have important design consequences.

The H-Oil Approach to the Production of Low Sulfur Fuel Oils

Several previous papers (2, 3, 4, 5) have reviewed the H-Oil process with respect to its principal characteristics and commercial performance. The major difference between H-Oil and the other processes for production of low sulfur fuels is a reactor system in which the oil and hydrogen are passed upflow through the reactor at a velocity sufficient to maintain the catalyst in a suspended or ebullated state. This reactor system offers several advantages. It is isothermal, it is not susceptible to pressure drop buildup from suspended materials contained in the feed, and catalyst can be added and withdrawn during operation to maintain a constant level of catalyst activity.

Reactor Staging. For practical purposes the H-Oil reactor can be considered as a completely back-mixed system. In such a reactor, the character of the reacting mixture is essentially identical to the material leaving the reactor. As a consequence of the second-order rate equation, $r = kc^2$ the reaction rate of the desulfurization reaction will be proportional to the square of the concentration of the effluent. As the process is required to produce a lower sulfur-content product, the reaction rate will decrease rapidly. As noted earlier the rate at 0.3% sulfur will be only one-tenth that at 1% sulfur. In theory then, a single reactor to produce a 0.3% sulfur product would be well over 10 times as large as one producing a 1% sulfur product, all other factors being equal.

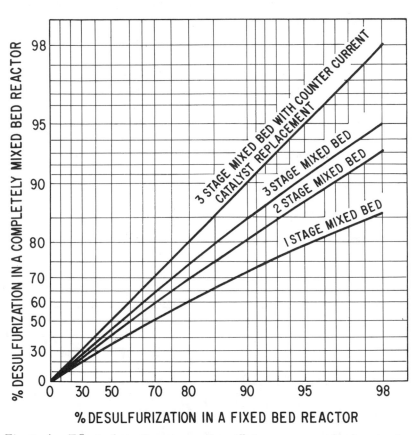

Figure 4. Effect of staging on reaction efficiency on completely mixed-bed reactors

In the H-Oil process this problem is solved by staging the reactor system by using two or more reactors in series. In this way the reaction takes place at several decreasing sulfur contents. This provides for higher reaction rates in those reactors in which the bulk of the desulfurization is occurring. Figure 4 illustrates this effect for the processing of Kuwait

atmospheric bottoms at various sulfur contents. Relationships are shown
for the desulfurization efficiency of one, two, and three stages in series
vs. a theoretical plus-flow reactor.

Catalyst Counterflow. A further area of design optimization relates
to the catalyst aging effects discussed earlier. If we use three H-Oil stages
in series in order to achieve a high degree of desulfurization, then there
is a distinct advantage in charging all of the makeup catalyst to the third
reactor stage. This material would then be withdrawn and charged to the
second stage, and in like fashion the second stage catalyst would be then
charged to the first reactor. We thereby achieve a counter-current flow
of oil and catalyst—the freshest catalyst is exposed to the cleanest oil in
the reactor which requires a high degree of catalyst activity because of
the low sulfur concentration present. At the same time the faster reactions take place in a reactor in which the catalyst has reached its final
equilibrium level before being discarded. The line for the back-staging
of catalyst in a three-stage system, shown in Figure 4, indicates that by
this approach virtual equivalence is attained between the H-Oil system
and a theoretical plus-flow reactor.

Split H$_2$ Recycle. A process flow scheme using the back-flow
catalyst/three-stage system is shown in Figure 5. This is basically the
reactor scheme which would be used within an H-Oil unit designed to
achieve very low sulfur contents. A further aspect of this system, shown
in Figure 5, is a split-recycle system. In this way, H$_2$S free-hydrogen
would be sent to the third reactor, thereby maintaining an extremely low
H$_2$S partial pressure at this critical point in the reactor system.

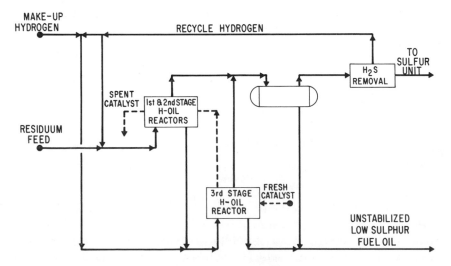

Figure 5.   Three-stage H-Oil system with catalyst back-flow

Residue Demetallization.   One of the most difficult problems associated with design of a facility to process a range of feedstocks has been the handling of those residues with a high concentration of organo-metallic compounds.   Figure 2 illustrates the rate at which H-Oil catalyst deactivates while processing a medium Venezuelan residual oil.   Operation with this feed to produce a low sulfur fuel would require a very high rate of catalyst addition.

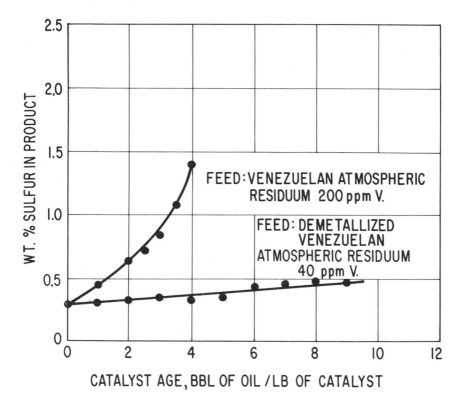

Figure 6.   Comparison of catalyst deactivation in desulfurizing virgin and demetallized Venezuelan atmospheric residues

A joint research program (Hydrocarbon Research, Inc.—Cities Service Research and Development Co.) has been underway for more than three years at the HRI laboratories to develop a demetallization procedure which would reduce the nickel and vanadium contents of fuel oils and thus produce an oil for further processing by H-Oil at low catalyst addition rates.   These research efforts have resulted in the development of solid adsorbent materials which are low in cost and which effectively remove the bulk of the organo-metallic compounds present in such oils. These solids are used in an H-Oil reactor with the conventional ebullated-

bed principle which is then followed by one or more H-Oil stages using conventional catalysts.

Figure 6 shows the effect of using this newly developed procedure in the processing of Venezuelan oil. The upper curve in Figure 6 shows the desulfurization of a medium Venezuelan residual oil as a function of catalyst age. The lower curve represents the performance of the same oil over the same catalyst after it has been processed through the newly developed demetallization procedure. The advantages of such an operation are obvious, and this procedure makes the processing of these oils at low rates of catalyst use practical. This procedure removes the limits previously placed on residue processing by metals content and all of the presently produced crudes can be considered for the production of low sulfur fuels.

New Catalyst Developments. In addition to the processing approaches discussed above, these two companies, together with several

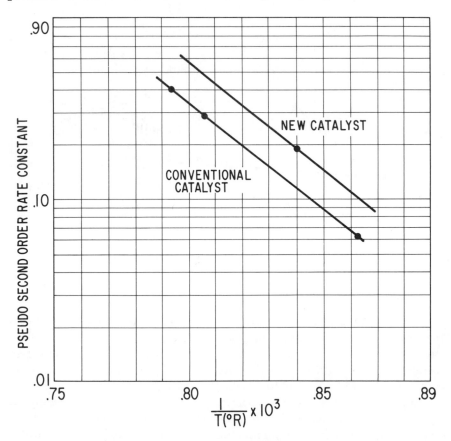

Figure 7. Comparison of new and conventional H-Oil catalysts, Kuwait feed

catalyst suppliers, have engaged in continuing development activities relating to improved H-Oil catalysts. These studies have covered catalyst composition, pore size distribution, catalyst size, *etc.* Figure 7 illustrates one of the more promising newer catalysts compared with the H-Oil catalyst which has been used in most commercial operations to date.

Characteristics of a Multi-Purpose Desulfurization Plant

We have noted earlier that a refiner or fuel processor must live in an uncertain environment. He is subject to the vagaries of the supply of crude, the requirements of the market, and the perpetual question of the future markets for residual fuel. We have developed a processing approach—using the H-Oil process—which provides the degree of flexibility necessary to cope with this uncertain environment. A schematic flow diagram of such a multi-purpose plant is shown in Figure 8. The basic feature of this plant, which has been designed for the production of 0.3% sulfur fuel oil from various atmospheric residues, is its flexibility with respect to feedstock, product specifications, and future alternative uses of the plant.

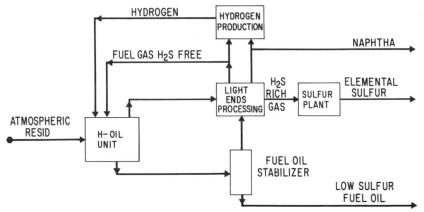

Figure 8.   Block flow diagram for multi-purpose desulfurization plant

The data developed in this illustration have been based on the conventional H-Oil catalyst. If one of the newer catalysts referred to earlier were used, the same results would be achieved at somewhat lower investment and at substantially reduced rates of catalyst use.

Base Operation. The feedstock flexibility of the plant is illustrated by the data in Table I. Using the identical plant, we show the ability of this facility to process Venezuelan, Kuwait, and West Texas atmospheric residues as well as West Texas vacuum residue to produce a 0.3% sulfur fuel oil product. The capacity of the plant varies with each of these stocks because of the varying sulfur contents and difficulty of processing the various raw materials. The refiner with such a unit should be able to change his source of supply amongst most of the commercially important crude sources, thereby optimizing his operation with respect to raw material supply.

When changing crude type, certain operational changes would be required. For example the optimum catalyst will vary with different crudes and for high metals stocks such as Venezuelan, the first reactor would be used for the demetallization procedure. These changes, however, would not require extensive shutdown and, apart from the change of catalyst type, the rest of the processing facility is completely adequate for all of the services.

Table I.   H-Oil Plant Performance—Manufacture of 0.3% Sulfur Fuel Oil from Various Feeds

	Feedstock			
Parameter	Kuwait Atmospheric Residuum	Medium Venezuelan Atmospheric Residuum	West Texas Atmospheric Residuum	West Texas Vacuum Residuum
Gravity, °API	17.0	17.2	17.7	10.5
Feed sulfur, wt %	3.8	2.2	2.2	3.2
Vol %, 975°F+	40.0	45.0	41	80.0
Plant throughout, BPSD	30,000	30,000	42,100	18,250
Total H_2 consumption, MM SCFD	21.9	21.9	21.9	21.9
H-Oil unit yields				
H_2S, wt %	3.7	2.3	2.1	3.4
C_1-C_3, wt %	1.6	2.3	0.8	2.8
C_4-350°F, vol %	7.8	9.6	3.9	11.5
350°F+fuel oil, vol %	95.0	94.0	98.7	94.9
Fuel oil sulfur, wt %	0.3	0.3	0.3	0.3
Catalyst replacement cost, $/bbl	0.15	0.16	0.04	0.18

Flexibility with Respect to Product Specifications. The same processing facility could, if it were desired for market reasons, readily produce a product of higher sulfur content or a variety of grades of products. In such a case, plant throughput would increase because hydrogen consumption per barrel of feed would be less. Should it be necessary to produce fuel oils having sulfur contents lower than 0.3%, this can be achieved in the same facility either by reducing flow rate through the plant or by separating some of the desulfurized vacuum residue for sales as bunkers thereby decreasing the sulfur content of the lighter product.

Future Applications. If nuclear power becomes more prevelant, or if stack gas-desulfurization processes are brought to the point of economic application, the market for low sulfur fuel oil may shrink and the price will decrease. Under either of these circumstances we would revert to the classic U.S. position in which high sulfur vacuum residue is a marginal product and a candidate for conversion to lighter materials.

The type of unit described here can, if desired, be used to convert vacuum residues to lighter materials or to prepare feed stock for low sulfur coke production. These applications of the process have been discussed in several previous papers. A good commercial example of this flexibility is shown in Table II. These data show operations of the Lake Charles H-Oil unit when processing for conversion and for desulfurization.

Table II. Commercial H-Oil Operations—Lake Charles, La.

Various West Texas Fractions

	Operation	
Parameter	Desulfurization	Conversion
Feedstock	sour atm residuum	vacuum residuum
°API	17.1	10.9
% Sulfur	2.80	1.95
% 975°F+	47.0	82.0
Goal achieved	100 vol % yield of stabilized 300°F+ fuel oil of 0.28% S	49% conversion of 975°F+ total product at 0.62% S

Table III. Fuels-Processing Complex—Investment and Operating Requirements (Operations Described in Table I)

	$
Investments,	
H-Oil unit	13,400,000
Light ends and gas processing	1,300,000
Hydrogen and sulfur plants	7,100,000
Offsites	5,500,000
Total investment	27,300,000
Operating Requirements	
Fuel, MMBtu/hr	—[a]
Power, kW	12,700
Steam, lbs/hr[b]	65,000
Cooling water, gal/min	4,750
Boiler feed water, gal/min	135
Catalyst and chemicals (other than H-Oil), $/day	225
Labor, men/shift	6

[a] Supplied from H-Oil gases and light ends.
[b] Net external steam requirement.

Fuel Oil Processing Costs. Figure 8 is a block flow diagram of the Lake Charles plant. Included are a hydrogen plant, a sulfur plant, and the H-Oil processing facility. The hydrogen plant is supplied with its fuel and raw material from the light products produced within the H-Oil system and therefore the entire complex requires no hydrocarbon raw material other than the fuel oil feed. This is a completely self-contained facility and is not dependent on the availability of natural gas or other hydrogen raw material.

Table IV.   Fuels-Processing Complex, Daily Processing Costs (Basis: 330 Days)

Items	$/SD
Investment-related costs at 20% of total capital	16,600
Labor-related items	1,440
Utilities[a]	3,550
Catalyst and chemicals (except H-Oil)	225
Total processing cost	21,815

[a] Utility unit costs: power 0.8c/kw hr, steam 70c/1000 lb, cooling water 0.3c/1000 gal, boiler feed water 3.0c/1000 gal. Hydrogen plant feed and fuel for the complex supplied from H-Oil gases, light ends, and 150 BPSD of product fuel oil.

Investment and operating requirements for the complex are presented in Table III, and in Table IV these factors have been converted into a daily processing cost exclusive of H-Oil catalyst. This latter item is specific to the feed in question. Unit processing costs are summarized for the various feedstocks in Table V which then shows the relationship between feed type and processing costs as well as the effect of product sulfur content on processing cost.

Fuels Refinery

The processing scheme just discussed uses atmospheric and vacuum residues as its raw material. Recently, consideration has been given to a fuels refinery concept in which whole crude oil is processed to yield only utility fuels. The processing sequence discussed in this paper would fit quite well into such a processing sequence. A block flow diagram of a fuels refinery is shown in Figure 9. Such a complex would produce low sulfur-content fuel oil, turbine fuel, and naphtha. The naphtha product could be a raw material for the production of either SNG or petrochemicals.

In summary, new developments in the H-Oil process have made it possible and practical to design a fuel-processing plant which would have

Table V. Feedstock Processing Cost

Feedstock	Charge, BPSD	Fuel Oil[a] Product, BPSD
Kuwait atm residuum	30,000	28,350
Lt. Venezuelan atm residuum	30,000	28,050
West Texas atm residuum	42,100	41,400
West Texas vac. residuum	18,250	17,165

Operating Cost (Ex. H-Oil Cat.), c/bbl Feed	H-Oil Catalyst Replacement Cost, c/bbl Feed	Total Processing Cost, c/bbl Feed
73	15	88
73	16	89
52	4	56
120	18	138

[a] After plant fuel consumption.

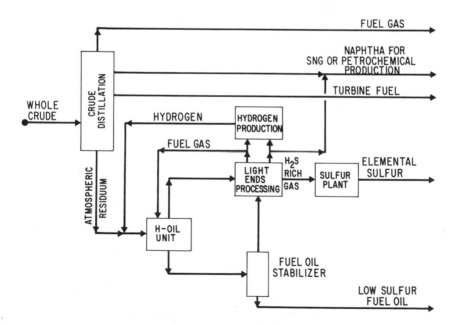

Figure 9. Fuels refinery

the flexibility necessary to handle raw crudes from various sources and to enable the processor to meet the varying requirements of the markets which may be imposed on him with changing product specifications and product requirements.

Acknowledgments

We express our appreciation to Hydrocarbon Research, Inc. and Cities Service Research and Development Co. for permission to publish this work, and we recognize the contributions of many members of the staffs of both companies to the development presented herein. Specifically, the contributions of M. C. Chervenak and L. M. Lehman of Hydrocarbon Research, Inc., and R. P. Van Driesen of Cities Service Research and Development Company are gratefully acknowledged.

Literature Cited

1. Beuther, H., Schmid, B. K., *World Petrol. Cong., Proc., 6th, Frankfurt,* 1963, Section III, paper 20–PD7.
2. Griswold, C. R., Van Driesen, R. P., *Amer. Petrol. Inst., Div. of Refining,* May 11, 1966, paper 53–66.
3. Van Driesen, R. P., Rapp, L. M., *World Petrol. Cong., Proc., 7th, Mexico City,* 1967, paper I.P. No. 32.
4. Johnson, A. R., Papso, J. E., Hippeli, R. F., Nongbri, G., *Amer. Petrol. Inst., Div. of Refining,* May 15, 1970, Houston, Tex., papers 48–70.
5. Johnson, A. R., Papso, J. E., Hippeli, R. F., Wolk, R., *Ann. Meetg., Nat. Petrol. Refiners Ass.,* March 21–23, 1971, San Francisco, Calif., paper AM–71–17.

RECEIVED February 15, 1973.

11

Low Sulfur Fuel by Pressurized Entrainment Carbonization of Coal

ROBERT J. BELT and MICHAEL M. RODER

Morgantown Energy Research Center, Bureau of Mines,
U.S. Department of the Interior, P.O. Box 880, Morgantown, W. Va. 26505

Coal containing 2.5% sulfur was processed into a char containing 0.7% sulfur, or 0.49 lb sulfur/MMBtu, by pressure carbonization of the coal at 1900°F and 400 psig in a gas consisting of 91% hydrogen and 9% nitrogen. Temperature, pressure, and hydrogen content of the entraining gas influenced the total and organic sulfur content of the char and the sulfur content per unit heating value; only temperature and pressure affected the pyritic sulfur content of the char. Sulfate sulfur was unaffected by any of the three variables. Relatively low carbonization temperatures produced a char with a high volatile-matter content, and vice-versa. Char yield decreased with increase in temperature; pressure and hydrogen concentration had no effect. Char heating value was virtually the same at all conditions. An empirical approach that included a mathematical model proved useful in predicting the sulfur content of chars produced over a specified range of operating conditions.

R apid entrainment carbonization of powdered coal under pressure in a partial hydrogen atmosphere was investigated as a means of producing low sulfur char for use as a power plant fuel. Specific objectives of the research were to determine if an acceptable product could be made and to establish the relationship between yields and chemical properties of the char, with special emphasis on type and amount of sulfur compound in the product. The experiments were conducted with a 4-inch diameter by 18-inch high carbonizer according to a composite factorial design (1, 2). Results of the experiments are expressed by empirical mathematical models and are illustrated by the application of response surface analysis.

Previous work with a 4-inch diameter by 12-inch high entrainment-type carbonizer showed that chars containing considerably less sulfur than the parent coals could be produced by rapid carbonization (3), and that the most important variables were temperature, pressure, and type of entraining gas. In the experiments with the 18-inch high carbonizer, all other variables—coal rate, size range and type, residence time, entraining gas rate, and run length—were held constant to determine the effect of the three main factors on char yield and voltaile matter concentration and the content of organic, pyritic, and sulfate sulfur in the char.

Equipment and Procedure

Carbonization runs were made with the equipment shown in Figure 1. The carbonizer was designed for temperatures to 2000°F, pressures to 500 psi, and coal rates to 500 grams/hr. Coal from a closed, pressure-equalized hopper was injected by a vibratory screw feeder into a gas stream that carried the particles at high velocity into the carbonizer. Another stream of gas entered the top of the carbonizer *via* a preheater that heated the gas to the carbonization temperature.

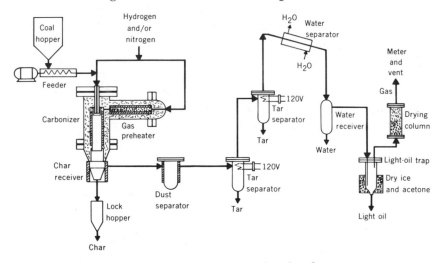

Figure 1.   Flow diagram of pressurized coal-carbonization system

The carbonizer was 4 inches in diameter by 18 inches long and was made of type 310 alloy steel, schedule 40 pipe. Three pairs of 6-inch long, semi-circular thermoshell heating elements enclosed the carbonizing tube. The preheater was a 4-inch diameter by 2-ft long coil of 1/4-inch stainless steel tubing surrounded by two pair of 12-inch long semi-circular thermoshell heating elements.

All solid and liquid products were recovered from the gas stream. Coarse particles of char were recovered in the lock hopper at the bottom of the carbonizer; char fines and carbon fines were extracted by a hot-dust knockout chamber. Tar and pitch were removed by two knockout chambers in series, and water and light oil were separated by means of a water condenser followed by solid CO_2 and silica-gel traps. Clean gas was passed through a pressure letdown system, metered, and vented. Yields of dust, tar, light oil, and gas were not determined.

The carbonizer was preheated to the desired (constant) temperature, the system was pressurized to the desired level, and the gas flows were set to the predetermined rates and compositions. Coal was then injected to begin the run. The carbonizer was designed to heat the coal particles rapidly as they passed through the 18-inch long hot zone. Pyrolization and devolatilization were effected in less than 1 sec. Two hundred grams/hr of 70%-through-200-mesh Pittsburgh-bed high-volatile A bituminous coal were processed in 2-hr runs. Entraining gas was admitted at a rate of 20 actual ft³/hr. During the run, char was periodically removed from the bottom lock hopper, and gas samples were removed for analysis.

Experimental Plan

Experiments in the carbonization of coal to produce low sulfur char were carried out and evaluated by means of a three-step procedure. Carbonization runs were first conducted to obtain data at various combinations of the three major independent variables. These data were then used to develop an empirical mathematical model that described the carbonization system. Finally, response surface analysis was used to interpret the empirical model and to predict the relationship between process variables and char yield and quality.

Table I.   Design of the Experiment

Factor	*Coded Design Coordinate*					Symbol
	−2	−1	0	1	2	
Temperature, °F	1500	1600	1700	1800	1900	X_1
Pressure, psig	0	100	200	300	400	X_2
Hydrogen in nitrogen, %	0	25	50	75	100	X_3

The carbonization runs were carried out according to a composite factorial design covering temperature, pressure, and entraining gas composition—each at five levels. Carbonization temperature was varied from 1500° to 1900°F in 100° increments and is represented by X_1. Operating pressure, X_2, was varied from 0 to 400 psig in 100-psig increments. Entraining gas composition (hydrogen in nitrogen), X_3, was varied from 0-100% H_2 at 25% intervals. Table I shows the levels of the operating conditions.

As illustrated by Figure 2, a three-dimensional coordinate system was assumed with temperature, pressure, and entraining gas composition as the axes. Points at the eight corners of the cube represent the two-level part of the factorial design; the remaining points represent the composite portion of the design. Each numbered point represents one experimental run, and the center represents five additional runs, totaling 19 runs. Computation of the variance of the system was based on the five runs shown at the center. Actual experimental conditions are shown in the table that accompanies the sketch.

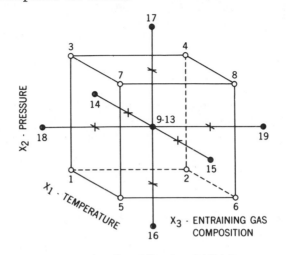

Location of Experimental Points

| Experiment | Operating Variables | | |
	Temperature, °F	Pressure, psig	Entraining gas composition [1]
1	1,600	100	25
2	1,600	100	75
3	1,600	300	25
4	1,600	300	75
5	1,800	100	25
6	1,800	100	75
7	1,800	300	25
8	1,800	300	75
9-13	1,700	200	50
14	1,500	200	50
15	1,900	200	50
16	1,700	0	50
17	1,700	400	50
18	1,700	200	0
19	1,700	200	100

[1] Volume-percent H_2 in N_2

Figure 2. Three-factor composite design

Results

The following results are based on the analyses of data by means of response surface analysis. The three-dimensional empirical models were developed at the 95% confidence level. In other words, 95% of the time the results obtained from the empirical model will match the actual data obtained.

As stated, char yield and char quality were of primary interest, the latter depending on the concentration of total sulfur, organic sulfur, pyritic sulfur, sulfate sulfur, and volatile matter, and on the heating value and ratio of sulfur content to the heating value. Concentrations of constituents in the char are given as a weight percentage. Table II gives the actual experimental data for runs at various combinations of operating conditions. Table III presents the mathematical model of the data including regression equations, reliability estimates, and maxima and minima within the experimental design limits.

Char Yield. Figure 3 shows predicted char yield plotted as a function of temperature, pressure, and entraining gas composition. Char yield values of 800, 880, 960 lbs/ton of coal are shown. Within the limits of the experiments, yields ranged from 654 to 1210 lbs/ton (Table III). Temperature had a considerable effect on char yield, as was also found in the prior work (3): Yields decreased with an increase in temperature. Although pressure variation alone had little effect on char yield, the *combined* effect of temperature and pressure was important. For example, yields were lower when temperature and pressure were both high and both low. However, when the temperature was the lowest and the pressure was the highest, yields were higher; this was also true when the temperature was the highest and the pressure was the lowest. The standard deviation and per cent variation indicate that the model is a good fit to the experimental data.

Char Quality. Sulfur does not occur as an element in coal or char; it is present in chemical combination in the form of organic compounds, iron sulfides, and sulfates (4). Total sulfur is the sum of the weight percentage concentrations of all three. As shown in Table III, total sulfur left in the char ranged from 0.7 to 2.8%, often a substantial decrease from the amount in the parent coal (2.55%). Figure 4 shows total sulfur surfaces for values ranging from 1.0 to 2.5%. Crowding of the curved surfaces in the upper left-hand corner of the cube clearly shows the decrease in amount of sulfur in the char with increase in the temperature, pressure, and per cent hydrogen in the entraining gas. Within the experimental limits, the models indicate that a char can be produced containing a minimum amount of sulfur (0.7%) at 1900°F, 400 psig, and 91% hydrogen in the entraining gas. Production of 0.7% sulfur char indicates more than a 70% reduction in sulfur from the original coal.

Organic sulfur accounts for about three-fourths of the total sulfur in the char. A three-dimensional plot of the values of organic sulfur as a function of temperature, pressure, and entraining gas composition is shown in Figure 5. By comparing this figure with the one for total sulfur (Figure 4), a similar relationship between the two plots can readily be

Table II.   Data Representing Char Yield and Quality

Run	X_1: Temp., °F	X_2: Pres., psig	X_3: H_2, %	S Content in Char, wt %			
				Total	Organic	Pyritic	Sulfate
1	1600	100	25	2.00	1.72	0.23	0.05
2	1600	100	75	1.98	1.67	0.27	0.04
3	1600	300	25	1.79	1.47	0.27	0.05
4	1600	300	75	1.72	1.44	0.24	0.04
5	1800	100	25	1.79	1.29	0.48	0.02
6	1800	100	75	1.88	1.33	0.51	0.04
7	1800	300	25	1.56	1.01	0.54	0.01
8	1800	300	75	1.16	0.66	0.49	0.01
15	1900	200	50	1.29	0.80	0.46	0.03
14	1500	200	50	1.83	1.22	0.56	0.05
17	1700	400	50	1.43	1.00	0.38	0.05
16	1700	0	50	2.28	1.60	0.64	0.04
19	1700	200	100	1.69	1.23	0.41	0.05
18	1700	200	0	2.16	1.73	0.39	0.04
9	1700	200	50	1.53	1.20	0.31	0.02
10	1700	200	50	1.64	1.19	0.43	0.02
11	1700	200	50	1.58	1.13	0.40	0.05
12	1700	200	50	1.62	1.29	0.27	0.06
13	1700	200	50	1.58	1.40	0.16	0.02

[a] Coal carbonized was Pittsburgh-bed high-volatile A bituminous with the following

observed. For instance, as in the case of total sulfur, an increase in temperature, pressure, and per cent hydrogen in the entraining gas decreased the amount of organic sulfur in the char. Theoretically, as indicated in Table III, carbonization at 1900°F, 400 psig, and 100% hydrogen in the entraining gas would produce a char containing virtually no organic sulfur. The reliability of the models for both total sulfur and organic sulfur is good, based on the variability shown in Table III.

Approximately one-fourth of the total sulfur in the char is in the form of pyritic sulfur. As shown by Figure 6, the amount of pyritic sulfur reached a minimum value of about 0.25% at 1650°F, 230 psig, and 50% hydrogen in the entraining gas. Increasing or decreasing values of the variables tend to increase the amount of pyritic sulfur. Pressure and temperature had a greater effect on pyritic sulfur than did per cent hydrogen in the entraining gas. The model for pyritic sulfur is not good as reflected by the high variation from the average. This may be the result of other factors varying randomly in the experiment or more likely an accumulation of sampling and analysis errors. A minimum value of pyritic sulfur is indicated within the experimental limits even though the model reliability is low.

as a Function of Variable Operating Conditions[a]

S/Heating Value, lb/MMBtu	Vol. Matter, % of Char	Heating Value, Btu/lb	Char Yield, lb/ton Coal
1.561	9.9	12,810	1010
1.549	9.9	12,790	922
1.398	8.3	12,800	1062
1.339	9.4	12,850	1012
1.450	5.7	12,350	916
1.482	8.0	12,690	934
1.166	4.8	13,380	908
0.926	5.5	12,530	854
0.997	5.7	12,940	752
1.434	10.6	12,770	858
1.092	7.3	13,100	914
1.811	10.4	12,590	890
1.290	10.8	13,100	936
1.701	7.7	12,700	1036
1.209	7.1	12,660	856
1.288	8.3	12,730	920
1.254	7.8	12,600	866
1.310	7.2	12,370	884
1.243	7.2	12,710	886

analysis: sulfur 2.55%, volatile matter 34.0%, and heating value 14,090 Btu/lb.

Sulfate sulfur is also inadequately described by the system model. The lack of significant coefficients in the regression equation and a high per cent variation (20.8%) of the results indicate that no valid conclusions may be drawn for this response. The low quantities of sulfate sulfur in both the coal and char place the analytical errors in the same order of magnitude as the variations between samples, and this fact limits the usefulness of the model for sulfate sulfur.

Char Sulfur Content Per Unit Heating Value. Probably the best way to express the amount of sulfur concentration of a fuel is in pounds of sulfur per million Btu heating value of the fuel (char). Ordinarily, this ratio would be a function of the amount of total sulfur in the char and the heating value of the char. However, since the heating value of the char changes very little within the experimental limits (discussed later in this paper), values for the amount of sulfur per heating value are essentially the same as those obtained for per cent total sulfur. Figure 7 shows that an increase in temperature, pressure, and per cent hydrogen in the entraining gas decreases the amount of sulfur per million Btu. Within the experimental limits, the model indicates that a char containing

Table III.   Mathematical

Response	Regression Equation[a]	Reliability Estimate[b]		
		Av.	Std Dev.	Av. % Dev.
Total sulfur, % of char	$1.592 + 0.066\ X_2{}^2 + 0.083\ X_3{}^2$ $-\ 0.136\ X_1 - 0.195\ X_2$ $-\ 0.084\ X_3 - 0.06\ X_1X_2$ $-\ 0.028\ X_1X_3 - 0.067\ X_2X_3$	1.59	0.04	2.4
Organic sulfur, % of char	$1.299 - 0.065\ X_1{}^2 + 0.053\ X_3{}^2$ $-\ 0.178\ X_1 - 0.164\ X_2$ $-\ 0.087\ X_3 - 0.059\ X_1X_2$ $-\ 0.028\ X_1X_3 - 0.046\ X_2X_3$	1.24	0.11	7.0
Pyritic sulfur, % of char	$0.262 + 0.056\ X_1{}^2 + 0.056\ X_2{}^2$ $+\ 0.0506\ X_1 - 0.0294\ X_2$	0.31	0.11	19.0
Sulfate sulfur, % of char	$0.0233 - 0.0088\ X_1$	0.03	0.02	20.8
Sulfur per heating value, lb/MMBtu	$1.264 + 0.047\ X_2{}^2 + 0.058\ X_3{}^2$ $-\ 0.106\ X_1 - 0.166\ X_2$ $-\ 0.069\ X_3 - 0.058\ X_1X_2$ $-\ 0.017\ X_1X_3 - 0.04\ X_2X_3$	1.26	0.04	2.5
Volatile matter, % of char	$6.84 + 0.25\ X_1{}^2 + 0.42\ X_2{}^2$ $+\ 0.51\ X_3{}^2 - 1.45\ X_1$ $-\ 0.74\ X_2 + 0.64\ X_3$ $+\ 0.22\ X_1X_3$	7.51	0.55	5.9
Heating value, Btu/10^{-4} lb	$1.259 + 0.006\ X_1{}^2 + 0.006\ X_2{}^2$ $+\ 0.008\ X_3{}^2 + 0.012\ X_2$ $+\ 0.010\ X_1X_2 + 0.007\ X_1X_3$ $+\ 0.014\ X_2X_3$	1.261	0.014	0.9
Char yield, % of feed coal	$46.7 - 1.29\ X_1{}^2 + 0.97\ X_3{}^2$ $-\ 1.89\ X_1 + 0.32\ X_2$ $-\ 1.17\ X_3 - 1.44\ X_1X_2$ $+\ 0.64\ X_1X_3$	44.12	1.22	3.0

[a] X_1, X_2, X_3 are temperature, pressure, per cent H_2 in N_2, respectively, in coded co-ordinates (see Table I).
[b] Based on replications at center of design.

Model Results

				Predicted Limits in Exptl Range				
	Minimum					*Maximum*		
		Conditions[c]					*Conditions*[c]	
Value	*Temp.,* °*F*	*Pres.,* *psig*	*EGC,*[d] *%*	*Value*	*Temp.,* °*F*	*Pres.,* *psig*	*EGC,*[d] *%*
0.73	1900 (2)	400 (2)	91 (1.64)	2.82	1500 (−2)	0 (−2)	100 (2)
<0.0	1900 (2)	400 (2)	100 (2)	1.90	1600 (−1)	0 (−2)	100 (2)
0.25	1650 (−0.5)	230 (0.3)	50 (0)	0.87	1900 (2)	0 (−2)	100 (2)
0.01	1900 (2)	300 (1)	25 (−1)	0.04	1500 (−2)	400 (2)	0 (−2)
0.53	1900 (2)	400 (2)	91 (1.64)	2.09	1600 (−1)	0 (−2)	100 (2)
4.09	1900 (2)	320 (1.2)	25 (−1)	16.3	1500 (−2)	0 (−2)	100 (2)
1.30	1770 (0.7)	0 (−2)	10 (−1.6)	1.49	1900 (2)	400 (2)	100 (2)
32.7	1900 (2)	400 (2)	55 (+0.2)	60.5	1500 (−2)	400 (2)	0 (−2)

[c] Coded coordinates are listed in parentheses.
[d] Entraining gas composition, hydrogen in nitrogen.

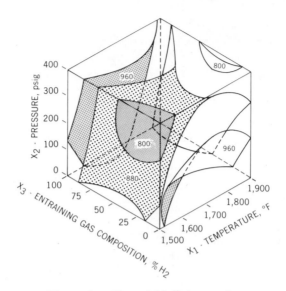

Figure 3.   Char yield, lb/ton coal

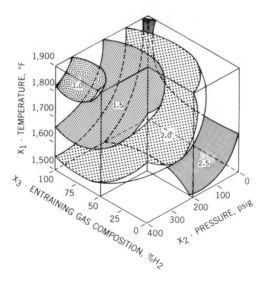

Figure 4.   Total sulfur in char, %

a minimum of 0.49 lb sulfur/MMBtu could be produced at 1900°F, 400 psig, and 91% hydrogen in the entraining gas.

Volatile Matter and Heating Value. As expected from the results of this experiment and prior work (3), char containing a maximum of volatile matter was produced at relatively low temperatures, and char containing the minimum was produced at higher temperatures. Pressure and type of entraining gas had little effect on the amount of volatile matter remaining in the char. Table III indicates that (within the experimental limits) char produced at 1900°F, 320 psig, and 25% hydrogen in the entraining gas would contain the minimum volatile matter—4.09%. Char produced at conditions that give the minimum total sulfur content (0.7%) would contain 7.38% volatile matter. Figure 8 is a graphic representation of predicted char volatile matter curves as a function of temperature, pressure, and entraining gas compositions.

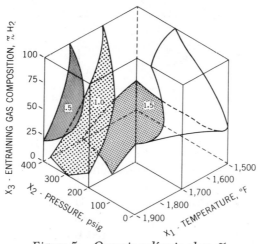

Figure 5.   Organic sulfur in char, %

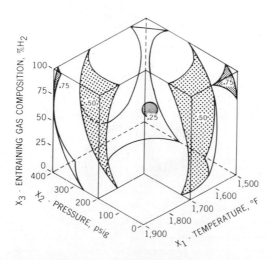

Figure 6.   Pyritic sulfur in char, %

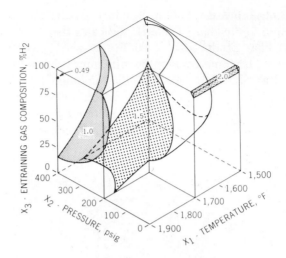

Figure 7.   Sulfur in char per unit heating value,
lb S/10⁶ Btu

As shown in Table II, char heating values ranged between 12,350 and 13,380 Btu/lb. In the three-dimensional plot (not shown), the portion of the curves that fell within the experimental limits was nearly flat. Because of the narrow range in the data and the flatness of the curves, it can be concluded that neither temperature, pressure, nor per cent hydrogen in the entraining gas affected the char heating value.

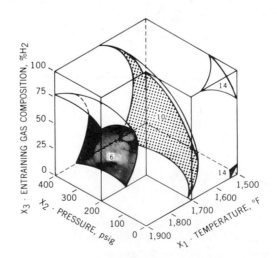

Figure 8.   Volatile matter in char, %

Summary and Conclusions

A low sulfur char was successfully produced by pressurized carbonization of coal, using hydrogen in nitrogen as a hot entraining gas. According to empirical models, a char containing 0.7% sulfur, or 0.49 lb sulfur/MMBtu, could be produced at 1900°F, 400 psig, and 91% hydrogen in nitrogen. Theoretical characteristics and properties of char produced under these conditions are compared with those of the parent coal in Table IV.

Table IV. Comparison of Pittsburgh Bed High Volatile A Bituminous Coal and Char Produced at 1900° F, 400 psig, and 91% H_2, 9% N_2 Entraining Gas

Characteristic	*Coal*	*Char*[a]
Char yield, wt %		34.0
Sulfur, wt %		
Total	2.55	0.70
Organic	1.49	0.00
Pyritic	0.93	0.77
Sulfate	0.13	0.038
Sulfur/Btu ratio, lb/MMBtu	1.81	0.49
Analysis, wt %		
Volatile matter	33.98	7.38
Ash	7.28	15.68
Hydrogen	5.23	2.19
Total carbon	76.4	80.3
Fixed carbon	53.51	76.41
Water	0.8	0.8
Calorific value, Btu/lb	14,300	13,300

[a] All values are theoretical. Sum of the organic, pyritic, and sulfate sulfur percentages will not necessarily equal the value for total sulfur.

Major conclusions drawn from this work are:

(1) Total sulfur and organic sulfur content of the char and sulfur content per unit of heating value decreased with increase in temperature, pressure, and hydrogen concentration in the entraining gas.

(2) Pyritic sulfur content depended only on the carbonization temperature and pressure.

(3) Sulfate sulfur was unaffected by temperature, pressure, or entraining gas composition.

(4) Carbonization temperature, as would be expected, was of prime importance in regard to the concentration of volatile matter in the resulting char; relatively low temperatures produced a char with a high volatile-matter content, and vice-versa.

(5) Char yield decreased with increase in temperature; pressure and entraining gas composition had no effect. Char heating value was not significantly influenced by any of the three variables.

An empirical approach that included a mathematical model was beneficial in predicting the sulfur content of chars produced from coal over a specified range of operation conditions. The technique was useful for predicting the conditions required for a specified product. For instance, the model for total sulfur indicates that a char containing less than 0.7% sulfur could probably be produced at temperatures and pressures higher than those investigated in this experiment.

Literature Cited

1. Davies, O. L., "Design and Analysis of Industrial Experiments," 2nd ed., Hafner Publishing Co., New York, 1967.
2. Himmelblau, D. M., "Process Analysis of Statistical Methods," John Wiley & Sons, New York, 1968.
3. Belt, R. J., Wilson, J. S., Sebastian, J. J. S., *Fuel* (1971) **50**, 381–393.
4. Walker, F. E., Hartner, F. E., *Bureau Mines Info. Circ.* **8301**, 1966, 51 pp.

RECEIVED February 15, 1973.

Wet Scrubbing of Sulfur Oxides from Flue Gases

M. R. GOGINENI, W. C. TAYLOR, A. L. PLUMLEY,
and JAMES JONAKIN

Combustion Engineering, Inc., Windsor, Conn. 06095

The controlling chemical reaction for the lime/limestone wet scrubbing SO_2 removal systems is calcium sulfite plus sulfur dioxide to form calcium bisulfite. Methods of preventing both calcium sulfite and calcium sulfate scaling are available. The marble bed is a good vapor–liquid contactor with a tray efficiency of 90–95%. The reaction tanks were designed using rate constants determined by Combustion Engineering, Inc. Full-scale C-E air pollution control systems that have been installed on utility steam generators consist of five furnace injection and three tail-end systems. Although many uses for the waste products produced in the air pollution control systems are being studied, land-fill and impounding are currently being used for waste disposal.

The need for removing SO_2 from stack gases of oil- and coal-fired combustion equipment has been and is being emphasized by the stringent emission limitations established by the Environmental Protection Agency and other government agencies. The EPA standards are 1.2 lbs/10^6 Btu for coal and 0.8 lb/10^6 Btu for oil. More stringent requirements in certain districts have been passed. An example is Clark County, Nev. which limits SO_2 emissions for a 1,500,000 kW steam-generating unit to 0.15 lb/10^6 Btu or one-eighth of the EPA requirement. To meet these requirements a high percent of SO_2 must be removed from stack gases produced from the combustion of most oil and coal fuels.

Figure 1 is a nomograph for determining the percent of SO_2 removal required for different fuels to meet a given standard. Even for the so-called low sulfur fuels it can be seen that in many cases SO_2 removal systems will be required to meet emission standards.

There are several ways to classify processes for the removal of SO_2 from stack gases: wet or dry, recovery or non-recovery, and absorption, adsorption, or catalytic oxidation. Except for catalytic oxidation, each of these has been described by others in this volume. In reviewing these processes and many others, Combustion Engineering (C-E) decided that wet lime/limestone scrubbing without recovery of sulfur was worth developing because of its simplicity and low cost.

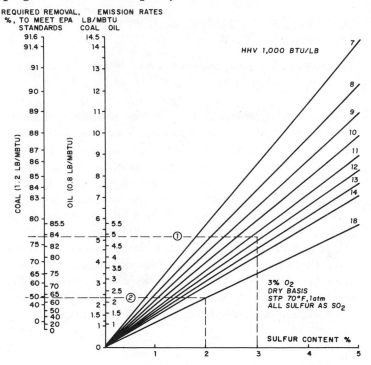

Figure 1.   Percent of SO_2 removal required for different fuels

The development of C-E's air pollution control system started in 1964 with the construction of a small pilot facility in our laboratories. A second pilot application on a Detroit Edison Co. unit in 1966 and 1967 followed. Table I lists the full-scale installations (1) that have been sold to date by C-E. In a move to accelerate further development, a large laboratory prototype unit of 12,500 cfm capacity was constructed and began operations in early 1970 (2).

The controlling chemical reactions for the lime/limestone wet scrubbing SO_2 removal systems have been established. In both the lime and limestone systems, the principal absorption reaction is calcium sulfite plus sulfur dioxide to form calcium bisulfite. Methods of preventing both calcium sulfite and calcium sulfate scaling are presented.

Chemistry of SO_2 Removal System

The possible reactions taking place within the wet lime/limestone SO_2 removal system have been studied. Our conclusions relative to the controlling reactions are based on consideration of theoretical equations in light of operating experience in both field and pilot systems. Because there is considerable difference in operating conditions required to provide adequate SO_2 removal in the absence of scale or deposit formation when utilizing lime or limestone as additives, the chemical reactions of the systems are treated separately. The essential reactions governing these systems are:

Calcium hydroxide or lime system reactions

$$CaO + H_2O \rightleftarrows Ca(OH)_2 \tag{1}$$

$$Ca(OH)_2 + SO_2 \rightleftarrows CaSO_3 + H_2O \tag{2}$$

$$CaSO_3 + SO_2 + H_2O \rightleftarrows Ca(HSO_3)_2 \tag{3}$$

$$Ca(HSO_3)_2 + Ca(OH)_2 \rightleftarrows 2CaSO_3 + 2H_2O \tag{4}$$

Calcium carbonate or limestone system reactions

$$CaCO_3 + CO_2 + H_2O \rightleftarrows Ca(HCO_3)_2 \tag{5}$$

$$2SO_2 + Ca(HCO_3)_2 \rightleftarrows Ca(HSO_3)_2 + 2CO_2 \tag{6}$$

$$CaSO_3 + SO_2 + H_2O \rightleftarrows Ca(HSO_3)_2 \tag{7}$$

$$2CaSO_3 + O_2 \rightarrow 2CaSO_4 \tag{8}$$

$$Ca(HSO_3)_2 + 2CaCO_3 \rightleftarrows 2CaSO_3 + Ca(HCO_3)_2 \tag{9}$$

Following the initial steps of hydration (Reaction 1) and formation of calcium sulfite (Reaction 2), removal of SO_2 in the lime or calcium hydroxide system depends on the formation of calcium bisulfite by reaction of suspended calcium sulfite with sulfur dioxide and water (Reaction 3).

The control of sulfite scaling requires that a minimum amount of free hydroxide ion be recirculated to the scrubber; therefore, fresh additive (lime or slaked lime) is added in the reaction tank external to the scrubber where calcium sulfite is formed (Reaction 4). An amount of calcium sulfite equivalent to the SO_2 removed (or the fresh $Ca(OH)_2$ added) is conveyed from the system to a pond or vacuum filter, and the remainder is recycled to continue the removal process.

The principal absorption reactions for the calcium carbonate system are shown in Reactions 5, 6, and 7. Sulfur dioxide reacts with the relatively soluble bicarbonate to form calcium bisulfite. In addition, solid

Name	Size, MW	Fuel
Furnace injection		
1. Union Electric, Meramec No. 2	140	coal
2. Kansas Power & Light, Lawrence No. 4	125	coal/gas
3. Kansas Power & Light, Lawrence No. 5	430	coal/gas
4. Kansas City Power & Light, Hawthorn Nos. 3 and 4 (each)	100	coal
Tail-end		
1. Louisville Gas & Electric, Paddy's Run No. 6	70	coal
2. Northern State Power, Sherburne Nos. 1 and 2 (each)	700	coal (low sulfur)

calcium sulfite recycled from the reaction tank reacts with SO_2 to form bisulfite.

The reactions in which sulfite is oxidized to sulfate (Reaction 8) and soluble bisulfite is converted to a insoluble calcium sulfite (Reaction 9) account for the waste products as well as the regeneration of the solid calcium sulfite reactant that is recirculated to the scrubber. The ratio of calcium sulfite to calcium sulfate found in the air pollution control system solid waste depends on the extent to which these reactions go to completion.

Deposit and Scale Formation

Calcium sulfite and calcium sulfate scaling in the system can be a problem for the lime/limestone wet scrubber systems. Scaling occurs when the solutions are supersaturated to a point where heterogeneous crystallization (crystallization on foreign surfaces such as the scrubber walls, overflow pots, marbles) takes place, resulting from nucleation. The ratios of the products of the activities (A) of Ca^{2+} and SO_4^{2-} or SO_3^{2-} to their solubility product constants (K_{SP}) as a measure of the degree of supersaturation are:

$$\left(\frac{A_{Ca^{2+}}\, A_{SO_4^{2-}}}{K_{SP(Ca\,SO4)}}\right), \left(\frac{A_{Ca^{2+}}\, A_{SO_3^{2-}}}{K_{SP(Ca\,SO3)}}\right) \quad \begin{array}{l} <1 \text{ subsaturation} \\ =1 \text{ saturation} \\ >1 \text{ supersaturation} \end{array}$$

Laboratory experiments have shown that heterogeneous crystallization is not significant until the ratio of the activity product to the solubility product constant reaches about 1.5 for calcium sulfate and about 7 for calcium sulfite.

Air Pollution Control Systems

Additive	Startup Date
calcium carbonate	late 1968
calcium carbonate	late 1968
calcium carbonate	March 1971 (gas);
	Nov. 1971 (coal)
calcium carbonate	late 1972
calcium hydroxide	late 1972
limestone slurry	early 1975

Heterogeneous crystallization is minimized by providing seed crystals for homogeneous crystallization (crystallization on the seed crystals) and by designing the reaction tanks so that the liquor leaving them is close to saturation and not highly supersaturated. This requires the knowledge of precipitation kinetics of calcium sulfate and sulfite.

Calcium Sulfite Deposition. Calcium sulfite ($CaSO_3 \cdot \frac{1}{2}H_2O$) is formed in the scrubber under those conditions that favor sulfite formation. These conditions are apparent when one considers the sulfite–bisulfite equilibrium and compares the relative solubilities of the corresponding calcium salts. As seen in Figure 2, extremely soluble bisulfite in solution changes to relatively insoluble sulfite when the solution pH shifts from 4 to 10. When SO_2 is absorbed, the scrubber solution is usually between pH 4 and 6 and, therefore, the predominant species is

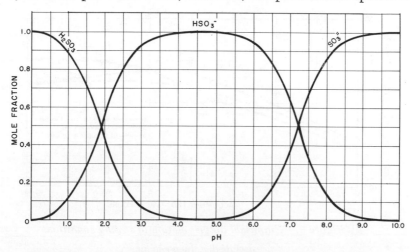

Figure 2. Mole fraction sulfurous acid-bisulfite-sulfite vs. pH

bisulfite. If the pH of the scrubber solution containing bisulfite is suddenly raised either in localized areas or in a reaction tank, the relatively energetic crystallization of calcium sulfite will occur.

Experimental work with lime scrubbing has shown that sulfite scaling occurs in the scrubber bed when free hydroxide is introduced. By proper control of the pH of the spray slurry (less than 10) entering the scrubber, calcium sulfite scaling will be prevented within the scrubber. In the calcium carbonate system, the buffering action of the carbonate–bicarbonate couple (Reaction 5) maintains a system pH between 5 and 6; thus sulfite scaling is not encountered.

Calcium Sulfate Deposition. The solubility of calcium sulfate is only slightly increased with increasing pH, and calcium sulfate scaling is related to the tendency of this material to form extensively stable supersaturated solutions. While chemical theory predicts that a given ionizable

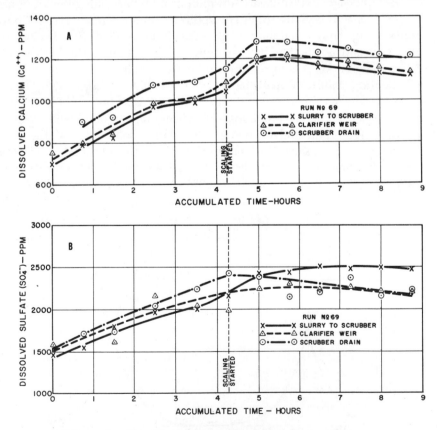

Figure 3.   Empirical determination of scaling conditions

a. For dissolved calcium
b. For dissolved sulfate

species will not remain in solution when the solubility product of its component ions has been exceeded, calcium sulfate may be held in solution to an extent twice that predicted before precipitation of calcium sulfate will occur (gypsum, $CaSO_4 \cdot 2H_2O$). The significance of this phenomenon to scrubber operation is that SO_2 removal can be accomplished while scrubbing with solutions containing more than the theoretical calcium and sulfite ion concentrations but less than some experimentally determined level at which precipitation will occur within the scrubber proper (Figure 3).

Crystallization from supersaturated solutions can occur by two processes, formation of new crystals or nucleation and growth on existing crystals. The internal surfaces of the scrubber can provide nucleation sites, thus resulting in scale formation. For many crystal systems, growth will occur without nucleation if sufficient seed crystals are provided. Work by other investigators (3) has shown that supersaturated calcium sulfate solutions can be effectively desupersaturated by circulation of 1–5% gypsum seed crystals.

By using this technique, operations free of calcium sulfate scaling have been demonstrated in laboratory and field installations. This seeding technique is the key to closed loop operation in which liquid leaves the system only by evaporation or in combination with the solid by-product of the scrubbing system. Disposal of this solid is discussed later.

Sulfate scaling is generally more prevalent in the calcium carbonate system than in the calcium hydroxide system because more sulfate is formed. The calcium hydroxide system reaches steady state below the saturation value of calcium sulfate.

System Design

The Air Quality Control Systems (AQCS) using lime/limestone wet scrubbing have three basic types of chemical process equipment: (1) scrubbers, (2) reaction tanks, and (3) solid–liquid separators, in addition to several auxiliary pieces of equipment such as pumps, demisters, and reheaters. The SO_2 in the flue gas is transferred into the liquid in the scrubber, the sulfur in the liquid is converted to solid calcium sulfite, and calcium sulfate in the reaction tanks and solid calcium sulfite and sulfate are separated from the liquid and disposed from the solid–liquid separators such as clarifiers, vacuum filters, and ponds.

The successful operation of the AQCS depends on the successful operation of the scrubber, reaction tanks, solid–liquid separators, and auxiliary equipment. It cannot be over-emphasized that the equipment should be designed to do the specific jobs. This section of the paper deals primarily with the principles and information needed to design the two most important pieces of equipment, namely, the marble bed scrubber and the reaction tanks. The design of solid–liquid separators is based on solids settling-rate data.

Scrubber. The primary function of the scrubber is to transfer SO_2 from the flue gas into the liquid. The SO_2 may remain in the liquid or be converted partially to solid sulfur compounds in the scrubber. Hence, knowledge of vapor–liquid mass transfer rates is important for scrubber design. The marble bed scrubber which has a turbulent layer acts as an absorption tray.

The vapor–liquid equilibrium line and the tray efficiency are needed to design a tray. The typical operating and equilibrium lines are shown in Figure 4. The operating line is the material balance line and has a negative slope of L/G, liquid-to-gas ratio.

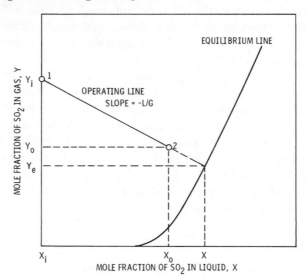

Figure 4.   Vapor–liquid operating and equilibrium lines

The inlet gas composition Y_i is known, and the SO_2 concentration in the incoming liquid X_i, which is usually zero, is also known. Hence, point 1 which represents the inlet condition is known. The operating line can be drawn through X_i, Y_i with a negative slope of L/G.

The intersection of the operating and equilibrium lines (X, Y_e) represents the scrubber outlet gas and liquid conditions for a theoretical stage which represents 100% overall tray efficiency. The overall tray efficiency E is defined as:

$$E = \frac{Y_i - Y_o}{Y_i - Y_e} \tag{10}$$

and is usually less than 100%. It can be seen from both Figure 4 and Equation 10 that the actual outlet liquid and gas compositions (X_o, Y_o) can be predicted using the tray efficiency and the point of intersection of the operating and the equilibrium lines. Laboratory tests show that the tray efficiency of the marble bed scrubber is 90–95%, indicating that the marble bed scrubber is a good liquid–gas contactor.

Once the tray efficiency is known, the number of marble beds needed to obtain the required SO_2 removal can be determined from the operating and the equilibrium lines. The equilibrium line is plotted using a computer program and the total alkalinity of the liquid available in the scrubber which is a function of the additive dissolution rate for slurry systems. For a specific L/G, the equilibrium line shown in Figure 4 moves to the left or right depending on the alkalinity of liquid available in the scrubber and, hence, affects the SO_2 removal efficiency. The SO_2 removal efficiency is defined as:

$$\eta = \frac{Y_i - Y_o}{Y_i} \tag{11}$$

If the additive dissolution rate is high enough to maximize the available alkalinity in the liquid in the scrubber, the equilibrium line will move to the far right in Figure 4 to a point where Y_e is zero. This represents the most favorable condition for SO_2 transfer from gas to liquid. Comparison of Equations 10 and 11 shows that the SO_2 removal efficiency, η, will approach the tray efficiency as Y_e approaches zero.

Reaction Tanks. The function of the reaction tanks is to provide: (1) dissolution of the additive in order to convert the highly soluble bisulfite in the liquid leaving the scrubber to relatively insoluble sulfite; (2) precipitation of calcium sulfate which is formed in the system (scrubber and/or reaction tanks) from the oxidation of sulfite; (3) precipitation of calcium sulfite. Proper design of the reaction tanks is important for eliminating the calcium sulfite and sulfate scaling problems in the lime/limestone wet scrubber systems.

Additive dissolution rates vary considerably with the type, origin, preparation, and concentration of the additive. At Combustion Engineering, a prototype scrubber system, pilot plant scrubber system, continuous flow stirred tank reactors, and batch reactors have been used to determine the dissolution rates for individual additives.

The following rate expression for the precipitation of calcium sulfate has been developed (3):

$$R = -KZ(C - C_e)^2 \tag{12}$$

The rate of desupersaturation, R, is proportional to the gypsum seed crystal concentration, Z. The difference between the actual concentration, C, and the equilibrium concentration, C_c of SO_4^{2-} or Ca^{2+} is the driving force. Although it is more accurate to express the driving force in terms of the activity and the solubility products, the driving force in Equation 12 is given in concentrations for convenience by including the factor for converting activities to concentrations in the rate constant K. With the rate constants determined by C-E, (4), the rate expression given by Equation 12 is used to design reaction tanks to relieve the calcium sulfate supersaturation.

Laboratory studies are in progress to determine the calcium sulfite precipitation kinetics and the oxidation kinetics of sulfite to sulfate. Until these reaction rate expressions are developed, the experimental data obtained from the pilot plant, prototype, and field units will be used to design the reaction tanks and scrubbers to eliminate calcium sulfite scaling.

Solid-Liquid Separators. Most of the SO_2 transferred from the flue gas into the liquid in the scrubber is converted to solid sulfur compounds in the scrubber and in the reaction tanks. The solid sulfur compounds and the fly ash collected in the scrubber have to be separated from the liquid and disposed of in a way that does not cause water pollution. Clarifier–thickeners, vacuum filters, ponds, etc., are being used as the solid–liquid separators. The liquid is returned to the system, and the solids are removed as waste.

The settling characteristics of the solid sulfur compounds produced in the lime/limestone scrubber systems vary considerably. Although the clarifier–thickeners are being designed by the vendors, C-E is developing a computer program that could be used to design the clarifier–thickeners for lime/limestone wet scrubber systems.

The solids concentration of the underflow from the clarifier–thickeners is between 20 and 40 wt % and is not concentrated enough for transportation by either trucks or railroad cars to the disposal areas. For this reason vacuum filters are usually used to concentrate the underflow to 60–80 wt % solids. Ponds are also being used to store solids and to accomplish solid–liquid separation. C-E is doing developmental work to determine the leaching characteristics of the sulfur compounds present in the sludge and also to determine the most suitable filtration system for lime/limestone wet scrubber systems.

C-E Air Pollution Control Systems

Two types of systems, tail-end and furnace injection, have been installed by C-E. Figure 5 is a schematic flow diagram of the tail-end APCS. During operation, a slurry of pulverized limestone or a slaked lime enters into the reaction tank. Recirculation pumps convey the scrubbing slurry from the reaction tank to underbed spray nozzles. The incoming gas, laden with dust and SO₂, contacts the sprayed slurry and continues to the bed. The removal of SO₂ and particulate matter occurs in the bed. The scrubbing cycle continues with the materials draining to the reaction tank which is designed to provide for completion of chemical reactions and precipitation of solids.

A bleed line provides for solids removal to a clarifier or pond. Here the solids settle, and clarified water is available for recirculation. The cleaned flue gas passes through a mist eliminator to remove moisture, and then it is reheated for fan protection and reduction of stack plume.

In providing for SO₂ removal, the tail-end system design adapts to a variety of situations by: (1) providing flexibility in the selection of the most suitable additives; (2) supplementing existing electrostatic precipitators on older units.

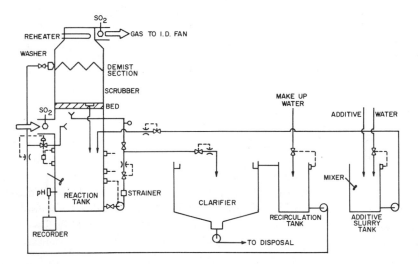

Figure 5.   C-E tail-end APCS controls schematic flow diagram

Results from operation of laboratory prototype units show that both particulate matter and SO₂ emissions can be reduced to acceptable levels. However, long-term operation on commercial-sized units must be demonstrated. Three types of C-E tail-end systems, as given below, are being installed by utilities on coal-fired units.

Calcium Carbonate—Low Sulfur Coal. Calcium carbonate systems will be installed at Northern States Power Co., 700 MW Sherburne County Units 1 and 2. These contracts are significant for two reasons: (1) they are the largest systems sold to date, and (3) the coal has a sulfur content less than 1%. Experience has shown that this latter fact is detrimental to the efficiency of electrostatic precipitators; therefore, the wet scrubber system was selected. The primary objective is particulate matter removal, although about one-half of the sulfur in the coal will be removed by the system. The fly ash contains sufficient additive to remove a portion of SO_2. Calcium carbonate will be added to control scaling and to meet SO_2 removal requirements. A 12,000-cfm prototype of this system is currently in operation at another Northern States power station.

Calcium Hydroxide System. A $Ca(OH)_2$ system is undergoing startup testing at Louisville Gas and Electric Co., Paddy's Run No. 6, on a 70 MW pulverized coal-fired boiler. This system uses carbide sludge, a waste calcium hydroxide material, as the additive for reducing SO_2 emissions. The utility is obtaining the carbide sludge from a local industrial firm which produces large quantities of it in the manufacture of acetylene.

Calcium Carbonate—High Sulfur Coal. These systems have been designed for a number of Midwestern utilities with units burning an average 3.5% sulfur coal, with 15% ash. The systems are installed following 80% or better removal of particulate matter by means of collection devices already on the boiler for retrofit systems, or by means of mechanical or wet collection devices supplied as part of the C-E system.

Furnace injection systems are similar to the tail-end design except the limestone additive is injected into the furnace and removed in the scrubber. Two of these units, one of 125 MW and another of 430 MW, are installed at the Lawrence Station of Kansas Power and Light Co. Two more units of this design, each of 100 MW, are installed at the Hawthorn Station of Kansas City Power and Light Co. although one is currently being operated as a tail-end system on low sulfur Wyoming coal.

In addition to the resolution of chemical scaling previously discussed, there have been a number of strictly mechanical problems encountered during the early operation of these systems. The various operating problems and subsequent modifications have been previously discussed (1, 5–9). A brief summary of significant modifications follows.

SOOTBLOWERS. The installation of half-track sootblowers at the scrubber inlet in 1969 eliminated the problem of massive inlet deposits. The sootblowers have been operating at normal blowing pressures and have not required any abnormal maintenance.

LADDER VANES. A system of ladder vanes can be used to improve the scrubber's gas distribution but not provide a large surface for deposition. In addition, sophisticated wash systems have been designed to prevent deposit growth.

SPRAY PIPING. Deposition on the underbed spray piping has been reduced dramatically by strategically placed wash nozzles and some quenching nozzles installed at the inlets of the scrubbers. The use of synthetic materials to prevent corrosion has led to the conclusion that the material best suited to the environment of the scrubber is glass fiber. Piping, either made from glass fiber or coated with glass fiber, has been installed in the existing field units. Glass fiber coatings on other scrubber surfaces have been successful.

NOZZLES. Underbed spray nozzle plugging has been another problem. Deposit formation in the bed area is directly related to improper operation of spray nozzles and maldistribution of spray water. Nozzle plugging with bits of scale and miscellaneous debris which happened to enter the spray water system, as well as a need for proper mixing of spray water and recycle slurry water, led to the development of a special nonclogging nozzle. There have been no serious plugging problems in field units since the new nozzles were installed.

MIST ELIMINATORS. The mist eliminators above the marble bed became coated with deposits during early runs. Laboratory studies were undertaken in 1971 to develop an improved mist eliminator appropriately located for optimum agglomeration of water droplets which would also lend itself to better washing than the existing demister. The evaluation showed that the double L-shaped demister would have considerably more throughput capacity than the existing design and that it could be washed more easily. These new demisters with appropriate washing devices are or will be installed in all systems at the optimum elevation.

REHEATERS. The reheaters have been plastered with deposits a number of times. The improvement in scrubber bed gas distribution and the installation of half-track sootblowers have made it possible to maintain the gas side pressure drop across the reheater. Our experience since the redesigned reheaters were installed has showed that the present reheater design, coupled with half-track sootblowers, is adequate if the demister is performing as designed. The overall throughput capacity of the scrubbers has also been somewhat reduced to provide more reliable operation and maintenance.

Waste Disposal

A comprehensive program for utilization of APCS by-products is currently underway. This five-phase program covers: (1) nationwide environmental survey of present waste products and ecological data relating to the needs of potential APCS customers; (2) determination of physical and chemical properties of waste products; (3) studies on direct disposal of both solid and liquid wastes; (4) beneficiation and use of liquid and solid waste products; (5) pilot plant studies of promising utilization procedures.

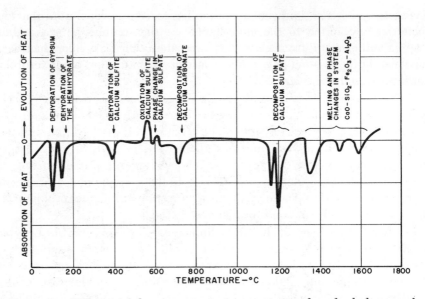

Figure 6.   Differential thermogram of a furnace injected mode sludge sample

A significant part of the physical and chemical property analyses is being carried out with x-ray diffraction and x-ray spectrographic equipment and thermal analysis techniques. Thermal analyses have been used to determine melting point, decomposition temperature, and sinterability of waste sludge from APCS operations (Figure 6). These properties are needed to determine applications of the material.

A number of areas for utilization of modified and unmodified fly ash are shown in Figures 7 and 8. These schemes range from production of light weight aggregate developed some years ago to compression and sintering of drain pipes, which is under laboratory development. Large volume usage of APCS sludge will be necessary because 2–3 tons/day/MW of sludge will be produced from a coal-fired boiler firing 3% sulfur coal with 10% ash.

Direct Disposal. Because of the potential volume of APCS sludge, or modified fly ash, the most promising methods for using this material are those requiring large quantities and a minimum of processing or handling. If we consider the current use of fly ash, the prospects for total utilization of APCS modified ash are not promising. Products such as fly ash light weight aggregate and fired fly ash brick have yet to gain a substantial portion of the market in which they are competing. Other possible fly ash products such as gas concrete and calcium silicate brick have not been marketed to any substantial extent in this country. The manufacture of cement appears to be technically feasible, but no actual study exists to evaluate its economics. Mineral aggregate and pozzolanic compacted materials appear to be the most promising areas of modified fly ash use.

POZZOLANIC BASE COURSE. Compacted pozzolanic materials have the potential for large scale use of fly ash or modified fly ash. Compacted base material usually consists of 10–20% fly ash, 0–10% lime, and the rest aggregate. The mixture is wetted to about 15% moisture for compacting to maximum density. It is then spread and compacted in place.

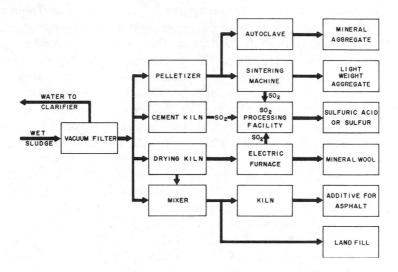

Figure 7.   Sludge disposal schemes for a single scrubber system

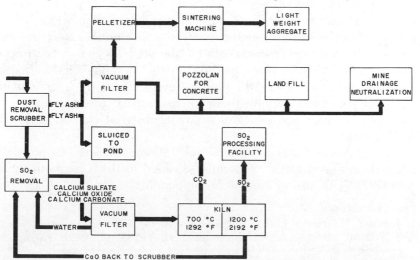

Figure 8.   Sludge disposal schemes for a dual scrubber system

A wear course of concrete or asphalt is placed on the base material. In 1971, 6.8% of the fly ash was used in this manner.

The G. & W. H. Corson Co. has also used mixtures of fly ash, lime, and sulfate sludge to produce compositions which can be used as paving and as pozzolanic base course. The material is currently being used in the paving demonstration at Dulles International Airport. A portion of the demonstration pavement was made with modified fly ash from the APCS at the Kansas Power and Light, Lawrence Station.

MINERAL AGGREGATE. Mineral aggregate is a manufactured aggregate which has a density greater than the upper limit of light weight aggregate (50 lbs/ft^3) but is generally less dense than naturally occurring aggregate. The Corson Co. has been able to produce a high quality mineral aggregate using fly ash, lime, and sludge from industrial acid waste sources. Mineral aggregate has also been produced by Michigan Technological University, using modified fly ash with 10% calcium hydroxide added. The aggregate was cured by autoclaving with saturated steam at 300 psi. The aggregate has a density of 58 lbs/ft^3 and an average crushing strength of 125 lbs.

It is difficult to ascertain the marketability of mineral aggregate because large quantities have not been manufactured. Mineral aggregate is not fired and should be less expensive to produce than sintered light weight aggregate. Another factor is the diminishing supply of conventional aggregate materials. Rising demand, limited resources, and increasing urbanization are combining to make natural aggregates increasingly more expensive in major market areas.

LABORATORY EVALUATIONS. A laboratory investigation of pozzolanic base course and pavement and mineral aggregate from APCS sludges from operating field units is underway. The main emphasis is to determine the unconfined compressive strength of laboratory specimens and to compare these values with those reported in the literature for base course materials and to determine the physical properties of the aggregate and the quality of concrete which can be made from the aggregate. The laboratory investigation indicates a paving material can be made with APCS sludge.

Using APCS wastes as land-fill and soil conditioners is a possibility that is being investigated. Presently, disposal methods for both fly ash and APCS sludge are by land-fill or impounding.

Literature Cited

1. Jonakin, J., Martin, J. R., "Applications of the C-E Air Pollution Control System." *Intern. Lime/Limestone Wet Scrubbing Symp., 2nd, New Orleans, Nov. 8–12, 1971.*
2. Plumley, A. L., Gogineni, M. R., "Research and Development in Wet Scrubber Systems," *Intern. Lime/Limestone Wet Scrubbing Symp., 2nd, New Orleans, Nov. 8–12, 1971.*

3. Lessing, R., "The Development of a Process of Flue Gas Washing Without Effluent," *J. Soc. Chem. Ind., London, Trans. Commun.,* (1938) **57,** 373–388.
4. Rader, P. C., "Bench Scale Studies of $CaSO_4$ Desupersaturation Kinetics," C-E Internal Reports, Windsor, Conn.
5. Jonakin, J., McLaughlin, J. F., "Operating Experience with the First Full Scale System for Removal of SO_2 and Dust from Stack Cases," *Proc. Amer. Power Conf.* (1969), **31.**
6. Green, G., "Installation and Initial Operation of Sulfur Dioxide Removal Equipment," Missouri Valley Electric Assoc., April 1969.
7. Miller, D. M., "Experience with Wet Scrubbing for SO_2 Removal at Lawrence Station of the Kansas Power and Light Company," *Amer. Inst. Mining Engr., Soc. Mining Engr.,* Sept. 1969.
8. "Modified SO_2 System Faces New Tests," *Elec. World,* Dec. 8, 1969.
9. Jonakin, J., Plumley, A. L., *Amer. Petrol. Inst., 37th Meetg., New York, May 1972.*

RECEIVED February 15, 1973.

13

Limestone Wet Scrubbing of Sulfur Dioxide from Power Generation Flue Gas for High and Low Sulfur Fuels

ROBERT J. GLEASON

Research-Cottrell, Inc., P.O. Box 750, Bound Brook, N.J. 08805

FRANK HEACOCK

Arizona Public Service, Phoenix, Ariz.

Limestone wet scrubbing is considered the most viable process approach for sulfur dioxide emission control on coal-fired power generation boilers. Systems under development have been concerned primarily with operational reliability. Sulfur dioxide absorption efficiency has been given secondary treatment. Pilot plant studies on high and low sulfur fuels using packed tower absorbers have shown the inlet SO$_2$ concentration and slurry composition as significant factors in the removal efficiency and operational reliability. Mass-transfer coefficients have been developed for a wetted film packing. Variable height packed absorbers can provide high absorption efficiency for both high and low sulfur fuels. Hence, compliance with State and Federal regulations can be achieved in the extreme low sulfur coal conditions.

The Environmental Protection Agency (EPA) through the Clean Air Act of 1967 and its amendments of 1970 has established the primary and secondary ambient air quality standards for sulfur dioxide and other pollutants. These standards were used to guide the State governments in developing their regional implementation programs (*1*). The primary air quality standards protect the public health while the secondary standards concern the national welfare (property, environment, *etc.*).

Background

Codes. The annual average short-term sulfur dioxide concentrations established for the air quality standards are given in Table I. Sulfur oxide concentrations at 0.03 and 0.02 ppm are the primary and secondary annual standards, respectively. To avoid short-term unhealthy or unsatisfactory conditions, the sulfur oxide must not exceed 0.1-0.14 ppm for more than one 24 hr period per year. To achieve these standards, EPA has proposed emission codes for new and modified industrial plants that are emitting sulfur oxides. For fossil-fired steam generators contracted for construction or modifications after August 17, 1971, the Federally mandated emission standards are 1.2 lbs SO_2/MMBtu for coal-fired and 0.8 lb SO_2/MMBtu for oil-fired generators. In Table II, these standard codes are also expressed in outlet concentrations, 620 ppm coal and 440 ppm oil.

Table I.   National Ambient Air Quality Standards for Sulfur Oxides

Time Averaging	Primary		Secondary	
	$\mu g/M^3$	ppm	$\mu g/M^3$	ppm
Annual	80	0.03	60	0.02
24 hr	360	0.14	260	0.1
3 hr			1300	0.5

Table II.   Standards for Sulfur Dioxide Emissions, New and Retrofit Abatement Systems (2)

Fuel	Emission Std, lbs SO_2/MMBtu	Approx. Flue Outlet SO_2 Concn, ppm (dry)
Coal	1.2	620[a]
Oil	0.80	440

[a] Assuming 15% excess air and no preheater leakage.

The State implementation programs for sulfur dioxide and other pollutants were submitted after January 1972 for EPA approval or rejection by May 1972. Each program plan was to achieve primary and secondary standards.

EPA has also recommended uniform pollution abatement for each region within the specific States; however, this recommendation has created some uncertainty and confusion (2). The electric utilities industries have found it difficult to anticipate the regional codes being adopted by the States or the acceptability of the plans by EPA. For example, this could require a coal-fired station burning low sulfur fuel to reduce the emissions to less than 150 ppm if 70 to 90% removal is adopted; however, a plant in the same region burning high sulfur fuel could be emitting as much as 400 ppm and achieving the same removal efficiency. Even today the emission codes in many regions are still controversial. Industrial plants burning low sulfur fuels could be unfairly equated with high sulfur fuel users on a percentage abatement basis where both are required to control the emissions.

Lime and Limestone Wet Scrubbing. The problem of atmospheric pollution by sulfur oxides has been given extensive attention by research and development firms in recent years and several process types are being proposed for full scale application. Lime and limestone wet scrubbing appears to be the most promising approach for immediate application. The major difficulty with the limestone or lime systems is solid deposition in the absorption device which could create unreliability and unscheduled shutdowns for the power plant.

In general, the power industry desires the following of a scrubbing device in a flue gas-cleaning system: operational reliability, a minimum of four-to-one turndown ratio, low pressure drop characteristics, high absorption efficiency potential, good alkali utilization, acceptable mist elimination, and future process adaptability.

Wet Scrubbing in Packed Towers. The packed absorption tower has been considered and used in lime and limestone scrubbing of SO_2. It has demonstrated its capabilities in most of the previously listed characteristics. However, commercially available packings have difficulty maintaining a reliable operation with calcium-based wet scrubbing because of scale deposition.

In England as early as 1930 and again in the 1950's an open grid-type packing was used for scrubbing SO_2 with limestone. The grids were constructed from wood strips or slats that allowed high liquid-to-gas ratio and low pressure drop. The absorber was tested over a period of years with minimal process difficulty. Over 3,500 hr of operation have been reported with scale-free conditions (3).

Presently, Research-Cottrell has developed a modern wetted film packing similar in many respects to the wood grid tower. The wetted film packing is constructed from corrugated sheets of neoprene-impregnated asbestos or several plastic types. The packing has high specific surface, low pressure, and high liquid rate capabilities. Tests on both high and low sulfur fuels have been successful. Controlled scaling has been reported under both fuel conditions. Longevity tests lasting three weeks on low sulfur coal have shown that little deposition takes place within the absorption device.

Process Description

The system used in conjunction with the tower is illustrated in Figure 1. Flue gas containing SO_2 and fly ash enters the FDS (S-1) where it is contacted concurrently with a limestone slurry which removes most of the fly ash and a fraction of the SO_2. The combined stream is then sent

to the cyclonic mist eliminator (TW-1) where the slurry is separated
from the gas. From the mist eliminator, the flue gas flows through the
packed absorber section where it is contacted countercurrently with
another limestone slurry stream. A significant portion of the remaining
SO₂ is removed here.

The tower absorber section is separated from the cyclonic mist
eliminator by a plate containing a conical hat. This arrangement allows
the flue gas to leave the cyclonic mist eliminator but prevents the slurry
leaving the packed absorption tower from combining with the slurry
stream leaving the FDS. Hence, most of the fly ash entering the system
is isolated from the absorption tower and is confined to the FDS slurry
stream.

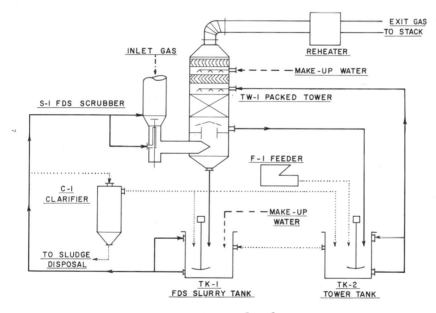

Figure 1.   Process flow diagram

Limestone is fed to the system through a variable-speed feeder
(F-1) which is mounted on top of the tower slurry tank (TK-2). Slurry
from this tank is pumped to the absorber section of the tower where it
is contacted countercurrently with the flue gas. The reacted slurry then
flows by gravity back to the primary tower slurry tank. An agitator
mounted on top of the tank maintains a uniform slurry suspension. To
prevent the buildup of reaction products, a small stream is bled from the
tower slurry tank (TK-2) and sent to the FDS slurry tank (TK-1).

Limestone slurry, which also contains fly ash, is pumped from the
FDS slurry tank to the FDS (S-1) where it is contacted with the incoming

flue gas. The combined stream of slurry and gas is separated in the cyclonic mist eliminator, and the slurry stream is cycled back to the FDS slurry tank. An agitator mounted on top of the tank maintains a uniform solids distribution.

Results and Discussion

Transfer Coefficient Calculations. The mass-transfer coefficients were calculated with the relationship developed by Chilton and Colburn (4):

$$N_{oG} = -\ln(1-Y) \tag{1}$$

$$N_{oG} = \frac{\bar{K} \, a \, P \, Z}{G} \tag{2}$$

Y = absorption efficiency, fraction
N_{oG} = number of overall gas-phase transfer units
$\bar{K}$ = overall mass-transfer coefficients, lb-mole/hr-ft²-atm
a = surface area per unit volume of packing, ft²/ft³
P = total pressure of the system, atm
Z = height of tower, ft
G = gas flow rate, lb-mole/hr-ft².

One assumes in using the above equation that the liquid is well mixed vertically, the chemical reaction is irreversible, the sulfur dioxide back pressure is negligible, and the interfacial area per unit of liquid volume is constant throughout the tower.

Table III. Mass-Transfer Coefficients for Low Sulfur Coal (0.5% Sulfur or 400 ppm) [a]

Material	Specific Area, ft²/ft³	Packing Ht, ft	Limestone Stoichiometry, % Theor.	Mass-Transfer Coeff., lb-Mole/hr (ft²)-atm
Neoprene-coated	43	5	77	0.31
Neoprene-coated	43	2	97	1.07
Neoprene-coated	68	5	85	0.96
Polypropylene	68	4	100	1.26
Neoprene-coated	43	5	91	1.09

L/G = liquid-to-gas ratio, 50–55 gal per 1000 ft³
P = 0.865 atm   limestone grind = 90%–200 mesh

[a] Mass-transfer coefficients calculated from average absorption efficiency. More than 10 measurements were averaged for each coefficient value.

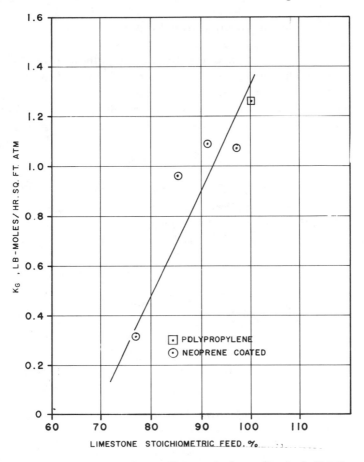

Figure 2.   Mass-transfer coefficients for low sulfur fuels (0.3% sulfur)

Low Sulfur Coal. In a pilot system sponsored by the Arizona Public Service, absorption tests with several types of Munters wetted film packing were performed using limestone as an alkali reagent. A high surface area packing, 68 ft^2/ft^3, and a low surface area packing, 43 ft^2/ft^3, were tested at several tower heights. Operating conditions were set at levels suitable for a stable and reliable process.

High mass-transfer coefficients were measured at packing heights between 2 and 5 ft. Limestone stoichiometric feed was varied from 77 to 100%. The calculated mass transfer coefficients and the operating conditions are given in Table III. Transfer coefficients between 0.31 and 1.26 were computed for the limestone stoichiometric range. The absorption efficiency follows almost directly the limestone feed rate as illustrated in Figure 2.

Absorption measurements with 0.2N sodium hydroxide solution and operating conditions approximately the same as for the low sulfur limestone tests gave a mass-transfer coefficient of 1.18 lb-mole/hr-ft^2-atm (5). This compares closely with the values measured with $CaCO_3$ at 100% stoichiometric feed. For sodium hydroxide/sulfur dioxide absorption, the liquid phase resistance can be considered negligible. This suggests that the limestone/SO_2 system at low sulfur coal conditions falls within a gas phase-resistant process. By selecting a tower height and a limestone feed, one could set the absorption efficiency at a level suitable for the emission codes.

High Sulfur Coal. Mass-transfer coefficients for high sulfur coal did not follow any simple pattern. Absorption efficiency varied with inlet SO_2 concentration, limestone stoichiometry, and limestone grind. For a sulfur dioxide concentration at 1000 ppm, the stoichiometry had a significant effect on the mass transfer. Limestone stoichiometry below 100% gave poor absorption; above 100%, the mass-transfer coefficient varied between 0.38 and 0.84 lb-mole/hr-ft^2-atm for limestone feeds between 100 and 140%, respectively (*see* Table IV). At higher levels of sulfur dioxide (1600 ppm), the calculated coefficients decrease sharply (6). The mass-transfer measurements at 100-140% stoichiometry gave values from 0.35 to 0.38 lb-mole/hr-ft^2-atm. At this higher SO_2 level, stoichiometry had little effect, indicating a significant liquid phase mass-transfer resistance.

**Table IV. Mass-Transfer Coefficients with High Sulfur Coal —
Limestone Scrubbing**

SO_2 Inlet Concn, ppm	Limestone Stoichiometry, %	Mass-Transfer[a] Coeff., lb-Mole/hr-ft^2-atm
1000	100	0.385
1000	120	0.510
1000	140	0.843
1600	100	0.252
1600	120	0.308
1600	140	0.385

[a] Packing = 68 ft^2/ft^3
    Height = 5 ft
        G = 70 lb-mole/hr-ft^2
        P = 1.0 atm
    Limestone grind = 75%-200 mesh
        L/G = 45 gal per 1000 ft^3.

This insensitivity to limestone feed is illustrated in Figure 3. At 1000 ppm, the SO_2 absorption is more than doubled as the limestone feed is increased from 100 to 140%, while at 1600 ppm the same limestone increase improved the absorption by approximately 50%.

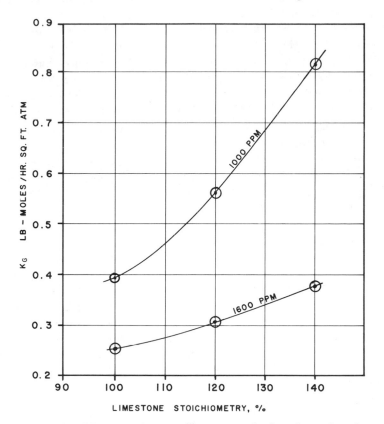

Figure 3. Mass-transfer coefficients of high sulfur dioxide concentrations

Table V. Mass-Transfer Coefficients with Limestone Mesh Size Variation

SO_2 Inlet Concn, ppm	Limestone Grind, %–mesh	Mass-Transfer[a] Coeff., lbs-mole/hr-ft²-atm
1300	89–325	0.665
1300	75–200	0.366
1300	60–200	0.287

[a] Packing = 68 ft²/ft³
   Height = 5 ft
   G = 70 lb-mole/hr-ft²
   P = 1.0 atm
Limestone stoichiometry = 115%.

Influence of Limestone Particle Size. The liquid phase resistance with limestone alkali is expected for the process conditions normally experienced with high sulfur coal. The solubility of $CaCO_3$ is much lower than demanded by flue gas containing above 1000 ppm, even at very high liquid flows through the absorbers (above 50 gal per 1000 ft³). Consequently, the controlling resistance would be the dissolution.

To determine the sensitivity of the dissolution rate, three limestone grind sizes were tested at similar process conditions. Material ground to 60%–200 mesh, 75%–200 mesh, and 89%–325 mesh gave coefficients at 0.287, 0.366, and 0.665 lb-mole/hr-ft²-atm, respectively. These results are summarized in Table V. By selecting the limestone grind, one could control the absorption in a given process over a range of SO_2 concentrations. For the finely ground limestone (89%–325 mesh), the absorption at 1300 ppm was about 95%, while the coarse grind (60%–200 mesh) allowed only 75% removal.

Conclusions

The mass-transfer coefficients measured with low sulfur coal for both limestone and sodium hydroxide were essentially the same. In a packed tower, limestone will absorb and react with SO_2 to the same extent as a strong alkali for flue gas concentrations less than 1000 ppm.

For both high and low sulfur fuels, the limestone stoichiometric feed allows control of the outlet SO_2 emission. Packed towers will allow flexible control of the SO_2 emission.

Mass-transfer for high sulfur coal applications is liquid phase resistant; the contact time and high surface exposure allowed in a packed tower reduces this adverse condition.

The limestone grind affects the absorption significantly at SO_2 concentrations above 1000 ppm. High absorption (95%) can be achieved with an 89%–325 mesh material at 1300 ppm.

Literature Cited

1. Jimeson, R. M., Gakner, A., 71st National Meeting, AIChE, February 1972.
2. Environmental Protection Agency, "Background Information for Proposed New-Scource Performance Standards," August 1971.
3. Berkowitz, J. B., 10th Monthly Report, EPA Contract No. 6802–0215.
4. Chilton, T. H., Coluburn, A. P., *Ind. Eng. Chem.* (1934) **26**, 1183.
5. Gleason, R. J., Final Report, EPA Contract No. EHS–D–71–24, October 1971.
6. Gleason, R. J., 2nd International Lime/Limestone-Wet Scrubbing Symposium, New Orleans, November 1971.

RECEIVED February 15, 1973.

14

Process Experience of the RC/Bahco Sulfur Dioxide Removal System

RICHARD S. ATKINS

Research-Cottrell, Inc., Bound Brook, N.J. 08805

The operating experiences of several Bahco SO_2 removal systems, are examined. Sulfur oxide removal technology developed by AB Bahco Ventilation, Enköping, Sweden, is being successfully applied in 19 commercial installations. Each of these units has exhibited on-stream reliability and high SO_2 absorption efficiency. Bahco design flexibility permits the use of Na and K bases, slurries of Ca and Mg bases, and less expensive materials such as dolomite, burned lime, limestone, sodium carbonate, and ammonia as potential scrubbing reagents. The process is amenable to by-product recovery of sodium sulfate, sodium sulfite, gypsum, and ammonium sulfate, which reduces the threat of discharging secondary pollutants. The possibilities of reverse fuel switching are also examined: the burning of high sulfur fuels in conjunction with an SO_2 scrubber and obtaining a more economic, less pollutant situation than switching to low sulfur fuels.

Pollution control is one of the major problems facing U.S. industry today. The ever-increasing concern about our environment and how it should be maintained has resulted in Federal and state antipollution codes. The Federal government, through the Environmental Protection Agency, has established the pace for pollution legislation and the means to enforce it.

As a result of the legislative action by the state and Federal governments, U.S. industry will begin to review the products it produces, their methods of production, its sources of raw materials and energy, and its means of disposing manufacturing waste and by-products. Therefore, during the next three years we will see domestic industries defining

161

their air pollution problems, selecting appropriate control processes or alternative nonpolluting processes, evaluating control economics, installing control systems, and starting up, debugging, and eventually operating their control systems.

Table I.   Nationwide Sulfur Oxide and Particulate Emissions, 1970 (1)

	Emissions, %			
Source	SO_2		Particulate	
Transportation	3.2		1.2	
Solid waste disposal	0.5		5.0	
Stationary fuel combustion	75.3		21.9	
Industrial boilers		16.4		6.5
Utility boilers		58.9		15.4
Industrial processes	20.4		50.0	
Miscellaneous sources	0.6		21.9	
Total	100		100	
Tons per year	46,850,000		36,280,000	

As illustrated in Table I, stationary fuel combustion contributes 75% of the sulfur dioxide and 22% of the particulates emitted into our atmosphere (1). One-quarter of the sulfur dioxide and one-third of the particulates from stationary fuel combustion are produced by industrial boilers. Again referring to Table I, we observe that industrial processes contribute 20% of the sulfur dioxide and 50% of the particulates. The combination of industrial processes and their energy sources is the single largest particulate polluter and the second largest source of sulfur dioxide.

Referring to Table II, we can observe that the petroleum, non-ferrous metallurgy, and sulfuric acid industries account for most of the industrial SO_2 emissions. However, particulate emissions are distributed among all industrial polluters.

This paper explores the operating experience of the Research-Cottrell/Bahco process specifically designed for handling the two major pollutants produced by the industrial sector of society, sulfur dioxide and particulate matter. The RC/Bahco process has demonstrated, in 19 units in Japan and Sweden, that it is capable of significantly reducing SO_2 and particulate emissions from industrial processes. This technology is currently being applied to the removal of SO_2 and particulates from the gases in a sintering plant, in a glass melt furnace, on oil-fired boilers, on a black liquor boiler, on two secondary sludge incinerators, and on a SCA-Billerud recovery process boiler. Negotiations are underway for Bahco systems on coal-fired industrial boilers and electric power boilers. Table III summarizes the location and service of these SO_2 removal installations, some of which will be discussed in detail.

Table II.   Nationwide Sulfur Oxide and Particulate Emissions from Industrial Sources, 1970 (1)

| Source | Emissions, 10^6 tons/year | |
	SO₂	Particulate
Asphalt batching		0.403
Cement		0.908
Coal cleaning		0.342
Grain plants handling		1.430
Feed		0.362
Gray iron foundries		0.260
Iron and steel		1.991
Kraft (sulfate) pulp		0.536
Lime		0.609
Petroleum refineries	3.010	0.241
Phosphate		0.350
Primary non-ferrous metallurgy		
Copper	3.335	0.314
Lead	0.213	0.39
Zinc	0.555	0.71
Aluminum		0.49
Secondary non-ferrous metallurgy		0.34
Sulfuric acid	0.92	0.38
Others not surveyed	1.530	10.15
Total industrial emissions	9.563	18.127

In 1964, AB Bahco Ventilation of Sweden initiated investigations of sulfur dioxide control using alkaline base scrubbing reagents (2, 3, 4). After several years of bench-scale screening studies, they developed a calcium-based scrubbing system. In 1966, AB Bahco installed a 1400 SCFM pilot unit on the boiler of their central heating plant. The initial pilot studies led to their first commercial installation in 1969 on an oil-fired boiler producing 75,000 lbs/hr of steam. In 1970, Bahco licensed their process technology rights in Japan to Marubeni with Tsukishima Kikai as a sub-licensee (5). In August 1971, Research-Cottrell acquired the rights to license the Bahco system in the United States and Canada (6,7).

Process Description

Figure 1 illustrates the major process equipment which comprises the RC/Bahco SO₂ removal system. The process is quite flexible and, with slight modifications to the basic design and equipment metallurgy, various scrubbing reagents can be used. The system has been commercially operated with hydrated lime, waste carbide sludge, and caustic soda. Pilot plant units have also used limestone, soda ash, and ammonia as scrubbing reagents.

Table III.   Installations of

Company	Location	No. of Units	Unit Capacity, SCFM at 32°F
Sodersjukhuset	Stockholm, Sweden	3	17,700
Daishowa Seishi Co.	Suzukawa, Japan	1	14,700
Daishowa Seishi Co.	Yoshinaga, Japan	5	44,200
Osaka City	Osaka, Japan	1	10,000
Hiroshima City	Hiroshima, Japan	1	10,000
Yahagi Iron Works	Nagoya, Japan	1	48,300
Taio Paper Co.	Iyomishima, Japan	1	83,000
Central Glass Co.	Sakai, Japan	1	31,300
Stora Kopparberg	Grycksbo, Sweden	1	17,700
Kanegafuchi Chemical[a]	Takasago City, Japan	2	79,500
Daishowa Seishi Co.[a]	Yoshinaga, Japan	2	66,400

[a] Startup late 1973.

Flue gas is supplied to the scrubbing system with a forced draft fan. Typically, the fan is designed for 20 inches of water pressure drop and is equipped with the typical draft control mechanism. A secondary damper is connected to the vacuum side of the fan. The secondary damper admits makeup air and thereby automatically maintains optimum gas flow in the scrubber during varying loads in the boiler operation.

Flue gases are treated in two stages, and the liquid-to-gas contact is achieved in an identical manner. The flue gas is forced into the scrubber inlet (1) where it is distributed and directed against a liquid reagent or slurry surface. There the gas must reverse direction and enter the throat of the first venturi stage (2). The gas velocity is accelerated in the venturi throat, causing extensive gas-liquid contacting and creating a vigorous cascade of droplets. The large gas velocity in the venturi throat causes the liquid droplets to be transported through the scrubber at a high concentration and turbulence. The droplets are separated from the flue gas in a centrifugal force drop collector (3). Liquid is returned to the first-stage contact zone and the gas passes to the second-stage venturi (4), where the gas liquid contact process is again repeated. In the second stage drop collector (5), the gas becomes free of droplets and exits through the chimney (6). The scrubbing liquid (13) is recirculated to the first stage contact zone (14).

In the case of a solid alkaline feed, such as hydrated lime and limestone, the raw material is fed from a bin (7) by a screw conveyor (8) through a mixer (9) into a dissolver (10). From the dissolver the reagent slurry is pumped to the second-stage impingement zone (11) where the liquid height is controlled by a level tank (12). The liquid overflow is recirculated to the mixer. The lower scrubber stage is provided with par-

the Bahco SO₂ Removal System

Service	Scrubbing Reagent	Inlet SO_2 Conc., ppm	SO_2 Removal Effic., %
oil-fired boiler	Ca(OH)₂	800–1500	97–99
oil-fired boiler	NaOH	900–1200	97–99
oil-fired boiler	NaOH	900–1000	97.5
secondary sludge incinerator	NaOH		
secondary sludge incinerator	NaOH		
sintering plant	Ca(OH)₂ waste carbide sludge	2500–4000	90–95
oil-fired boiler	NaOH	1000–1500	98
oil-fired boiler	NaOH	1000–1500	98
glass furnace	NaOH	1200 (25% SO₃)	98
black liquor boiler	CaO and CaCO₃ dust	4000–6000	70
oil-fired boiler	NaOH		
SCA-Billerud recovery boiler	NaOH		

tially spent reagent from the two drop collectors. The second stage overflow returns to the dissolver which is also the level tank for the first stage. A regulator keeps the level constant in the dissolver by supplying fresh water.

A fraction of the return flow from the first drop collector (16) is continuously separated by a concentration regulator (17) into a thickener (18) which automatically feeds viscous waste sludge to a large bin (19). The sludge can then be pumped to facilities for further chemical processing, filtered for producing a dried waste product, or disposed of by truck transport to a waste dump. Alternatively, the sludge can be pumped to a settling pond or disposed of directly.

Commercial Bahco SO₂ Removal Installations

As previously indicated, there are 18 commercial installations of the Bahco system in Sweden and Japan. Three of the Swedish units treat flue gas from oil-fired boilers, using hydrated lime as the scrubbing reagent. Each boiler produces 75,000 lbs/hr of steam and about 29,000 ACFM of flue gas at 300°F. The boilers burn 2.4% sulfur fuel oil, producing an off-gas containing about 1500 ppm SO₂. About 97–99% of the SO₂ is removed. Particulate emissions are controlled to 0.01-0.025 grain/ SCFD. The gas exits to the atmosphere through a stack without any reheating. Hydrated lime is delivered to the facility in 22 ton pneumatic trucks. Sludge is removed in a tanker truck to the Stockholm dump. Tests performed at the disposal site indicate that the waste sludge has no harmful effects on the ground or surface water in this area.

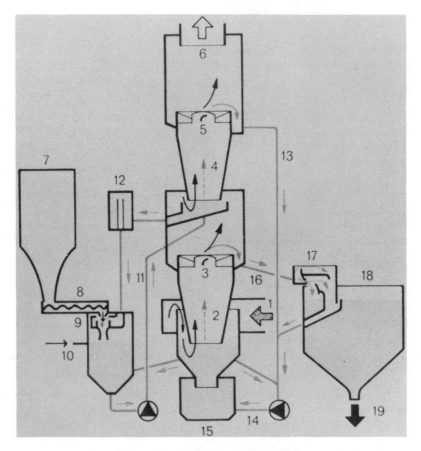

Figure 1.   RC/Bahco SO$_2$ scrubber

Eight of the Bahco scrubbers are located on oil-fired boilers in pulp
mills. The boilers range in size from 50,000 to 375,000 lbs/hr of steam
and produce 10,000–145,000 ACFM of off-gas at about 340°–360°F. Each
of these units operates with caustic soda as the scrubbing reagent. The
units operate at a controlled pH of 6.5 which maximizes the production
of sodium bisulfite and limits unwanted sulfate oxidation. The soluble
bisulfite product is utilized in the pulping operation. Particulate and
mist concentrations are held to about 0.02 grain/SCFW and SO$_2$ levels
are reduced by 97–99% from about 1500 to about 30 ppm. These units
have operated continuously without any operational upsets.

Bahco units have been installed on municipal waste treatment facilities in two Japanese cities. These units will be part of a total pollution
abatement facility. The units are operational and are awaiting the completion of the secondary sludge incinerators. The units will be operated
with caustic soda.

A Bahco system, using waste carbide sludge from an acetylene manufacturing plant, is treating the off-gases from a pelletizing and sintering furnace. This unit operates on a schedule governed by the steel manufacturing operation. The unit treats off-gases containing as much as 4000 ppm SO_2 with 95% removal efficiency. Outlet SO_2 concentrations are about 200 ppm SO_2. The units are pH-controlled to minimize reagent consumption and to maximize the production of calcium sulfite. The calcium sulfite is later oxidized under controlled conditions to form long gypsum crystals (calcium sulfate). The gypsum is used commercially.

A Bahco unit has been operating since October 1972 on a black liquor boiler at a Swedish pulp mill. The system is designed to handle about 30,000 ACFM of off-gases containing 4000–6000 ppm SO_2. This operation is treating flue gases containing about 6.5–8.5 grains/SCFD of particulates. The particulate is composed of calcium sulfite, sulfate, and carbonate salts. Some of the particulate matter is used as scrubbing reagent; the remaining alkali is waste lime ($\approx$50% CaO) and limestone. Pilot studies on this unit indicate that greater than 85% SO_2 removal efficiency could be expected. Presently the commercial installation is removing 99% of the particulates but only 70–75% of the SO_2. This unit has operated continuously since its installation without any scale-formation problems. The blowdown from the system is vacuum-filtered and the waste process sludge is disposed of as landfill at a concentration of 50 wt % solids.

As can be attested to by the above-mentioned installations, the Bahco SO_2 removal process is being successfully operated on many different

Table IV.   Typical Material Balance for the RC/Bahco CTB-100 Module

Material Balance	Low Sulfur Fuel	High Sulfur Fuel
Inlet gas		
Vol, ACFMW	170,000	170,000
Temp, °F	350	350
SO₂, ppmw	1,000	4,000
Dust load, grains/SCFD	2.15	2.15
Outlet gas		
Vol, ACFMW	134,000	134,000
Temp, °F	131	131
SO₂, PPMW	20	185
Dust load, Grains/SCFD	0.023	0.023
Raw materials		
Pebbled lime (92% CaO), tons/hr	0.6	2.3
Water, gal/min	62	82
Sludge (50% solids), tons/hr	4.5	12.7

types of processes using various scrubbing reagents. The reasons for the success of this process are as follows:

ON-STREAM RELIABILITY. The process can maintain continuous operation in the sodium systems and several months of prolonged operation in the calcium-based systems before brief cleanup periods are required.

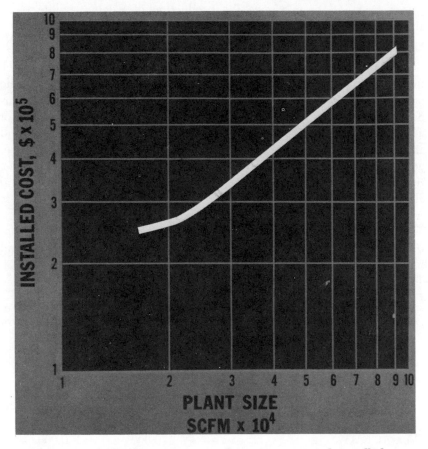

Figure 2. RC/Bahco SO₂ removal system estimated installed cost vs. capacity (carbon steel modules less turnkey)

EASE OF OPERATION. This system does not require large quantities of sophisticated instrumentation or expert manpower. Because of good mechanical design, most commercial units are operated by the same personnel who operate the sister flue gas-producing units.

FAVORABLE ECONOMICS. The RC/Bahco process has an annualized cost of 8–16¢/MMBtu and 17–24¢/MMBtu, respectively, for inlet SO_2 concentrations of 1000 and 4000 ppmw.

RC/Bahco Economics

Typical material balances and process economics are developed in this section of the paper and related to the annual operating costs for the process. A consistent set of data was used in developing the following information.

Material Balance. Material balances for a low and high sulfur content gas to the RC/Bahco CTB-100 module are illustrated in Table IV. Operating data from actual installations indicate 93–99% SO_2 removal and particulate emissions as low as 0.01 grain/SCFW. Scrubbing reagent consumption is about 1.1 times the stoichiometric amount.

Capital Investment. Standard module units are available in five sizes for gas flows from 18,000 to 90,000 SCFM, corresponding to roughly 60,000–300,000 lbs/hr of boiler capacity. For large capacities, two or more modules can be installed in parallel.

The initial capital investment for different capacity modules is illustrated in Figure 2. Represented here are the estimated budgetary selling prices for installed carbon steel units. However, unique installation costs, like site preparation, unusual foundations or support structures, interconnecting duct work, utility connections, or remote instrumentation are excluded.

Operating Costs. The annualized cost for processing 170,000 ACFM of flue gas at 350°F containing 4000 ppmw SO_2 is approximately $826,000 per year as calculated in Table V. However, at an inlet SO_2 concentration

Table V.   **Estimated Annual Operating Costs for the RC/Bahco CTB-100 Module (High Sulfur Flue Gas)**

Utilities	Quantity Required		Cost, $/unit	Annual[a] Cost, $/yr
Power	600	kw	$ 0.008/kw hr	42,050
Makeup water	82	gal./min	$ 0.30/1000 gal.	12,950
Chemicals				
Pebbled lime (92% CaO)	2.3	tons/hr	$22 /ton	443,250
Sludge disposal	12.7	tons/hr	$ 1/ton	111,250
Other operating costs				
Operators	0.5	man/shift	$ 4/hr	17,500
Supervision	25%	operating labor		4,400
Maintenance	3%	investment		22,500
Taxes and insurance	2%	investment		15,000
General overhead	100	of L&M		44,400
Depreciation	15%	investment		112,500
			Annualized cost:	$825,800

Assumes 8760 hr/yr.

of 1000 ppmw, the annualized cost of the process is about $410,000 per year. The annualized cost includes the cost of utilities, chemicals, waste removal, labor, maintenance, taxes, insurance, general overhead, and depreciation. As with other throwaway scrubbing systems, raw material consumption is the largest single cost item. A comparison of the operating costs for treating low and high sulfur fuel gases is illustrated in Figure 3. It can be observed that in both instances raw material consumption and sludge disposal represent significant expenditures.

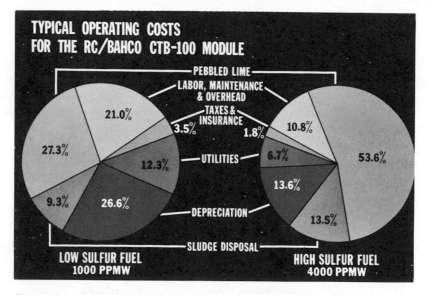

Figure 3. Typical operating costs for the RC/Bahco CTB–100 module

Figure 4 illustrates the annualized cost of operating an RC/Bahco SO_2 scrubbing system for various flue gas SO_2 concentration levels and unit sizes. As illustrated in Figure 4, a different fuel price of $4/ton of coal and $1/barrel of oil is approximately equal to 16¢/MMBtu. The current differential between high and low sulfur coal and oil are, respectively, $6–8/ton and $1.5–2/barrel or about 24–32¢/MMBtu. Coupled with the increased demand for low sulfur fuels will be an increase in price and a decrease in availability. Therefore the RC/Bahco process is an economic alternative which permits the use of available fuel sources.

Perspective

The pollution control industry has developed many different SO_2 removal systems to meet individual industry needs. There are systems recovering SO_2 to produce incremental sulfuric acid and sulfur. There

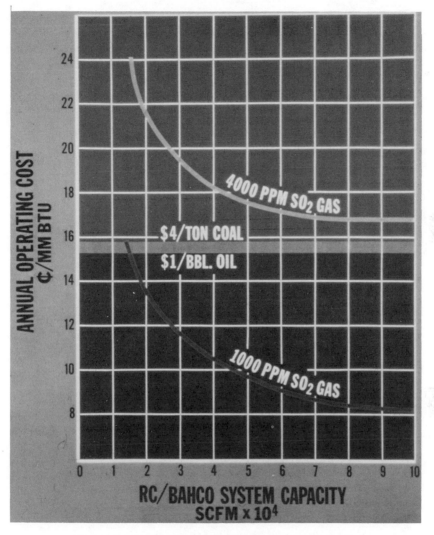

Figure 4.   Annualized cost/fuel switching comparison

are by-product systems which produce sodium bisulfite, gypsum, ammonia bisulfite, etc. However, the chemical industry is already producing
more than adequate supplies of sulfur, sulfuric acid, ammonium sulfite,
sodium sulfite and -bisulfite, and gypsum. Therefore it will only be in
rare circumstances that operators of SO$_2$ removal facilities will be able
to sell their by-products.

Without the commercial sale or internal consumption, it is necessary
to find a non-polluting means of disposing of the reaction products. The
reaction products from sodium and ammonia scrubbing are quite soluble

and will result in a water pollution problem if disposed of as a liquid blowdown or as a leachable solid waste product. Likewise the production of sulfuric acid, unless it can be consumed or sold, represents as much or more of a problem than the sulfur dioxide.

However there is a distinct advantage in operating a sodium- or acid-producing system. These systems operate with solutions rather than slurries and thereby avoid the problems or worries associated with most slurry systems. As a result of the advantages of operating a liquid phase system and the disadvantages of disposing of by-products, several control systems employ combined technology. Some units scrub with sodium salts and regenerate with calcium, forming a relatively insoluble by-product. Some units produce weak acid and neutralize it with limestone as a means of disposal.

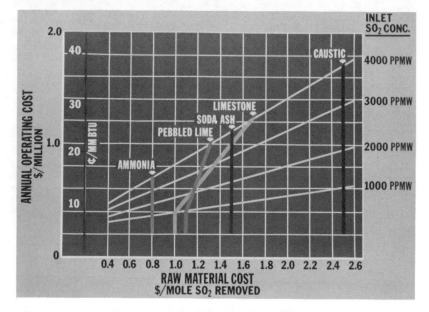

Figure 5. Annual operating cost vs. *raw material cost for an RC/Bahco CTB–100 module*

The RC/Bahco system can operate as a by-product recovery system. However it is also capable of scrubbing with slurries and avoiding many of the problems of its competitors. Figure 5 illustrates the economics involved in using various scrubbing reagents in this process. When operating a by-product system, the cost of SO_2 scrubbing is about 10¢/MMBtu of fuel burned. When it is necessary to produce a disposable by-product which will not contribute additional pollution, the cost is more likely to be 20¢/MMBtu.

Literature Cited

1. Economics of Clean Air, Annual Report to the Congress, February 1972.
2. Gustavsson, K. A., 1st International Lime/Limestone Symposium, Pensacola, Fla., March 1970.
3. Gustavsson, K. A., 1st International Lime/Limestone Symposium, Pensacola, Fla., March 1970.
4. Karvegard, I., Swedish Technical Week, Japan, 1972.
5. Nakayama, E., Swedish Technical Week, Japan, 1972.
6. McKenna, J. D., Atkins, R. S., 2nd International Lime/Limestone Symposium, New Orleans, La., November 1971.
7. Atkins, R. S., McKenna, J. D., *Power Engineering* (May 1972) 50–51.

RECEIVED February 15, 1973.

15

The Chemistry of the Molten Carbonate Process for Sulfur Oxides Removal from Stack Gases

S. J. YOSIM, L. F. GRANTHAM, and D. E. McKENZIE

Atomics International, A Division of Rockwell International Corp., P.O. Box 309, Canoga Park, Calif. 91304

G. C. STEGMANN

Consolidated Edison Co. of New York, Inc.

In the molten carbonate process a molten eutectic mixture of lithium, sodium, and potassium carbonates removes sulfur oxides from power plant stack gases. The resulting molten solution of alkali metal sulfites, sulfates, and unreacted carbonate is regenerated in a two-step process to the alkali carbonate for recycling. Hydrogen sulfide, which is evolved in the regeneration step, is converted to sulfur in a conventional Claus plant. A 10 MW pilot plant of the process has been constructed at the Consolidated Edison Arthur Kill Station on Staten Island, and startup is underway.

The Atomics International molten carbonate process for removal of sulfur oxides from power plant stack gases has been under development since 1966. Construction of a 10 MW pilot plant has been completed, and startup is underway. This paper describes the process chemistry, the pilot plant, and the process economics.

Process Description

In the molten carbonate process, a molten eutectic mixture of lithium, sodium, and potassium carbonates is used to scrub the power plant gas stream. The sulfur oxides in the gas stream react with the carbonates to form sulfites and sulfates which remain dissolved in excess unreacted carbonate melt. The molten carbonate-sulfite-sulfate mixture is then treated to convert the sulfite and sulfate back to carbonate and to recover the sulfur as elemental sulfur. The regenerated carbonate is then recirculated to the scrubber to repeat the process cycle.

The carbonate is regenerated in two steps: (1) the sulfite and sulfate are reduced to sulfide by reaction with a form of carbon, such as petroleum coke and (2) the sulfide is converted to carbonate by reaction of the melt with steam and carbon dioxide, liberating hydrogen sulfide. The hydrogen sulfide is then converted to elemental sulfur in a Claus plant.

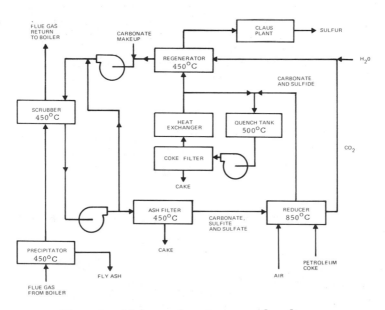

Figure 1. Molten carbonate process flow diagram

The process flow diagram is shown in Figure 1. The process steps are as follows:

1. The gas to be treated is removed from the boiler at about 450°C and, if the boiler is burning coal, the gas passes through a high temperature, high efficiency electrostatic precipitator where essentially all the fly ash is removed. The gas then passes through the scrubber, where the sulfur oxides are removed by contacting the gas stream with a spray of molten carbonate at 450°C. This gas-liquid contact removes 95% or more of the sulfur oxides and most of the remaining ash from the gas stream. The cleaned gases are then returned to the boiler for further heat recovery and eventually pass out the stack.

2. The molten salt stream containing carbonate (M_2CO_3, where M = the mixture of Na, K, and Li), sulfite (M_2SO_3), sulfate (M_2SO_4), and ash from the scrubber is pumped to a purification system and filtered

to remove the ash. The ash filter cake is subsequently treated to recover the contained lithium carbonate.

3. The filtered melt is fed into the reducer and reacts with carbon. The melt temperature is raised from 450 to about 850°C by heat from the combustion of part of the carbon with air, and the sulfite and sulfate in the melt are completely reduced to sulfide (M_2S).

4. The melt stream from the reducer is passed into a quench tank where its temperature is lowered from 850 to 450°C by mixing with cooler melt and by passing through a heat exchanger. The effluent from the quench tank is filtered to remove unreacted coke and coke ash and then is passed to the regenerator.

5. In the regenerator the reduced melt reacts with carbon dioxide (produced in the reduction step) and steam in a multi-stage, counter-current sieve-tray column. The sulfide in the melt is completely regenerated to carbonate (M_2CO_3), and the sulfur is released as hydrogen sulfide (H_2S). The hydrogen sulfide is passed to the Claus plant where it is converted to elemental sulfur.

6. The regenerated melt is recirculated to the scrubber, and the small filter melt losses are replaced by adding fresh carbonate.

Chemistry of the Process

The alkali carbonate eutectic melt (1) used in the process is a mixture of 32 wt % lithium carbonate, 33 wt % sodium carbonate, and 35 wt % potassium carbonate. The physical properties of the eutectic are given in Table I.

Table I. Physical Properties of the Alkali Carbonate Eutectic Melt

Property	Magnitude	Reference
Melting point	397°C	2
Molecular weight	100 gram/mole	2
Heat of fusion	6.6 kcal/gram-mole at 397°C	2
Density	2.12 gram/ml at 450°C	3
Viscosity	9.82 cp at 450°C	4
Heat capacity	40.39 cal/gram-mole at 450°C	2
Surface tension	236.9 dynes/cm at 450°C	3

The melt has several chemical and physical properties which are advantageous for scrubbing sulfur dioxide from flue gas. It is a liquid which is easy to handle, pump, and transport, and it has a negligible vapor pressure so that it is not lost by evaporation and does not require high pressure equipment. It is a strong base; therefore, it reacts rapidly with acidic sulfur oxides so that scrubbing contact time can be short. Because the entire liquid is a strong base, it has a high capacity for sulfur oxides, and the amount of melt which must be regenerated continuously is relatively small. The great affinity of the melt for sulfur oxides leads to the removal of large percentages of the sulfur oxides from even very dilute gas streams. Using this melt in the scrubber at 450°C neither cools the gas stream nor saturates it with water vapor. Finally, the carbonate will react with the other acidic gaseous pollutants such as NO_2 and HCl; therefore, laboratory tests suggest that the potential exists for control of other pollutants such as NO_x by the same process. The chemistry of each step of the process has been studied in detail and is summarized below:

The Scrubbing Step. The reactions taking place in the scrubber are

$$SO_2(g) + M_2CO_3(l) \rightarrow M_2SO_3(l) + CO_2(g) \tag{1}$$

$$SO_3(g) + M_2CO_3(l) \rightarrow M_2SO_4(l) + CO_2(g) \tag{2}$$

$$M_2SO_3(l) + 1/2\ O_2(g) \rightarrow M_2SO_4(l) \tag{3}$$

Absorption of SO_2 and SO_3 (Equations 1 and 2) is very rapid. For example, in the laboratory when pure SO_2 is bubbled through 2 inches of melt, no odor of SO_2 can be detected in the exit gas (CO_2). The presence of O_2, CO_2, N_2, H_2O, and fly ash does not affect the SO_2 removal. Melt which was regenerated 3 times in a series of cyclic tests was equally effective in removing SO_2. These results are not surprising in view of acid-base considerations in which the acidic SO_2 is neutralized by the basic alkali carbonate melt.

In an actual plant good contact must be made between the large volumes of flue gas and the relatively small melt stream. However, power plant integration requirements make it important to impose as small a pressure drop as possible on the gas stream. Because of this, a spray contactor has been selected as the molten salt scrubber concept. The spray contactor uses spray nozzles to break up the melt into small droplets for good gas-liquid contact and a very efficient mist eliminator to prevent the gas stream from carrying melt mist out of the scrubber.

For example, in bench-scale tests when hot synthetic flue gas containing 2000 ppm SO_2 was forced past a single melt spray nozzle at 25 ft/sec, sulfur oxide removal efficiencies of 97-100% were obtained at molar gas-to-liquid ratios of 0.01-0.30; little (if any) melt in the exit gas could be found. The oxidation of M_2SO_3 (Equation 3) does not appear to be very rapid at the scrubber temperature. For example, when synthetic flue gas containing 1 vol % O_2 and 0.1 vol % SO_2 was bubbled through molten carbonate eutectic at 450°C, only 18, 31, and 44 wt % of the sulfite (formed from the absorbed sulfur dioxide) were oxidized to sulfate in 4, 7, and 14 hrs, respectively. When the synthetic flue gas contained 5 vol % O_2 and 0.3 vol % SO_2, 42, 49, and 55 wt % of the absorbed sulfur oxide were oxidized to sulfate at similar times. Neither water nor fly ash had any appreciable effect on the oxidation rate; however, it is anticipated that NO_x absorption will increase oxidation of sulfite.

The Reduction Step. The principal reactions occurring in the reduction step are disproportionation (Equation 4) and reduction (Equations 5 and 6).

$$4M_2SO_3(l) \rightarrow 3M_2SO_4(l) + M_2S(l) \tag{4}$$

$$2M_2SO_3(l) + 3C(s) \rightarrow 3CO_2(g) + 2M_2S(l) \tag{5}$$

$$M_2SO_4(l) + 2C(s) \rightarrow 2CO_2(g) + M_2S(l) \tag{6}$$

The disproportionation rate of sulfite to form sulfide and sulfate (Equation 4) has been measured. Rate measurements indicate that disproportionation is a first-order reaction which is not important at the scrubber temperature (450°C) but is rapid at reduction temperatures (850°C). Therefore the major sulfur compound undergoing reduction in the process is sulfate.

The sulfate (Equation 6) and sulfite (Equation 5) can be reduced by numerous substances. Fluidized coke is particularly good for this application because it is relatively inexpensive and has a low ash content. Depending on the sulfate to carbonate ratio, about 1.5-2 lbs of coke are consumed per pound of sulfur reduced. This includes coke consumed in the reaction and coke burned to cover heat of reaction, heat required to increase salt temperature to reducing temperature, and heat losses from the system. The reaction rate increased by about 2 to 3 for each 50°C temperature rise; reduction times of 170, 30, 15, and 4 min were observed at 700, 800, 875, and 950°C, respectively. Therefore, the reduction reaction is carried out at about 850°C or above.

In order to raise the temperature from 450° to about 850°C and to supply the endothermic heat of reduction ($\sim$ 40 kcal/mole), considerable heat must be supplied. Because of materials limitations at this high temperature, the most feasible way to supply the heat of reaction is to generate the heat internally by the combustion of carbon with air. This eliminates the need for heat transfer surfaces operating at high temperatures in a corrosive environment.

The Regeneration Reaction. Two important reactions occur in the regenerator: absorption of carbon dioxide (Equation 7) and regeneration of carbonate (Equation 8).

$$M_2S(l) + CO_2(g) \rightarrow M_2CO_2S(l) \tag{7}$$

$$M_2S(l) + CO_2(g) + H_2O(g) \rightarrow M_2CO_3(l) + H_2S(g) \tag{8}$$

Carbon dioxide is readily absorbed by molten melts containing sulfide. The amount of carbon dioxide absorbed increases as the temperature decreases and as the carbon dioxide partial pressure increases. Although thiocarbonate intermediates (M_2CO_2S, M_2COS_2 and M_2CS_3) have not been identified in the melts, the chemistry involved indicates that the formation of these substances is the most likely explanation for carbon dioxide absorption. These intermediates are quite stable at temperatures of about 450°C and even appear to exist to some extent at temperatures as high as 950°C. Depending on the carbon dioxide partial pressure, about 0.5-1.5 moles of CO_2 are absorbed per mole of sulfide at 450°C. These absorption reactions are exothermic (15 to 20 kcal/mole) and are reversible.

Both carbon dioxide and steam must react with the melt before regeneration occurs (Equation 8), although a substantial amount of carbon dioxide must be absorbed (Equation 7) before any evolution of hydrogen sulfide begins. However, because the intermediate has not been identified, the overall regeneration reaction is given in Equation 8. This reaction is rapid and complete, particularly at about 450°C. The regeneration reaction is exothermic; therefore the melt must be cooled during regeneration in order to maintain optimum regeneration temperatures (450-500°C). The concentrated hydrogen sulfide stream evolved from the regenerator is fed to a Claus plant for conversion to sulfur.

Lithium Recovery. The melt used in this process is relatively inexpensive except for the lithium carbonate which comprises approximately 84% of the salt cost. Therefore it is desirable to recover the lithium from the process filter cakes. An aqueous process has been developed for this purpose. The filter cakes are slurried with water and filtered to extract the very soluble sodium and potassium carbonates; lithium carbonate remains with the ash because it is relatively insoluble under these conditions. The ash-lithium carbonate cake is slurried in water and the lithium is solubilized by conversion to the bicarbonate. The ash is removed by filtration and the soluble bicarbonate in the filtrate is precipitated as the carbonate. The lithium carbonate is separated by filtration and returned to the process stream; the saturated lithium carbonate filtrate is recycled to conserve lithium. Laboratory tests have demonstrated that more than 90% of the lithium can be recovered by this technique.

Materials and Components. A test program to select materials of construction which resist corrosion by the process melts has been underway for more than 5 years. At first, all of the common metals, alloys, and ceramics were screened. Successful candidates were then subjected to long-term tests, including one-year tests in rotating capsules.

After the preliminary selection of 300 series stainless steel, these alloys were subjected to further tests to study the effect of stress in the presence of chloride, oxygen, and water vapor, the effect of sensitization, and the rate at which the alloying constituents are leached and transported under the influence of a temperature gradient. A molten salt loop has been in operation for nearly a year as a part of these tests. The results indicated Types 304 and 347 stainless steel were the best of the conventional alloys for service below 550°C. High density alumina was very corrosion-resistant even at 950°C; therefore alumina bricks will be used to line the pilot plant reducer vessel.

The success of the Type 300 series stainless steel in molten carbonates is a result of the protective $LiCrO_2$ film which forms a compact, tenacious, and self-healing layer. This film forms in about 500 hrs and decreases the corrosion rate to a few mils per year. It has been shown that this film is essentially chromium oxide, with the vacant interstices filled with lithium. Lithium is the only stable ionic species present in the melt which is capable of filling the vacant interstice without expanding the oxide lattice (5). Thus a stable diffusion barrier is formed which limits further corrosion.

Figure 2. Molten carbonate process pilot plant at completion of construction, Mar. 30, 1973

Economical Evaluation of the Process

Updated economic analyses of the process have been done to estimate the capital and operating costs of a large commercial plant (6, 7). The economic analyses were made for a plant treating the gas stream from an 800 MW generating station, operating at a 70% plant factor and burning coal containing 3% sulfur. A penalty charge for the high-temperature electrostatic precipitator was assessed. The cost of the Claus sulfur plant was also included. The total capital requirement (1973 dollars) is about $24 million or about $30 per kilowatt of generating capacity. This cost appears to be quite competitive with that for any other stack gas treatment process which recovers the sulfur in useful form.

The estimated annual operating cost for the 800 MW plant, assuming capital charges of 14% per year, is 1.0 mills/kW hr without any credit being taken for the by-product sulfur produced. A return of $20/long ton for the sulfur is equivalent to a credit of 0.18 mills/kW hr, reducing the operation costs to about 0.8 mills/kW hr. This compares quite well with present estimates of 0.7-1.4 mills/kW hr for low sulfur or desulfurized fuels.

A thorough engineering and economic evaluation of the molten carbonate process was completed by Singmaster and Breyer in 1970, under contract to EPA (8). For the same plant situation, their cost estimates (based on 1970 dollars) were $16.81/kW for the capital investment (not including the Claus plant) and 0.95 mills/kW hr for operating costs without by-product credit.

Pilot Plant Program

The pilot plant, funded by Consolidated Edison, Northeast Utilities, and Rockwell International, will process a side stream of stack gases from a 335 MW boiler at the Consolidated Edison Arthur Kill Station on Staten Island. It is planned to vary the SO_2 concentration at the inlet to the scrubber in order to map process performance over a range of conditions. The side stream will correspond to approximately 10 MW equivalent of gas.

The gases, at 125°C, will be heated to about 450°C by an in-line burner firing the same fuel as the boiler. The flue gases produced by the boiler when burning the fuel oil presently specified will contain about 200 ppm sulfur oxides. This concentration is low when compared with the 2000 ppm typical of gases produced by boilers burning coal containing 3% sulfur. In order to provide the flexibility needed to operate over a range of sulfur oxide concentrations, the pilot plant will be designed to recycle some sulfur dioxide from its Claus plant.

Construction of the pilot plant is complete (7); a photograph is shown in Figure 2. Plant startup is currently underway. A one-year test program is contemplated. During this period all system and component performance tests and optimization studies can be completed.

Literature Cited

1. Janz, G. J., "Molten Salt Handbook," Academic, New York, 1967.
2. Janz, G. J., Neuenschwander, E., Kelly, F. J., *Trans. Faraday Soc.* (1963) 59, 841.
3. Ward, A. T., Janz, G. J., *Electrochim. Acta* (1965) 10, 849.
4. Janz, G. J., Saegusa, F., *J. Electrochem. Soc.* (1963) 110, 452.
5. Grantham, L. F., Shaw, P. H., Oldenkamp, R. D., in "High Temperature Metallic Corrosion of Sulfur and Its Compounds," Z. A. Foroulis, Ed., The Electrochemical Society, New York, 1970.
6. Botts, W. V., Oldenkamp, R. D., *Ann. Meetg., Air Pollut. Contr. Ass.*, June 18–22, 1972, paper 72–115.
7. Botts, W. V., Oldenkamp, R. D. *Ann. Meetg., Air Pollut. Contr. Ass.*, June 25–29, 1973, paper 73–305.
8. Drobot, W., Finkler, S., Whitlock, D. R. EPA Contract CPA–70–76, Singmaster and Breyer, 235 East 42nd St., New York, 1970.

RECEIVED February 15, 1973. A portion of this work was performed under Contract No. CPA 70–78 with the U.S. Environmental Protection Agency.

Recovery of Sulfur Dioxide from Stack Gases as Elemental Sulfur by a Dry, Fluidized Activated Carbon Process

F. J. BALL, G. N. BROWN, J. E. DAVIS, A. J. REPIK, and S. L. TORRENCE

Westvaco Corp. Research Center, Box 5207, N. Charleston, S. C. 29406

A dry, fluidized activated carbon process is being developed for recovery of SO_2 from waste gases as elemental sulfur. The SO_2 is removed at 150–300°F as H_2SO_4 sorbed on carbon. Sorbed H_2SO_4 is converted directly to sulfur by reaction with internally produced H_2S. The product sulfur is vaporized at 1000°F and recovered as molten sulfur. Remaining sorbed sulfur reacts with hydrogen at 1000°F to produce the required H_2S. Adsorption of SO_2 has been demonstrated on power boiler flue gases and simulated Claus tail gas at rates as high as 25,000 ft^3/hr. Carbon can be economically regenerated at acceptable rates of reaction.

In 1970, 20 million tons of sulfur dioxide emitted from steam electric-power plants. Without control measures these emissions will increase to 40 million tons by 1980. With typical SO_2 concentrations in stack gas currently in the range of 1000–2000 ppm, target levels for future control legislation correspond to 50–150 ppm SO_2 in the stack, and there are not sufficient low sulfur fuels to meet these standards. To fill the gap between projected supplies of low sulfur fuels and our nation's energy requirements, an economical, high efficiency process to remove SO_2 from the flue gases of power plants is required. Such a process must also recover SO_2 in a form which can be readily handled and sold, in recognition of the quantities involved. Furthermore such a process must be compatible with the many constraints public utilities face in its installation and operation.

Westvaco has, over the past six years, developed a sulfur dioxide removal process using activated carbon that operates after the usual low temperature electrostatic precipitators. This process incorporates the features of compact size, recovery of SO_2 as elemental sulfur, minimal power train interruption, capability of reducing stack gas SO_2 to below 50 ppm, and economic advantage over fuel desulfurization. The active carbon, which has a tremendous surface area, acts as a catalyst to increase the rate of reaction of SO_2 with the flue gas oxygen and moisture to form sulfuric acid which remains adsorbed within the carbon's pores. This catalytic effect is so great that virtually complete SO_2 removal can be obtained in a fraction of a second contact between the flue gas and the carbon. In contrast only about 1% of the SO_2 is oxidized to SO_3 in the power boiler and the conversion of SO_2 in the atmosphere may take hours or days.

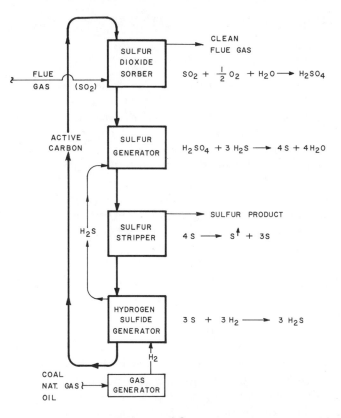

Figure 1. Westvaco SO₂ recovery process

The feasibility of using activated carbon as a catalyst and adsorbent for SO_2 removal is demonstrated in processes currently in use in other countries. A series of carbon-based SO_2 recovery installations have been operated with continuous recycling for up to two years in West Germany.

Also two carbon-based SO_2 recovery demonstration plants are now in operation in Japan on power plants of greater than 50 MW. All of these processes use fixed-bed or plug-flow adsorption columns and recover the sulfur as dilute sulfuric acid or as concentrated SO_2 at the expense of consuming the carbon. However the Westvaco sulfur dioxide recovery process employs fluidized beds of active carbon both to remove the sulfur dioxide and to regenerate economically the carbon while producing sulfur as a by-product. Fluidized granular activated-carbon technology has been progressively developed on a large plant scale for cyclic recovery of low concentration solvent contaminants from high volume air streams and for by-product purification in petro-chemical processing. Air streams of up to 50,000 ft³/min, which is equivalent to that emitting from a 250 MW boiler, are currently being purified in this manner.

The sulfuric acid formed in the sorption step is reduced to sulfur on the carbon by a reaction sequence using hydrogen. This sulfur is then stripped from the carbon. The overall chemistry of the sulfur recovery is:

$$3H_2 + SO_2 + \frac{1}{2}O_2 \rightarrow S + 3H_2O \tag{1}$$

This paper describes the development of the process with particular emphasis on the sulfur recovery sequence. Previous papers have covered the background and process development (1), kinetics of fluid-bed SO_2 sorption (2), and process application to Claus plant tail gases (3).

Although the process discussed pertains to power boilers, the inherent flexibility in the process allows its application to Claus plants, sulfuric acid plants, and smelters with the option of either elemental sulfur or SO_2 as the product. There appear to be some unique advantages of this process in simplifying the production of pipeline gas from coal flowsheets.

Process Description

The basis of the process is to use activated carbon to recover SO_2 in a salable form. The process flowsheet and chemistry are summarized in Figure 1. All steps of this dry, cyclic process are performed in continuous, countercurrent, multi-stage fluidized-bed equipment. In the SO_2-removal step the carbon catalyzes the reaction of the SO_2 with oxygen in the flue gas to form SO_3, which is hydrolyzed to sulfuric acid that remains sorbed

$$SO_2 + \frac{1}{2}O_2 + H_2O \xrightarrow{\text{activated carbon}} H_2SO_4 \text{ (sorbed)} \tag{2}$$

in the carbon pores (Reaction 2). The carbon is regenerated by the reaction of sulfuric acid on the carbon with hydrogen sulfide to form elemental sulfur (Reaction 3).

$$H_2SO_4 \text{ (sorbed)} + 3H_2S \xrightarrow[\text{carbon}]{\text{activated}} 4S \text{ (sorbed)} + 4H_2O \qquad (3)$$

One-fourth of the elemental sulfur, the amount derived from the sulfuric acid, is recovered from the carbon by direct vaporization in the sulfur stripper. The remaining elemental sulfur is allowed to react with hydrogen in the hydrogen sulfide generator to provide hydrogen sulfide (Reaction 4).

$$H_2 + S \text{ (sorbed)} \xrightarrow[\text{carbon}]{\text{activated}} H_2S \qquad (4)$$

The hydrogen for the hydrogen sulfide generator is supplied by a gas producer or reformer. The hydrogen sulfide generator provides the gas needed for the sulfur generation step (Reaction 3). In the overall Reaction 1, SO_2 is removed from the power plant flue gas at the expense of hydrogen consumption and yields elemental sulfur as a useful by-product.

Process Development

The SO_2 recovery process is being studied in both bench-scale and fluid-bed pilot equipment (1, 2, 3). Initial feasibility tests were conducted in small fixed-bed reactors to determine the most effective carbon for SO_2 removal and to evolve the regeneration sequence for minimum carbon loss. Continuous operation of the various process steps was evaluated under simulated conditions in fluidized-bed pilot equipment.

Removal of SO_2 from actual boiler flue gas was first tested in a 1500 ft^3/hr, 6-inch diameter unit operating on a slipstream from a 50 MW oil-fired boiler. This equipment was operated satisfactorily around-the-clock for periods as long as one week. Scaled up 18-inch diameter adsorbers, capable of handling gas rates of 20,000 ft^3/hr, also have been operated satisfactorily on flue gas from an oil-fired boiler and on simulated Claus tail gas. Data from these continuous units showed SO_2-removal capabilities to as low as 50 ppm.

Reactor Design

Process development has progressed from initial measurements of overall reaction rates under expected commercial conditions to the development of equilibrium and kinetic models for all process steps. The most emphasis has centered on the SO_2 sorber because this is by far the largest and most expensive piece of equipment.

SO_2 Sorber. In applying of the Westvaco process to boilers, Claus units, smelters, *etc.*, a variety of waste gases will be encountered. Therefore, to estimate reactor size differential, sorption rate studies were made with simulated flue gases. Stepwise regression techniques were then applied to obtain a rate expression (Equation 5). A more detailed discussion of the rate models considered and the quality fit of the model

$$\text{Rate} = \frac{dX_v}{dt} = 1.59(10^{-4}) \exp^{5520/T} (y_{SO_2})^{0.4} (y_{O_2})^{0.63} (y_{H_2O})^{0.73} \left(1 - \frac{X_v}{0.38}\right) \quad (5)$$

where t = time, min
   T = temperature, °R
   y = volume fraction in gas phase
   X_v = acid loading, gram H_2SO_4/gram carbon

chosen is given elsewhere (*4, 5*). This model gives the rate of SO_2 sorption with activated carbon as a function of temperature, SO_2, O_2, and water concentrations up to 2, 3.5, and 15%, respectively. Figure 2 shows graphically the effects of these variables on SO_2 sorption rate. Note that the rate of reaction increases by about an order of magnitude as the temperature decreases from 300 to 150°F. Although inlet gas temperatures above 300°F may be encountered, experiments have shown that the gas temperature is readily lowered and accurately controlled by spraying water directly into the fluidized carbon. At the high heat transfer rates in the well mixed fluid bed the water rapidly evaporates, cooling both the gas and the fluidized carbon. In addition to savings of up to 25% in projected capital costs of the total process, direct cooling allows lower sorber temperatures and results in better control than indirect heat exchangers. Although the additional water added to the stream by the sprays is only a small per cent of the flue gas, it also increases the sorption rate (Figure 2). These data were taken with gas streams which contained more than 50 ppm nitric oxide, as would be the case for power boilers. For nitric oxide concentrations below 50 ppm, the reaction rate increases sharply to 2½-3 times the values shown.

The sorption rate and kinetic model gave good agreement with data on actual flue gas from an oil-fired boiler in both the 1500 and 20,000 ft³/hr continuous fluid-bed SO_2 sorbers (Figure 3). Rates somewhat higher than the model at higher SO_2 concentrations suggest a higher reaction order for SO_2 than that found in bench-scale work. A computer program incorporating this model has been developed for sorber design.

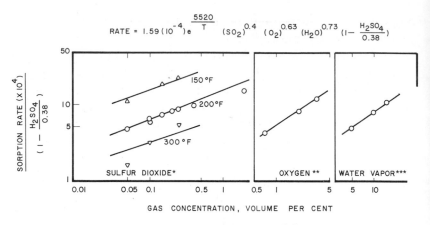

Figure 2. SO_2 sorption rate model

*SO_2 concentration and temperature were varied as shown and the O_2 and H_2O concentrations were constant at 2 and 10 vol %, respectively. **O_2 concentration was varied as shown and the SO_2 and H_2O concentrations were constant at 2000 ppm and 10 vol %, respectively. The temperature was held constant at 200°F. ***Water vapor concentration was varied as shown and the SO_2 and O_2 concentrations were constant at 2000 ppm and 2 vol %, respectively. The temperature was held constant at 200°F.

Sulfur Generation. During the SO_2 removal step the gaseous SO_2 is converted to nonvolatile sulfuric acid which remains sorbed in the carbon's pores. Conversion of this sulfuric acid to SO_2 or elemental sulfur by reaction with hydrogen sulfide has been studied in bench scale.

A series of experiments were performed in a different reactor to develop a kinetic model for the sulfur generation step; *see* Reaction 2. The progress of the reaction was followed by analyzing the carbon for acid and sulfur content. Each run was made at a different combination of inlet hydrogen sulfide concentration and temperature. The ranges of variables tested were: 250-325°F, 0-40% H_2S, 0-30% H_2O, and 0-24 lbs H_2SO_4/100 lbs carbon. A rate equation was developed from these data by multiple-regression techniques:

$$\text{Rate} = \frac{dXS}{dt} = 23.57 \ \exp^{-2644/T}(y_{H2S})^{0.58}(X_v)^{0.67} \qquad (6)$$

where X_S = sulfur loading, gram S/gram C
      y_{H2S} = volume fraction of H_2S

The fit of the differential reactor data to the model is shown grapically in Figure 4. Moisture, which is generated in the sulfur generator as hydrogen sulfide reacts with the sulfuric acid, has the effect of decreasing the rate of reaction predicted by Equation 6. Work is continuing to find the appropriate function to describe the observed effect of water. The

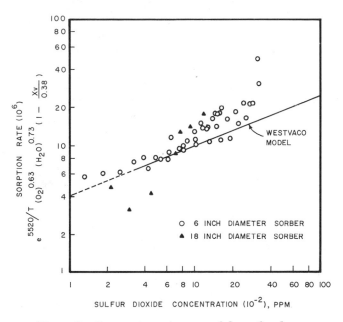

Figure 3. Comparison of rate model to pilot data

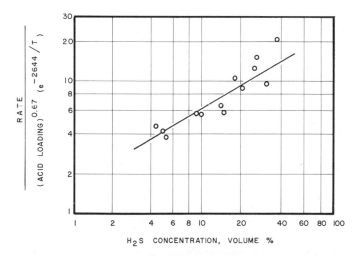

*Figure 4. Comparison of the sulfur-generation rate model
with the experimental data for 250° to 325°F*

reaction shown in Equation 7 can cause a premature evalution of SO₂ at
temperatures near 350°F so the sulfur generation step is carried out at
300°F.

$$2H_2SO_4 + S \rightarrow 3SO_2 + 2H_2O \qquad (7)$$

The validity of rate Equation 6 will be tested with a pilot unit. If it is adequate, it will be used for design of the sulfur generator.

Sulfur Stripping. One-fourth of the sorbed sulfur coming from the sulfur generator is removed from the carbon in the sulfur-stripping step. The sulfur is stripped by a recirculating inert gas stream in a multi-stage fluidized-bed stripper. The sulfur is recovered from the inert gas by a condensing circuit that is similar to equipment and instrumentation currently used in Claus plants. The molten sulfur product that is withdrawn from the condensing circuit can be stored and shipped as the liquid product or additional product inventory may be handled by either sulfur blocks or sulfur flakes. Various methods of solvent extraction and steam stripping were also evaluated prior to the choice of inert gas as the preferred stripping medium. In addition, inert gas-stripping of sulfur from activated carbon has been proved commercially on tail gas units on Claus plants currently recovering 3,000 tons of sulfur/day.

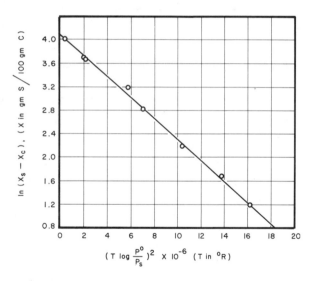

Figure 5. Polanyi-Dubinin plot of sulfur adsorption equilibrium on activated carbon

Sorbed sulfur on the active carbons used for SO_2 sorption is in three categories. Sulfur down to a loading of 7 grams/100 grams carbon is readily removed by the inert gas. Sulfur in the range 7 to 1-3 grams/100 grams carbon is more strongly held or chemisorbed but is removed as hydrogen sulfide by the hydrogen treatment at 1000°F. This hydrogen treatment is also very beneficial in maintaining high catalytic activity for SO_2 adsorption. Sulfur below this level behaves as an integral part of the carbon matrix.

In the sulfur-stripping step, the physically adsorbed sulfur is removed with the carbon leaving the stripper at a loading about 18 grams sulfur/100 grams carbon. Because the vapor pressure of sorbed sulfur would be expected to be much less than that of free sulfur, equilibrium adsorption data for sulfur vapor on the activated carbon were obtained by bench-scale, fixed-bed experiments. From these data, the equilibrium loading of physically sorbed sulfur is represented as a function of temperature and sulfur vapor pressure by the Polanyi-Dubinin adsorption equation. The fit of the equation with constants derived graphically from the experimental data is shown in Figure 5. The results are summarized by the best linear fit, Equation 8:

$$\ln(X_s - X_c) = 4.10 - 0.179 \left(T \log \frac{P^\circ_s}{P_s} \right)^2 \times 10^{-6} \tag{8}$$

where X_s = total equilibrium sulfur loading in gram S/100 grams C
   X_c = 7.3 grams S/100 grams C
   P°_s = saturation vapor pressure of sulfur in torr at temperature T
   P_s = equilibrium vapor pressure of sulfur over carbon in torr

The range of experimental data included temperatures of 650-1000°F, sulfur vapor pressures of 1.55-1.38 torr, and sulfur loadings of 10.6-63 grams sulfur/100 grams carbon. An isotherm constructed from the above equation at 1000°F, Figure 6, gave good agreement with the experimental data.

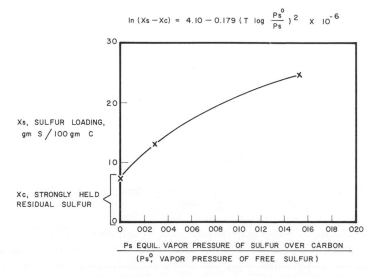

Figure 6.   Sulfur isotherm for Westvaco carbon at 1000°F, Polanyi-Dubinin model

Because it is desirable to operate at high space velocities (low contact times) in the sulfur stripper, operating data from a continuous pilot unit having a contact time per stage of only 0.17 sec were analyzed to determine if the removal of physically sorbed sulfur was diffusion limited. The data showed an average approach to equilibrium of 80% over the eight-stage unit. Much closer approaches to equilibrium would be expected at the longer contact times used in studies on large-scale units. Experimental data at intermediate contact times are being analyzed to develop a quantitative relationship.

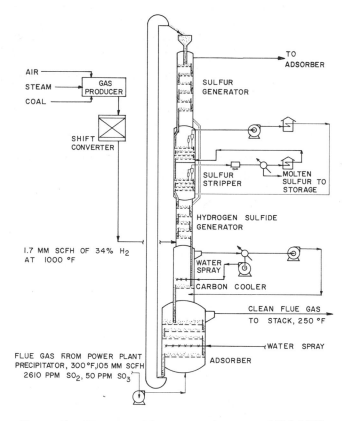

Figure 7.   Westvaco SO_2 *recovery process, 1000 MW unit*

The stripping vessel may be designed by applying standard graphical (6) or stage-by-stage techniques similar to those used for distillation calculations to determine equilibrium stages. Experimentally determined approaches to equilibrium may then be applied in the same manner as stage efficiencies to determine the actual stages required.

The sulfur removal during stripping is controlled to leave the required amount of sulfur on the carbon for conversion to hydrogen sulfide by hydrogen at 1000°F in this subsequent H_2S generation step. The kinetics of hydrogen sulfide generation on carbon will be covered in a subsequent paper.

Future Development

Pilot studies are currently underway on all process steps at the 20,000 ft³/hr flue gas level. While concluding these studies, the reactors are being integrated to study cyclic operation and evaluate long-term effects in continuous equipment. Following these pilot studies installation of a 10 MW, 20,000 ft³/min or larger prototype on a coal-fired boiler is projected by Westvaco. This size is also approximately comparable to expected gas volumes from a 200 ton/day Claus unit.

After initial tests have established satisfactory operation of the prototype unit, a full-scale demonstration unit of 200 MW could be installed. At the conclusion of this latter work, the process should be applicable to virtually any size utility boiler. A conceptual design module, one of four required for a 1000 MW power plant, is shown in Figure 7.

In summary then, an all-dry process is being developed which uses fluidized beds of activated carbon to remove SO_2 from waste gases and recover either concentrated SO_2 or elemental sulfur. Scale-up is currently directed for power-boiler installations to solve existing emission problems. Applications to Claus plant tail gas might proceed more rapidly because of the smaller equipment size required. Consideration has been given to the needs of the electric utility industry in developing a process which is compact in size, economical in installation and operation, and capable of meeting the most stringent SO_2 regulations proposed, and which can fill the gap between available supplies of low sulfur fuels and our nation's energy requirements.

Literature Cited

1. Ball, F. J., Torrence, S. L., Repik, A. J., *J. Air Pollut. Contr. Ass.* (1972) **22**, 20-26.
2. Brown, G. N., Torrence, S. L., Repik, A. J., Stryker, J. L., Ball, F. J., *Chem. Eng. Progr.* (1972) **68**(8), 55-56.
3. Ball, F. J., Brown, G. N., Davis, J. E., Repik, A. J., Torrence, S. L., *Prepr., Amer. Petrol. Inst., Div. Refining, Midyear Meetg.*, 137, May 9, 1972. paper **17-72**.
4. Brown, G. N., Torrence, S. L., Repik, A. J., Stryker, J. L., Ball, F. J., *Prepr., Amer. Inst. Chem. Eng., Nat. Meetg.*, 71st, Feb. 20, 1972, paper **25B**.

5. Westvaco Corp., Charleston Research Center, *Progr. Rept. Air Pollut. Contr. Off.*, Contract No. **68-02-0003,** Mar. 1-Apr. 30, 1971.
6. Kunii, D., Levenspiel, O., "Fluidization Engineering," John Wiley & Sons, New York, 1969.

RECEIVED February 15, 1973.

17

Ammonia Injection: A Route to Clean Stacks

C. C. SHALE

Morgantown Energy Research Center, Bureau of Mines,
U.S. Department of the Interior, P.O. Box 880, Morgantown, W. Va. 26505

Previously reported results of laboratory research have dem-
onstrated essentially complete removal of sulfur dioxide
from mixed gases by ammonia injection; the simulated stack
gas contained 4200 ppm of the contaminant which is equiva-
lent to combustion of coal containing 6.0% sulfur. Con-
tinuation of this work using gases from a small coal-fired
combustor confirms earlier findings for removal of sulfur
dioxide to less than 100 ppm and shows that ammonia can
be regenerated on a continuous basis for re-use with mini-
mal loss. Product sulfur-bearing salts and remaining ash
are removed effectively from the gas in a wet scrubber,
apparently assisted by the process of nucleation. The
ammonia-injection process could provide effective control of
sulfur dioxide from coal-burning power plants.

Reduction in SO_2 emissions from coal-burning power plant stacks is essential to minimize atmospheric pollution from this source. Projections of energy demand show that by 1980 coal will account for about 25 million tons of total sulfur oxides output, mostly SO_2, unless effective control methods are developed.

A vapor-phase ammmonia-injection process for SO_2 removal is being developed at the Morgantown Energy Research Center. In laboratory research with simulated stack gas containing 4200 ppm SO_2 (equivalent to 6.0% sulfur in coal), essentially complete removal of SO_2 from the gas phase was effected by ammonia injection (1). Preliminary work has since proceeded with a small pilot-scale installation in which the sulfur products from the vapor-phase reaction are removed in a water scrubber. This paper presents additional data from the laboratory work and the pilot-scale installation.

Description of Process

In the vapor-phase ammonia-injection process, water (or steam) and gaseous ammonia are injected into the stack gas while the gas is at some temperature ($>160°F$) above the decomposition temperature of ammonium sulfite, the principal product (140° to 158°F) (2). After the water is vaporized and the reactants are thoroughly mixed, the gas is cooled below 140°F and the finely divided salt particles separate from the gas as a smoke or fume ($d_p = 0.01\text{-}1.0\mu m$). The entrained solids, salt particles, and fly ash are then recovered concurrently.

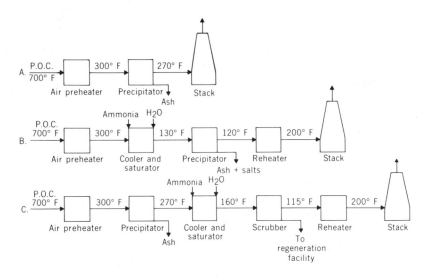

Figure 1. Proposed modifications for stack gas-clearing methods

The process offers high versatility in the removal of the entrained solids. They can be removed in either a dry or wet state, and if removed by a wet method, several alternatives are available for regenerating ammonia for re-use. Furthermore, each salt particle could contain over a million SO_2 molecules, so removal of SO_2 as a solid salt could provide more effective gas cleaning at reduced capital and operating costs. For example, the usual method for cleaning stack gas in modern power plants is depicted in Figure 1A; after partial recovery of heat, ash is removed in an electrostatic precipitator prior to release of the gas to the atmosphere. Proposed modifications to this mode of cleaning in conjunction with ammonia injection also are shown for dry removal of the salt particles along with the ash in a precipitator as indicated in Figure 1B, or by dry removal of ash followed by wet removal of the salts and residual ash as indicated in Figure 1C. Results of qualitative tests 1 ι a precipitator indicate the salts are collectable in the dry state, as suggested, but no attempts have been made to secure quantitative data. These salts might also be collected in a bag filter if the gas stream is maintained dry. If collected dry, the salt-ash mixtures could be utilized as a soil conditioner or low-grade fertilizer and regeneration of ammonia would not be necessary.

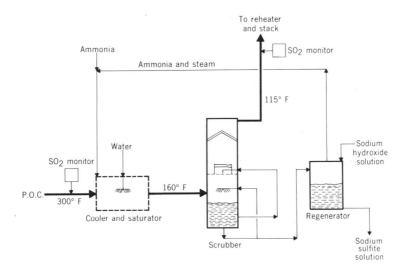

Figure 2. Flow diagram for pilot-scale SO₂-removal system

If a wet method for collection is selected, such as a wet electrostatic precipitator, fiber-type self-draining mist eliminator, or wet scrubber, ammonia can be regenerated from the salt solution by reaction with a readily available metal oxide such as lime or zinc oxide with formation of a stable sulfur product for disposal. These metal oxides, however, as well as their reaction products, are insoluble and could cause deposition on heat transfer surfaces and/or clogging in the regenerating equipment. Therefore, as indicated in Figure 2, to ensure continuity and reliability of the process, a soluble metal oxide was utilized (in the form of sodium hydroxide solution) to regenerate the ammonia in the experimental work described. This procedure also allows more effective utilization of the metal oxide; the soluble oxide (NaOH) can be regenerated in batch equipment outside the continuous portion of the process by reaction with either the aforestated insoluble reactants, lime, or zinc oxide. Better control is afforded in a batch reactor with more efficient use of reactants. However, in full-scale equipment undersirable deposition of reactant and product may be controllable so that batch operation may not be necessary.

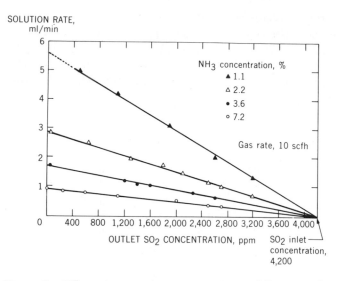

*Figure 3. Effect of ammonia concentration on SO$_2$ removal
from gas phase*

Laboratory Data

Published data (*1*) from the laboratory work on the vapor-phase reaction as well as unpublished data on kinetics of the reaction are presented for purposes of clarity. Figure 3 shows the effect of adding various quantities of ammonia to an SO$_2$-laden gas stream in the presence of an excess of water vapor in the laboratory-scale equipment. Essentially complete removal of SO$_2$ from the gas phase is effected when ammonia additions are actually slightly less than the calculated stoichiometric quantity for sulfite formation. For example, at a gas flow of 10 standard ft^3/hr (scfh) the calculated rate of ammonia addition for 3.6% solution is 1.86 ml/min for removing all SO$_2$ from a gas containing 4200 ppm, but no SO$_2$ was detected at the rate of 1.74 ml/min. Apparently, some bisulfite salt is formed in the reaction of SO$_2$ with ammonia and water vapor. The kinetics of the reactions are indicated to be adequate for commercial utilization by the curves given in Figure 4; residence time in the reactor was less than 0.4 sec at a gas flow of 70 scfh, the highest tested.

Pilot-Scale Equipment

The entire pilot-scale installation consists of a coal combustor, cyclone separator, two heat exchangers, scrubber, regenerator, and exhaust fan. The scrubber and regenerator are equipped with heat-transfer coils, and all equipment in contact with the scrubber liquid is made of stainless steel. Gas-sampling ports are installed upstream and downstream of the scrubber. Process data are provided by three recording instruments: a liquid conductivity meter, a pH analyzer, and a flame photometric SO_2 analyzer. This type of analyzer detects sulfur regardless of the compound in which it occurs.

Combustion gas is generated by burning coal at rates as high as 10 lb/hr. A portion of the gas is cooled to about 400°F, is passed through the cyclone to remove most of the fly ash, and is further cooled (to about 160°F) before entering the scrubber vessel above the liquid level as shown previously in the flowsheet of Figure 2. A liquid spray in the lower portion of the vessel cools the gas to about 130°F prior to actual scrubbing. After scrubbing, the clean gas, saturated with water vapor, flows through a mist eliminator to a stack at about 115°F. Sulfur dioxide content of the gas is monitored at the cyclone outlet (before reactant injection) and at the scrubber outlet.

Most of the scrubber liquor is cooled (105°F) and recycled in the raw state. Part of the cooled liquor is filtered to remove accumulated ash particles and flows through the pH meter, conductivity meter, and then the cooling spray. Another portion (without cooling) is filtered and flows to the regenerator at a controlled rate. As shown, sodium hydroxide solution also flows to the regenerator at a controlled rate. The mixture of solutions is heated to about 220°F, and chemical reaction releases the ammonia and steam; these products return to the system under the force created by their vapor pressures.

Prior to use of sodium hydroxide, lime and zinc oxide slurries were tested successfully for regenerating ammonia, but these insoluble metal

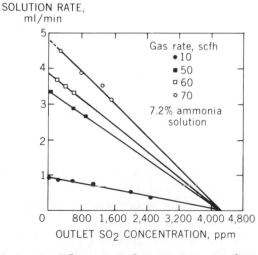

Figure 4. Effect of gas flow rate on removal of
SO₂ by ammonia

oxides could not be effectively maintained as a suspension. Both reactant and product settled in the regenerator to ruin heat transfer and/or clog the liquid drain. Therefore, as stated earlier, sodium hydroxide was used to promote continuity and reliability to the system.

Pilot-Scale Operations

Total liquid in the scrubber system in the pilot equipment is maintained at about 16 liters. The raw solution in the scrubber is recycled to the distribution plate at rates from 0.2 to 0.7 gal/min. The filtered portion that flows through the monitoring instruments and the cooling spray are maintained constant at a rate of 0.2 gal/min. Flow of solution to the regenerator is controlled from 0 to 4.2 liters/hr, depending on the rate at which ammonia is needed for the vapor-phase reaction.

At the start of an operation, water or ammonium sulfite solution can be used as the scrubbing liquid. If water is used, primary ammonia and steam must be injected to the gas and the scrubbing operation must continue for several hours prior to regeneration of any ammonia. This builds up a salt solution. If a sulfite solution is used (3.0%), ammonia regeneration can begin immediately.

Preliminary tests with the pilot-scale unit confirmed laboratory results and showed that essentially complete removal of SO_2 from the gas phase could be achieved in the larger equipment by injecting ammonia and steam. Many other tests were conducted to isolate the effects of some operating variables, including minimal development of the water scrubber. Results of these tests, however, are not described; the data are outside the scope of this paper.

Final selection of scrubbing medium allowed provision for a liquid reservoir on a distribution plate as described by Kempner et al. (3) and indicated in Figure 2. Single or multiple layers of 50-mesh screen were used to obtain liquid–solid contact and to cause wetting and removal of the solids. Results of selected tests of a few hours duration are given in Table I. In these tests, unless otherwise noted, 1.0 scfh ammonia and 2.0 lb/hr steam were injected into a flow of 500 scfh combustion gas. Under these conditions mass flow rate was about 350 lb/hr-ft². Calculated salt content of the gas was 0.13 gram/ft³ based on an SO_2 concentration of 900 ppm, as determined by wet chemical analysis (analyzer not installed). Ash content was determined by sampling the gas at the specified isokinetic rate. Because of comubustor limitations, higher mass flow rates could not be tested on a continuous basis.

As shown, the scrubber removes greater than 90% of the salt and residual ash particles, using a single screen atop the liquid reservoir. This degree of removal is attainable at a pressure loss of less than 2 inches of water and demonstrates that the solids are removed with very short contact time in the cleaning equipment.

After installation of the sulfur analyzer, continuous monitoring was provided. Results of a continuous operation using this scrubber concept in the pilot-scale unit, covering 105 consecutive hours (4.4 days), are summarized in Table I. During this period the scrubber was off-line only one hour for cleaning of a clogged line. At the start of the operation the scrubber contained a 2.9% solution of ammonium sulfite which had been prepared and used previously for almost 8 hrs. During extended tests, pressure loss through the scrubber ranged from 2.0 to 2.2 inches of water. The liquid/gas ratio was about 5.0 lb/lb. Throughout the test all ammonia was regenerated from the scrubber liquor using sodium hydroxide solution except for a single 3-hr span during which 1.0 scfh of ammonia was added to test the effect of higher pH in the scrubbing liquid. Operation during the final 20 hrs is not representative. This period was devoted to obtaining specific essential data for other purposes.

Table I.   Scrubber Operating Data

Test	Scrub. Medium, No. of Screens	Liq. Recycle Rate, gal/min	Pres. Loss, inches H_2O	Resid. Salt, grams/ft³ $\times 10^{-3}$ [a]	Resid. Ash, grains/ft³ $\times 10^{-3}$ [b]	Removal Eff., % Salt	Removal Eff., % Ash
1	none [c]	0.4	1.5	15.5	23	88.1	92.8
2	1	0.4	2.5	6.8	13	94.8	95.9
3	1	0.4	2.5	6.4	20	95.1	93.7
4	1 [d]	0.2	1.8	6.6	0.6	94.9	99.8
5	1 [d]	0.4	2.9	5.8	0.3	95.5	99.9
6	2	0.2	3.5	4.8	11	96.3	96.6
7	3	0.2	4.0	5.5	11	95.8	96.6
8	3 [d]	0.4	4.6	5.6	12	95.7	96.2
9	3 [e]	0.2	3.8	5.5	15	95.8	95.3
10	3	0.4	5.5	5.4	9	95.8	97.2

[a] Calculated salt produced, 0.13 gram/ft³
[b] Ash concentration inlet gas, 0.32 grain/ft³.
[c] Distribution plate only, 0.1-inch holes.
[d] Steam rate, 3.0 lb/hr.
[e] Steam rate, 4.0 lb/hr.

From prior calibrations we found that pH of the solution denoted the sulfite/bisulfite salt ratio and conductivity data were related to the concentration of salts in solution. From these data the quantity of ammonia that was regenerated could be calculated. A calculated ammonia balance over the first 83 hr of operation showed 4.23 gram-moles ammonia loss from all causes, which is representative of a maximum stack loss of 3.53 ft³ of ammonia. Since a total of 41,500 ft³ of gas was processed, ammonia loss was about 85 ppm. On a once-through basis this represents about a 4% loss, using an average SO_2 inlet of 1050 ppm with 90% removal. Other potential losses can occur as solid salts out the stack, unregenerated salt solution, and leakage. Sulfur dioxide concentration in the effluent gas remained consistent, always ranging below about 220 ppm (usually below 100 ppm) and demonstrating a removal efficiency greater than 77%. This removal effectiveness was accomplished at a pH that never exceeded 5.4 and usually was in the range 3.5 to 4.5.

Table II. Representative Data on Continuous SO_2 Removal by NH_3 Injection

Cumu-lative Time, hr	pH Scrubber Soln	Soln Conduct., mhos $\times 10^4$	SO_2, ppm Inlet	SO_2, ppm Outlet	Soln Regen. Rate, ml/hr	Removal Effic., %
3.0	5.20	5.40	1000	150	2400	85
9.5	4.85	5.40	1000	45	2000	95
15.0	4.30	5.18	1000	120	1056	88
20.0	4.45	5.01	1225	130	1440	89
24.0	4.30	5.10	1250	90	1056	93
29.0	4.18	5.30	1250	220	1056	82
35.0	5.02	5.50	1650	220	1056	87
43.0	4.30	4.89	885	25	600	97
47.0	3.80	4.80	1030	39	240	96
51.0	3.03	4.83	930	51	240	94
55.0	4.23	4.11	910	20[a]	2100	97
61.0	4.39	3.69	910	210	2100	77
67.0	5.42	3.49	1000	10	0	99
72.0	4.02	4.45	930	0	0	100
76.0	3.16	4.74	1090	0	1056	100
83.0	4.54	3.90	1200	0	2100	100
89.0	4.29	3.50	1100	0	2100	100
93.0	4.02	2.90	1030	220	2400	79
97.0	2.90	3.05	780	760	2700	3
101.5	3.98	1.93	780	505[b]	>4200	35
102.0	3.78	1.80	1030	505	>4200	50
104.0	4.72	1.55	1400	590	>4200	58
105.0	3.95	1.50	1900	910	>4200	52

[a] Analysis by wet chemical method, 30 ppm.
[b] Analysis by wet chemical method, 510 ppm.

Further analysis of the data in Table II reveals apparent irregularities in performance of the process. For example, at an elapsed time of 61 hr, scrubber solution was being regenerated at a rate of 2.1 liters/hr to supply ammonia for the vapor-phase reaction. Removal efficiency was only 77%. Six hours later, while SO_2 content of the inlet gas was higher (1000 *vs.* 910 ppm), scrubber solution flow rate to the regenerator was zero, but the SO_2 content of the purified gas was only 10 ppm; removal efficiency was 99%. Other similar examples can be isolated. These conflicting data indicate some of the complexities of the process:

1. If all SO_2 is not converted to a solid salt, part or all of the remainder is absorbed during the scrubbing operation. The degree to which this action occurs appears to be directly proportional to the pH of the scrubbing solution and the rate at which scrubber solution is recycled to the distribution plate.

2. At any given flow rate of scrubber solution to the regenerator, the volume of ammonia regenerated appears to vary directly with solution pH, salt concentration, and regenerator temperature (up to about 220°F).

3. Excess sodium hydroxide solution (metal oxide) must be available at all times in the regenerator for reaction with the scrubber solution.

Process Chemistry

Initial chemical reactions in the vapor state are postulated as

$$2NH_3 + SO_2 + H_2O \rightleftarrows (NH_4)_2SO_3 \tag{1}$$

$$NH_3 + SO_2 + H_2O \rightleftarrows NH_4HSO_3 \tag{2}$$

After the scrubbing operation, the solution of salts is exposed to sodium hydroxide solution; chemical reaction releases ammonia and steam for recycle.

$$(NH_4)_2SO_3 + 2NaOH \rightleftarrows Na_2SO_3 + 2NH_3 + 2H_2O \tag{3}$$

$$NH_4HSO_3 + NaOH \rightleftarrows NaHSO_3 + NH_3 + H_2O \tag{4}$$

During the scrubbing operation some of the sulfites are oxidized to sulfates; the oxidation products appear to be continuously removed from the scrubbing liquor by similar reactions in the regenerator.

$$(NH_4)_2SO_4 + 2NaOH \rightleftarrows Na_2SO_4 + 2NH_3 + 2H_2O \tag{5}$$

$$NH_4HSO_4 + NaOH \rightleftarrows NaHSO_4 + NH_3 + H_2O \tag{6}$$

Moreover, it is evident that sulfur trioxide also is removed from the gas as shown by the analyses listed in Table II (0 ppm SO_2, 72-89 hr). Ammonia can be regenerated from the sulfates as shown in Reactions 5 and 6. Other reactions that may occur could remove selected components from the combustion gas, such as NO_2 or CO_2, but the high reactivity of the sodium ion should induce reaction with the ammonium salt produced and thereby minimize this potential loss of ammonia.

As previously indicated, other chemical means are available for regenerating ammonia, such as reaction with lime or zinc oxide slurries, both of which have been tested successfully in the pilot installation. These reactions are demonstrated by the equation

$$CaO + (NH_4)_2SO_3 \rightleftarrows CaSO_3 + 2NH_3 + H_2O \qquad (7)$$

In this reaction, however, both the reactant and the sulfur product are insoluble and could interrupt process continuity by deposition and clogging if installed in the continuous portion of a recycle system. Furthermore, the sodium salt solution from the regenerator can be isolated for batch reaction with an inexpensive insoluble metal oxide, such as lime slurry.

$$Na_2SO_3 + Ca(OH)_2 \rightleftarrows CaSO_3 + 2NaOH \qquad (8)$$

$$Na_2SO_4 + Ca(OH)_2 \rightleftarrows CaSO_4 + 2NaOH \qquad (9)$$

After concentration, the sodium hydroxide can be recycled. In addition, all disposable salts can be oxidized to the most stable state, e.g., calcium sulfate.

Another means for disposal of a sulfur product could involve reaction of hydrogen sulfide with either the ammonium or sodium sulfite solution to produce elemental sulfur. Additional processing is required, but the weight of disposable product could be reduced by a factor of about four. Moreover, under select conditions sale of sulfur could offset at least part of the processing costs.

Discussion

The vapor-phase reaction between water, ammonia, and SO_2 is essentially instantaneous in the presence of an excess of water vapor. The reaction occurs when the mixture is cooled below the decomposition temperature of the product compound(s). In the presence of adequate ammonia virtually complete removal of SO_2 is available, providing that the reactants are thoroughly mixed prior to the cooling operation.

The apparent cause for such effective removal of the finely divided salt particles ($d_p = 0.01$ to $1.0 \mu m$) and the residual ash particles is the process of nucleation that occurs when excess water in the gas condenses on the solids during the cooling operation. This process allows the soluble particles to be dissolved in the scrubbing liquid and the insoluble ones to be enlarged for easier capture. Theoretically, the ash particles could serve as condensation nuclei for the salt particles; the ash particles then could be wetted by dissolution of the adhering salts and could cause effective size growth in the insoluble solids with concurrent ease of removal.

Scrubber liquid can be recycled to obtain a salt solution of any desired concentration prior to regeneration of ammonia from the solution. The upper limit on solution concentration presumably will be controlled by the vapor pressures of the components, ammonia and sulfur dioxide. At high pH, ammonia vapor predominates; at low pH, sulfur dioxide is the dominant vapor. Therefore, optimum recycle of the scrubber liquid will be controlled at low pH and dilute solution concentration concurrent with and relative to equipment (capital) and operating costs. A solution having low pH (*e.g.*, < 6.0) requires stainless steel or protected carbon steel to prevent corrosion.

The process of nucleation apparently is dominant in removal of the entrained solid salts, whereby most of the residual ash also is removed by scrubbing liquid with low contact time. Whatever the reason, the process is effective at low pressure loss.

Batch processing of the sodium salt solution from the regenerator allows more effective utilization of lime. However, disposal of product salts remains a problem. Furthermore, after ammonia injection, effective removal of SO_2 as a solid salt can be accomplished with water or a dilute salt solution. As exemplified by work conducted at Tennessee Valley Authority (4) for removal of SO_2 by scrubbing with ammoniacal solution, the scrubber solution must have high pH ($\sim$6.4) and must be relatively concentrated to provide the required driving force for effective absorption. Under these conditions at least one additional stage of scrubbing is required (with increased pressure loss) to prevent gross loss of ammonia.

Literature Cited

1. Shale, C. C., Simpson, D. G., Lewis, P. S., *Chem. Eng. Prog. Symp. Ser.* (1971) **67**, No. 115, 52–58.
2. Weast, R. C., Selby, S. M., Hodgman, C. D., "Handbook of Chemistry and Physics," 45th ed., p. B–152, The Chemical Rubber Co., Cleveland, 1964.
3. Kempner, S. K., Seiler, E. N., Bowman, D. H., *Jour. Air Pollut. Contr. Ass.* (1970) **20**, 139–143.
4. Tennessee Valley Authority, "Sulfur Oxide Removal from Power Plant Stack Gas; Ammonia Scrubbing," *Conceptual Design Cost Study Ser., Study No. 3, Nat. Air Pollut. Contr. Ass.*, **PB 196804**, Sept. 1970, pp. 58–61.

RECEIVED February 15, 1973.

18

Aqueous Scrubbing of Nitrogen Oxides from Stack Gases

G. A. CHAPPELL

Government Research Laboratory, Esso Resesarch and Engineering Co., Linden, N.J. 07036

A screening program compared various aqueous solvents for removing NO_x from flue gases. Slurries of $CA(OH)_2$, $Mg(OH)_2$, and $Zn(OH)_2$ were inefficient for removing NO and NO_2 from a flue gas containing NO_x but no SO_2. NaOH solution was also inefficient whereas concentrated amine solutions were very effective. Concentrated aqueous ammonia and 2-aminoethanol absorbed 74 and 48%, respectively, of the NO. Sulfite solutions are excellent NO_2 absorbants but poor NO absorbants. Alkaline hydroxide slurries and solutions are effective NO_2 absorbers if SO_2 is present in the flue gas. The sulfite formed during SO_2 absorption enhances NO_2 removal. $Mg(OH)_2$ slurry absorbed 58% of the NO_2 and 100% of the SO_2 from a flue gas containing 830 ppm NO_2 and 2460 ppm SO_2. NO_2 removal is enhanced by adding an anti-oxidant such as hydroquinone to the scrubber. Combined NO_x–SO_x absorption is possible provided the NO in flue gases can be oxidized to NO_2 upstream from the scrubber.

The oxides of nitrogen, NO and NO_2, are essential components in the formation of photochemical smog, in addition to being pollutants themselves. Large fossil fuel-fired boilers, such as those found in electric power-generating plants, are major sources of these oxides. In such boilers, the nitrogen oxides are formed by the reaction of molecular nitrogen and oxygen in the high temperature combustion zone of the furnace. The immediate product of this reaction is the thermodynamically favored NO. As the combustion gases cool, part of the NO, typically less than 10%, oxidzes to NO_2. The two oxides are generally considered together as NO_x. If the fuels contain organically bound nitrogen, as do coal and oil, part

Table I.   Typical Compositions of Flue Gases

Component	Vol % Combustion of		
	Coal[a]	*Oil*[b]	*Gas*[c]
N_2	76.2	77.0	72.3
CO_2	14.2	12.0	9.1
H_2	6.0	8.0	16.8
O_2	3.3	3.0	1.8
SO_2	0.2	0.15	—
NO_x	—	0.07[d]	—
Particulates, gram/ft³	0.5[e]	0.01	—

[a] Calculated for burning with 20% excess air a typical high volatile, bituminous coal of the following composition: 70.1% carbon, 6.6% oxygen, 4.9% hydrogen, 1.4% nitrogen, 3.0% sulfur, 12.7% ash, 1.3% water.

[b] Calculated for a typical residual fuel oil of the following composition: 86.5% carbon, 10.3% hydrogen, 2.5% sulfur, 0.7% nitrogen, with 20% excess air.

[c] Calculated for burning natural gas with 10% excess air.

[d] This is an average value. Actual values range from 0.01 to 0.15%.

[e] Assumes 90% particulate removal.

of this nitrogen is also converted to NO during combustion. The composition of different flue gases is shown in Table I.

In a 1969 report (*1*), Esso Research and Engineering Co. assessed the various NO_x control techniques. One promising procedure was aqueous alkaline scrubbing of the flue gas to which NO_2 had been added. Nitric oxide, the chief NO_x constituent, does not combine with water or with basic solutions. Absorption of NO requires NO_2. A mixture of NO and NO_2 reacts to form a small amount of N_2O_3.

$$NO + NO_2 \rightleftarrows N_2O_3 \tag{1}$$

Sherwood and Pigford (*2*) found the rate of absorption of $NO + NO_2$ by a 46% NaOH solution to be approximately proportional to the first power of the N_2O_2 concentration, indicating it to be the reacting species. Mirev *et al.* (*3*) found that the completeness of the reaction between an NaOH solution and NO–NO_2 mixtures reached a maximum at a 1:1 molar ratio of the oxides.

The N_2O_3 hydrolyzes rapidly in basic solutions to form nitrous acid and nitrite salts.

$$N_2O_3 + H_2O \xrightarrow{\quad OH^- \quad} 2HNO_2 \longrightarrow 2NO_2^- + 2H_2O \tag{2}$$

Based on the potential of aqueous alkaline scrubbing, a flue gas-scrubbing apparatus was constructed and used to screen a large number of potential scrubbing solutions. The original NO_x levels were 350 ppm each of NO and NO_2 with no SO_2 present. The SO_2 was eliminated to simplify the scrubbing chemistry; SO_2 would also be absorbed by the alkaline scrubbers.

The results of the early work led to a second phase directed toward NO_2 absorption by aqueous solutions, notably sulfites. This effort presumed the prior oxidation of NO to NO_2 by a suitable technique such as ozone addition or catalysis. In these latter scrubbing studies, SO_2 was usually present in the flue gas and was found to be beneficial for NO_2 absorption. The results from the second phase are quite promising and indicate the technical possibility of simultaneous NO_2/SO_2 scrubbing.

Experimental

The scrubbing apparatus consisted basically of a flue gas-blending system and the gas scrubbers. The blending system was capable of producing a variety of flue gas compositions by mixing the pure components in different proportions. The flue gas passed through heated lines to the scrubbers where the NO_x and SO_2 were absorbed and the effluent gases were carried by heated lines to the gas analyzers for the determination of the residual NO, NO_2, and SO_2.

Flue Gas-Blending System. The blending system was designed to produce a heated flue gas from the various components contained in cylinders. The flue gas contaminants SO_2, NO_2, and NO were contained in separate high pressure gas cylinders at 5 mole % (50,000 ppm) with nitrogen constituting the balance. Other cylinders contained pure oxygen, pure CO_2, and pure nitrogen. Each gas was delivered through 0.25 inch od stainless steel tubing to a calibrated rotameter for flow measurement prior to mixing. Steam was available in the laboratory but it was wet. The steam was dried by passing it through heated aluminum coils. The dry, hot steam also passed through a calibrated rotameter before mixing with the other components. Figure 1 shows a schematic of the gas-blending system. The order of mixing was important for minimizing gas phase reactions between NO_2 and SO_2.

$$NO_2 + SO_2 \longrightarrow NO + SO_3 \qquad (3)$$

After passing through their respective rotameters, N_2, CO_2, O_2, and SO_2 fed into a common line which passed through the heated steam box, where steam was added to the mixture. At this point the dewpoint of the gas was about 46°C and the lines were maintained at approximately 93°C. The NO and NO_2 were added and the entire mixture was passed through a heated rotameter to determine the total flow rate. The synthetic flue gas was delivered through heated lines to the gas scrubbers. The composition of a typical blend was 350 ppm NO, 350 ppm NO_2, 2400 ppm SO_2, 3 mole % O_2, 12 mole % CO_2, 10 mole % steam, and the balance N_2. In all experiments the total gas flow rate was equivalent to 3200 ml/min at 20°C and 1 atm. The actual line pressure was slightly above 1 atm.

We observed that the heated steel lines initially underwent a conditioning process by the flue gas. The composition of gas exiting from the system varied for 10–20 min before stabilizing. If the system was not used for several days, the lines had to be reconditioned.

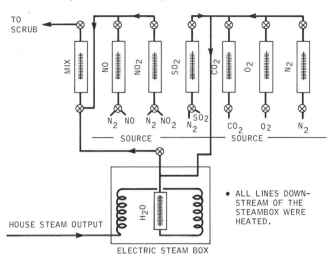

Figure 1. Gas-blending system

No gas phase reactions were observed. Nitric oxide (NO) was not oxidized to NO_2 in the lines, and NO_2 did not react with SO_2 at these low concentrations.

Flue Gas Scrubbers. The gas scrubber was a 2 liter round-bottom glass flask containing 1 liter of scrubbing solution or slurry. A Teflon-coated magnetic stirring bar agitated the solution. The scrubber temperature was maintained by an electric heating mantle which was controlled by a thermocouple immersed in the solution. The thermocouple was clad with stainless steel. The hot flue gas was introduced into the absorbing solution (49°–55°C) through a porous glass frit located approximately 4 inches below the surface. The gas exiting from the scrubber was carried by heated lines to the gas analyzers which measured the NO, NO_2, and SO_2 levels.

Analysis. The heated line carrying the scrubber effluent entered a junction from which three lines exited. These lines transferred the hot gas to the analyzers for measurements of the NO, NO_2, and SO_2 levels.

The SO_2 and NO_2 were analyzed independently by two DuPont 400 spectrophotometers. These were double-beam instruments containing analyzer cells maintained at 212°F. The flue gas passed through the cells continuously. The two analyzers were totally separate except that they shared the same light source; the two gas cells were perpendicular to each other. The signals from the NO_2 and SO_2 analyzers were recorded continuously by strip-chart recorders.

The NO analysis involved considerable problems. Eventually we used a Beckman NDIR (non-dispersive infrared) for NO measurements because of good signal stability and because the instrument read NO directly, not total NO_x. However all of the water had to be removed from the gas because moisture was recorded as NO. The $NO–NO_2–H_2O$ interaction was eliminated in the water trap by removing the NO_2 before the trap. After trying several approaches, we finally used a saturated solution of sodium sulfite at room temperature as the NO_2 absorber because of its capacity to remove *all* traces of NO_2. Part of the NO was also removed by the Na_2SO_3 trap, but the fraction of the NO absorbed depended on the amount of NO_2 in the gas stream. The sulfite trap was calibrated with known gas mixtures so that the NO level before the sulfite trap could be calculated from the NDIR reading, the NO_2 reading, and the calibration chart. In the final arrangement for NO analysis, the flue gas passed through the Na_2SO_3 solution and then entered a cold trap chilled with solid CO_2 and methanol. The dry gas warmed to room temperature before entering the NDIR. The cold trap was packed with glass beads to increase surface area and to reduce the dead volume. The sulfite trap also removed all SO_2 from the gas stream, which eliminated the possibility of condensation in the cold trap.

As the nitrogen oxides are absorbed by the alkaline scrubbing solution, nitrite and nitrite ions are produced.

$$N_2O_3(g) + H_2O(l) \longrightarrow 2HNO_2(aq.) \tag{4}$$

$$HNO_2 + OH^- \longrightarrow H_2O + NO_2^- \tag{5}$$

$$2NO_2(g) + H_2O(l) \longrightarrow HNO_2(aq.) + HNO_3(aq.) \tag{6}$$

$$HNO_3 + OH^- \longrightarrow H_2O + NO_3^- \tag{7}$$

At first we used a specific ion electrode for nitrate ion measurements. While this procedure worked well with dilute solutions, interference became a problem with concentrated salt solutions. Fortunately a spectrophotometric procedure developed by Wetters and Uglum (4) was satisfactory for most of our solutions.

Results

NO_x Absorption by Metal Hydroxide Solutions and Slurries. The hydroxides of sodium, calcium, magesium, and zinc were screened for NO_x scrubbing potentials, using an SO_2-free flue gas. Table I contains the results. In most of the runs the NO_2 absorption was only slightly improved over pure water but the NO absorption was definitely greater

Table II. NO_x Scrubbing

		Initial	*Input, ppm*	
Run	*Absorbant*	*pH*	*NO*	*NO_2*
11–19–71	5N NaOH	14	350	400
1–19–72	50 wt % NaOH	14	345	330
2– 8–72	$Ca(OH)_2$ slurry	11.5	353	365
12– 7–71	NaOH	11.5	311	360
2– 9–72	$Mg(OH)_2$ slurry	8.9	330	350
12–17–71	NaOH	8.9	404	370
2– 9–72	ZnO slurry	7.5	353	370
11–10–71	water	6.8	400	390

[a] NO generated by hydrolysis of NO_2.

with the metal hydroxides. The ability of NaOH to absorb NO in the presence of NO_2 increased with pH. At the higher pH levels NaOH removed approximately equimolar NO and NO_2 which is consistent with N_2O_3 being the reactive species.

NO_x material balances were measured for several experiments and the results are contained in Table III. The high solution level for run No. 12–17–71 is probably a result of dissolved carbonate ion which interferes with the spectrophotometric procedure. This species is produced by the CO_2 in the flue gas. In general the balances are acceptable.

NO_x Absorption by Ammonia and 2-Aminoethanol Solutions. The best NO removal observed during the project occurred with concentrated aqueous ammonia (28 wt % NH_3) as the scrubbing solution. Here 74% of the NO and 80% of the NO_2 were absorbed. Table IV contains these results in addition to scrubbing data from a similar system, 2-aminoethanol.

The vapor pressure of NH_3 above the NH_4OH scrubber dictated that the process proceed at room temperature. A water scrubber (1 liter of water at 21°C) was placed downstream from the NH_4OH scrubber to trap NH_3 vapors for continued scrubbing. Thus the data in the table result from two scrubbers in series. When the water scrubber was by-passed, the per cent absorption changed to 54% for NO and 58% for NO_2. We placed a flask containing dilute H_2SO_4 downstream from the water scrubber to protect our analyzers from ammonia vapor. The H_2SO_4 trap was saturated with NO_x before putting the NH_4OH scrubber on line. The interdependence of NO–NO_2 absorption was shown by varying the input levels of each species. If the NO_2 input is halved, the absorption of NO decreases from 74 to 49%. If, however, the NO input is reduced to zero, the NO_2 absorption decreases from 80 to 51%. The problems associated with the high NH_3 vapor pressure led us to consider another amine for scrubbing.

The vapor pressure of 2-aminoethanol (2AE) is much lower than

with Metal Hydroxides

Absorption, %		Soln. Temp.,	Run Time,
NO	NO₂	°C	min
20	18	52	180
28	23	49	30
20	21	51	130
10	29	49	130
6	23	52	60
6	24	49	90
7	16	50	130
−5[a]	18	52	220

Table III.   NO$_x$

Run	Absorbant	Time, min	NO$_x$ Absorption, ppm ΔNO	ΔNO_2
12–17–71	NaOH (pH 8.9)	70	30	95
12–20–71	Ca(OH)$_2$ soln	300	32	125
12–13–71	Mg(OH)$_2$ soln	80	25	100
12–15–71	ZnO soln	90	25	115

^{a} Concentration unit = mmole/liter.

Table IV.   NO$_x$

Run	Absorbant	Input, ppm NO	NO$_2$
1–26–72	concd aq. NH$_3$	330	355
2– 3–72	2AE^a	340	320
2– 4–72	50% 2AE^b	340	330
2– 4–72	25% 2AE	347	350

^{a} 2AE = 2-aminoethanol.

that of 28 wt % NH$_4$OH. The pure amine has a vapor pressure of 7 torr at 66°C, whereas the NH$_3$ partial pressure over the ammonia solution is 570 torr at 21°C. The 2AE in the scrubber did not eliminate the need for a dilute H$_2$SO$_4$ trap. The small amount of amine vapor emanating from the NO$_x$ absorber had to be removed before the gas stream entered the analyzers. The mist which formed above the scrubbing fluid when NO$_2$ was present in the flue gas was removed from the effluent by the H$_2$SO$_4$ trap. Before we recorded data, this trap was saturated with NO$_x$. As Table V shows, the 2AE soluitons were excellent NO$_x$ scrubbers but did not remove as much NO, as did the ammonia solution. We observed that the 2AE temperature increased if CO$_2$ was present in the flue gas indicating that CO$_2$ is reacting with the solution. This is to be expected

Table V.   NO$_x$ Absorption

Run	Absorbant	Input, ppm NO	NO$_2$
12– 5–71	4.1m (NH$_4$)$_2$SO$_3$	328	350
1–17–72	6m NaOAc	340	360
1–18–72	8.4m NH$_4$Cl	330	350
1–24–72	8.4m NH$_4$OAc	362	360
2–15–72	2.5m Na$_2$SO$_3$	358	350
2–10–72	1.0m ammonium citrate	358	350
3– 7–72	CaSO$_3$	390	380

Material Balance

Soln. Anal.		Total Dissolved NO$_x$ Calc. from	
NO$_3^-$	NO$_2^-$	Gas Anal.	Soln Anal.
0.3[a]	1.3[a]	1.1[a]	1.6[a]
0.4	4.6	5.9	5.9
0	0.9	1.2	0.9
0.3	1.4	1.6	1.7

Scrubbing with Amines

Absorption, %		Soln. Temp.,	Run Time,
NO	NO$_2$	°C	min
74	80	21	40
40	91	53	95
48	88	53	120
48	86	53	110

[b] 50 vol % 2AE and 50 vol % water.

because this type of compound is used commercially for scrubbing CO$_2$ from gas streams. The 2AE solutions changed from colorless to orange as the runs progressed. A variety of products may result when a primary amine reacts with N$_2$O$_3$ (NO + NO$_2$). These include molecular nitrogen (N$_2$), alkyl ammonium nitrites and nitrates, and alkyl nitrites and nitrates. Secondary amines form dialkylammonium nitrites and dialkyl N-nitroso compounds which are colored. It therefore seems reasonable that 2AE could react with NO$_x$ to produce highly colored products. The reactions are most likely irreversible. An attempt to determine the nature of the reaction was inconclusive.

NO$_x$ **Absorption by Salt Solutions.** A number of aqueous salt solutions have been screened for NO$_x$ scrubbing potential and some of these

by Salt Solutions

Absorption, %		Soln. Temp.,	Run Time,
NO	NO$_2$	°C	min
23	100	44	150
80	25	48	100
27	49	51	80
31	39	51	160
16	100	53	60
25	26	52	90
33	60	52	40

appear promising. Table V summarizes the experimental data. The results show that soluble sulfites are excellent NO_2 absorbers but are not effective for NO removal.

At this stage it seemed reasonable to explore the simultaneous absorption of NO_2 and SO_2 using various sorbents. It is technically possible to oxidize the NO in flue gas to NO_2 prior to absorption, and the sulfite required to absorb the NO_2 can be produced from the SO_2 already present in the gas stream.

NO_2–SO_2 Absorption by Hydroxides and Carbonates. Several metal hyroxide slurries were screened for NO_2–SO_2 scrubbing potential. In addition a limestone ($CaCO_3$) slurry was investigated. Magnesia, lime, and limestone scrubbing systems are under consideration for SO_2 scrubbing, so our results on the combined scrubbing are pertinent. A summary of the data is contained in Table VI.

Table VI. NO_2–SO_2 Absorption

Run	Scrubber, grams/liter	NO_2	SO_2
		Input, ppm	
3–17–72	Ca(OH)$_2$ slurry (10)	740	0
3–17–72	(continuation of 3–17–72)	730	800
4– 7–72	Ca(OH)$_2$ slurry (18)	680	2460
3–22–72	Mg(OH)$_2$ slurry (7.4)	830	2460
4–10–72	ZnO slurry (10)	700	2490
4–14–72	CaCO$_3$ slurry (10)	650	2280

These slurries are inefficient for NO_2 removal in the absence of SO_2 as indicated by the two runs numbered 3–17–72. Only 19% of the NO_2 was absorbed in the absence of SO_2 whereas 50% was removed in its presence. Thus the sulfite formed during SO_2 scrubbing becomes the absorber of NO_2.

A NO_x material balance was measured at the end of run 3–22–72. Gas analysis indicated 6.9 mmoles of NO_2 removed. Solution analysis showed 6.1 mmoles of NO_3^- and 2.0 mmoles of NO_2^- were produced. Nitrate ion is the main product of NO_2 absorption from flue gas.

All of the slurries demonstrated roughly equal scrubbing efficiency on the full flue gas. If oxygen is eliminated from the gas stream, the scrubbing efficiency improves markedly. For example, during run 4–10–72 the O_2 was removed from the stream, and the NO_2 removal increased from 63 to 90%. When the oxygen flow resumed the NO_2 removal decreased to 69%. Similar effects were observed with the other slurries. The presence of hydroquinone, an antioxidant, diminishes the negative influence of oxygen on NO_2 absorption. Run 4–18–72 provides an example.

A flue gas containing 670 ppm NO_2 and 2400 ppm SO_2 but no O_2 was bubbled into an $Mg(OH)_2$ slurry. All of the NO_2 and SO_2 was absorbed. When 3% oxygen was added to the flue gas, the NO_2 absorption decreased 57% while the SO_2 continued to be totally removed. The addition of 1.0 gram of hydroquinone to the slurry instantly caused the NO_2 absorption to increase to 93% in the presence of oxygen. The hydroquinone was still effective 200 min later when the run was terminated. Similar effects were observed with other slurries but were not as dramatic. An endurance run (5–5–72) was made with a slurry containing 15 grams of $Mg(OH)_2$ and 1.0 gram of hydroquinone. The flue gas contained 675 ppm NO_2, 2280 ppm SO_2, and 3% O_2 in addition to the normal constituents. The SO_2 absorption was complete for the full 390 min of the run. The NO_2 absorption was about 100% during the first 200 min but gradually decreased to 82% at the end of the experiment. The

by Hydroxides and Carbonates

Absorption, %		Soln.	pH		Run Time,
NO_2	SO_2	Temp., °C	Initial	Final	min
19	—	56	11.2	6.6	50
50	81	56	6.6	6.0	70
56	100	52	11.2	6.5	40
58	100	52	8.7	7.8	110
63	100	52	7.5	6.3	40
46	100	53	7.5	6.2	100

slurry slowly turned yellow as the run progressed. The hydroquinone is acting as an antioxidant but undergoes slow degradation, perhaps by reaction with NO_2.

Sulfate Formation During NO_2–SO_2 Scrubbing. Several experiments were conducted to determine sulfate formation during $Mg(OH)_2$ scrub-

Table VII.   Sulfate Formation in $Mg(OH)_2$ Slurries

Sulfate Formation	$Mg(OH)_2$[a]	$Mg(OH)_2$[b]	$Mg(OH)_2$[c]
Wt % SO_4^{-2} ($t = 0$ min)	0.005	0.019	0.0079
Wt % SO_4^{-2} ($t = 100$ min)	0.181	0.230	0.202
Wt % SO_4^{-2} formed in 100 min	0.176	0.211	0.194
mmoles SO_4^{-2} formed/liter	18.6	22.2	20.5
mmoles NO_2 absorbed/liter	5.2	4.9	8.7
mmoles SO_2 absorbed/liter	31	30	31

[a] Contained 15 grams $Mg(OH)_2$/liter; SO_2 absorption was 2400 ppm; NO_2 absorption was 400 ppm of 700 ppm input.

[b] Same as *a* except that SO_2 absorption was 2300 ppm; NO_2 absorption was 380 of 640 ppm input.

[c] Same as *a* except that NO_2 absorption was 670 ppm of 670 ppm input and flue gas contained no oxygen.

bing. These results are compared in Table VII. Absorber c, which scrubbed an oxygen-free flue gas, formed as much sulfate as the other $Mg(OH)_2$ slurries did in the presence of 3% oxygen. However c absorbed almost twice as much NO_2 as each of the other scrubbers so that the number of sulfates formed per unit NO_2 absorbed is smaller than in the other two. The data show that two-thirds of the SO_2 absorbed by the magnesia scrubbers is converted to sulfate.

Conclusions

A comprehensive screening program evaluated the capability of various aqueous systems to scrub NO_x from the flue gases emitted by stationary power plants fired with fossil fuels. These are the conclusions of this study:

With NO and NO_2 present in the flue gas but no SO_2:

(a) Slurries and solutions of calcium, magnesium, and zinc hydroxide are inefficient NO_x absorbers.

(b) Strong bases (NaOH) are poor NO_x absorbers.

(c) Concentrated amines (ammonia and 2-aminoethanol) are efficient NO_x scrubbers but have excessive vapor pressures and may form exotic products such as alkyl nitrites and nitrates, and nitro and nitroso compounds which are difficult to regenerate and could not be introduced safely into the environment.

(d) Sulfite solutions and slurries are excellent NO_2 but poor NO absorbers. The soluble sulfites are more effective NO_2 scrubbers than the insoluble slurries because of the higher sulfite levels attained in solution.

(e) In general, NO_2 recycle and addition to flue gas to achieve equimolar NO–NO_2 is not attractive. While the presence of NO_2 does increase the absorption of NO, the magnitude of the increase is insufficient for developing a practicable process.

With NO_2 and SO_2 present in the flue gas but no NO:

(a) Calcium, magnesium, and zinc hydroxides are effective NO_2 and SO_2 scrubbers. The sulfite formed when SO_2 is absorbed is vital to NO_2 scrubbing.

(b) Limestone is an effective NO_2–SO_2 absorber.

(c) Sulfite solutions and slurries are efficient NO_2–SO_2 absorbers.

(d) NO_2 scrubbing is enhanced by removing oxygen from the flue gas or by adding an antioxidant such as hydroquinone to the scrubber.

(e) A portion of the absorbed SO_2 is oxidized to sulfate.

(f) Combined NO_x–SO_x scrubbing is possible using any of several hydroxide or carbonate systems provided NO can be oxidized to NO_2 upstream from the scrubber.

(g) Separate NO_2 absorption is feasible using the sulfite solution or slurry produced in the SO_2 scrubber.

Several scrubbing systems appear promising with a high degree of flexibility available in their application. However this hypothesis must be supported by further research aimed at obtaining scale-up information in addition to spent-solution regeneration data.

Acknowledgments

The advice and assistance of Alvin Skopp, Victor Engleman, and Henry Shaw are gratefully acknowledged. The technical assistance of William Moss in the laboratory is sincerely appreciated.

Literature Cited

1. Bartok, W., Crawford, A. R., Cunningham, A. R., Hall, H. J., Manny, E. H., Skopp, A., Esso Research and Engineering Co., Final Report GR–2–NOS–69, Contract No. PH 22 68 55 (PB 192 789), Nov. 1969.
2. Sherwood, T. K., Pigford, R. L., "Absorption and Extraction," Chem. Eng. Ser., McGraw-Hill, 1952.
3. Mirev, D., Valarev, K., Boyadzhiev, L., Lambiev, D., *Compt. Rend. Acad. Bulgare Sci.* (1961) **14,** 250–262.
4. Wetters, J. H., Uglum, K. L., *Anal. Chem.* (1970) **42,** 335–340.
5. Environmental Protection Agency, Reports EPA–R2–72–051, Sept. **1972, and** EPA–R2–73–051a, June 1973.

RECEIVED February 15, 1973. Work conducted by Esso Research and Engineering Co. under EPA Contract No. 68–02–0220.

19

The Chemistry of Nitrogen Oxides and Control through Combustion Modifications

D. W. PERSHING and E. E. BERKAU

U. S. Environmental Protection Agency, Office of Research and Monitoring, National Environmental Research Center, Research Triangle Park, N.C. 27711

The chemistry of NO_x formation during atmospheric pressure, hydrocarbon combustion is reviewed. During natural gas combustion, NO_x forms via a thermal fixation mechanism. During heavy oil and coal combustion, NO_x is formed via the fixation mechanism and through the conversion of bound nitrogen in the fuel to NO. The fixation mechanism depends strongly on both the local gas temperature and the local stoichiometry; therefore, temperature-reduction techniques such as flue gas recirculation and water injection and reductions in oxygen availability through low excess air firing or staging are effective in practical NO_x control. The conversion of fuel nitrogen seems to depend on the amount of nitrogen present in the fuel and oxygen availability.

The Air Quality Act of 1967 (Public Law 90-148 as amended) and the Clean Air Amendment of 1970 (Public Law 91-604) assigned to the Environmental Protection Agency (EPA) the responsibility of (a) developing emission standards for existing sources to be enforced by the States, and (b) setting performance standards for new sources to be enforced by EPA. Under these laws, EPA published in the Apr. 30, 1972, *Federal Register* the "National Primary and Secondary Ambient Air Quality Standards," which set the maximum acceptable ambient nitrogen oxides (NO_x) concentration at 55 parts per billion (annual arithmetic mean measured as nitrogen dioxide).

In an effort to guide the States in meeting this ambient level, EPA recently published the following as "Standards of Performance for New Stationary Sources" (*Federal Register,* vol. 36, No. 247, Dec. 23, 1971):

	Fuel Burning Emissions, lbs/MMBtu		
	Gas	*Oil*	*Coal*
New sources	0.2	0.3	0.7

Nitrogen oxides—primarily nitric oxide (NO) and nitrogen dioxide (NO_2)—are formed during the combustion of fossil fuels with air. Table I shows source estimates developed for EPA. These estimates of pollutant emission rates are based on emission factors developed by past stack-sampling data, material balances, and engineering appraisals of other sources similar to the listed sources.

As Table I indicates, almost half of the total national NO_x emissions result from stationary fuel combustion. In principle, NO_x emissions from fossil fuel-combustion systems can be reduced by three methods: fuel cleaning (removal of the fuel nitrogen), combustion modification, and flue gas treatment. Combustion modification appears to be by far the easiest and most economical of the three. Therefore, EPA has assigned to the Control Systems Division's, Combustion Research Section (CRS) the responsibility for assisting industry in developing technology to re-

Table I. Estimates of NO_x Emissions in the U. S. by Source, 1968 (1, 2)

Source	NO_x Emissions, tons/yr	Per Cent of Total
Mobile fuel combustion		40
Motor vehicles		
Gasoline	6,600,000	
Diesel	600,000	
Aircraft	40,000	
Railroad	400,000	
Vessels	300,000	
Non-highway users	300,000	
Stationary fuel combustion		48
Coal	4,000,000	
Fuel oil	1,110,000	
Natural gas	4,640,000	
Wood	230,000	
Solid waste		11
Open burning	450,000	
Conical incinerators	18,000	
Municipal incinerators	19,000	
On-site incinerators	69,000	
Coal waste banks	190,000	
Forest burning	1,200,000	
Agricultural burning	280,000	
Structural fires	23,000	
Industrial processes	200,000	1
Total	20,669,000	100

duce stationary-source emissions through changes in the combustion system. The purpose of this paper is to review the chemistry of NO_x formation in flames, to explain what CRS is presently doing to advance the understanding of this chemistry, and to relate the chemistry to existing control technology.

Chemistry of NO_x Formation from Thermal Fixation

Nitrogen oxides are formed during the combustion of coal, oil, natural gas, *etc.*, by two mechanisms. The first mechanism is high temperature thermal fixation of molecular oxygen and nitrogen present in the combustion air; the second mechanism is the reaction of atmospheric oxygen with nitrogen-containing compounds introduced in the fuel. Both mechanisms result primarily in NO because the residence time in most stationary combustion processes is too short for the oxidation of NO to NO_2, even though NO_2 is thermodynamically favored at lower temperatures (3). NO, however, does oxidize in the atmosphere to NO_2, which is a primary participant in photochemical smog.

For many years it was generally assumed that the thermal fixation of NO occurred according to the mechanism suggested by Zeldovich *et al.* (4).

$$O + N_2 \rightleftarrows NO + N \qquad (1)$$

$$N + O_2 \rightleftarrows NO + O \qquad (2)$$

Until recently it was further assumed that the hydrocarbon oxidation reactions have equilibrated prior to the onset of NO formation because the NO reactions are relatively much slower (5) at temperatures of stoichiometric hydrocarbon-air combustion and because they take place over an extensive portion of the mixing region. Fenimore (6) and Harris *et al.* (7) have conducted recent experimental studies of NO formation in atmospheric flat flames; their data support this simplified picture for *post*-combustion-zone formation. However, Fenimore (6) noted a substantial amount of NO was formed very rapidly in the flame front of methane-air and ethylene-air flames but not in CO-air or H_2-air flames. Figure 1 shows Fenimore's data on NO formation in four ethylene-air flames as a function of reaction time from the burner surface to the probe tip. The positive intercepts are indicative of flame zone or "prompt NO." Fenimore subsequently postulated that reactions such as

$$CH + N_2 = HCN + N \qquad (3)$$

$$C_2 + N_2 + CN + CN \qquad (4)$$

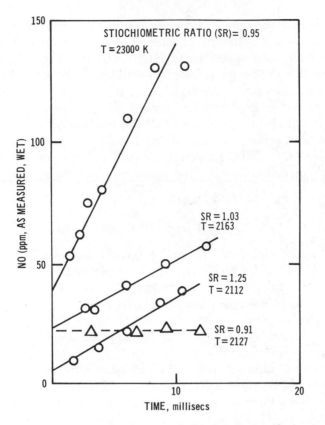

*Figure 1.   NO formation in ethylene-air flames above
a porous plate burner*

may be responsible for the breaking of the N-N bond. Subsequent reactions of HCN and other molecules containing a single nitrogen atom could easily lead to NO. To test the Fenimore conjecture of prompt NO through a cyanide route, Sternling and Wendt (8) proposed a model for methane combustion involving, in addition to the Seery and Bowman (9) combustion reactions, the following:

$$CH_3 + OH = CH_2 + H_2O \qquad 7.71 \times 10^{14} \exp (4{,}180/RT) \quad (5)$$

$$CH_3 + N_2 = HCN + NH_2 \qquad 4.60 \times 10^{15} \exp (19{,}000/RT) \quad (6)$$

$$CH_2 + N_2 = HCN + NH \qquad 2.04 \times 10^{15} \exp (41{,}700/RT) \quad (7)$$

$$CH_2 + O_2 = HCO + OH \qquad 7.38 \times 10^{14} \exp (1{,}700/RT) \quad (8)$$
(units in cc, mole, °K, cal)

To establish the *maximum* possible rate of N_2 fixation by the cyanide route, the highest conceivable rates (steric factor of unity) were utilized for Reactions 5 through 7. Reaction 8 was assigned a rather low rate. For the test case of isothermal burning of methane at 2100°K and 114.2% theoretical air, large quantities of HCN, NH, and NH_2 were produced, indicating that the Fenimore proposal could possibly be significant if the unknown reaction rates were high.

An alternative explanation of prompt NO proposed by several investigators is as follows: it is known that the combustion reactions proceed by a chain-branching mechanism involving the rapid buildup of such species as H, OH, and O to high levels, in some cases considerably above the values predicted by assuming equilibration of the reactions:

$$O_2 = \quad O + O \tag{9}$$

$$H_2O = OH + H \tag{10}$$

These "superequilibrium" radical concentrations would cause large amounts of NO to form very quickly by Reaction 1 because of the high oxygen level. Edelman and Economos (10) and Marteney (11) both conducted recent theoretical studies which proved that coupled finite-rate kinetic calculations do predict free radical concentrations considerably in excess of those calculated by assuming equilibrium for Reactions 9 and 10.

At present, although there is no absolute consensus regarding the mechanism behind prompt NO, the evidence that it occurs continues to increase. Since Fenimore's report it has been observed experimentally by many others (12, 13, 14, 15, 16, 17, 18). Figure 2 shows Lange's experimental results. In this investigation, NO was measured above a premixed, flat flame burner during methane combustion. The non-zero intercept is again taken as indicative of the prompt NO which was beyond the resolution of the sampling apparatus.

Attempts to correlate total NO_x emissions on an absolute basis have met with varying degrees of success. However, all investigators found that correlation required a system more detailed than the two-step Zeldovich scheme—Reactions 1 and 2—and equilibrium hydrocarbon chemistry. Thompson et al. (15) obtained satisfactory agreement with experimental NO formation in an oscillating combustor by using the Zeldovich reactions in conjunction with a more advanced hydrocarbon scheme. He assumed an equilibrium of the following reactions and used them with measured H_2 concentrations to calculate [O] for the NO formation:

$$H \quad + O_2 \quad = OH + O \tag{11}$$

$$H \quad + OH = H_2 \quad + O \tag{12}$$

$$OH + H_2 \quad = H \quad + H_2O \tag{13}$$

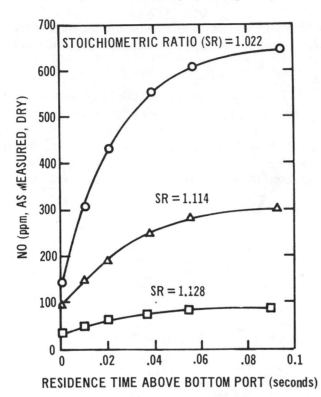

Figure 2. Experimental nitric oxide concentration above a Meeker burner

Sarofim and Pohl (*16*) used this same technique and found fair agreement with their data on premixed, atmospheric pressure flat flames. Iverach *et al.* (*17*) used a similar partial equilibrium assumption to correlate their data on hydrocarbon flames and found good agreement under fuel-lean (excess air) conditions. Poor agreement was observed under fuel-rich conditions; unreasonably large radical concentrations were required to make the Zeldovich mechanism account for the measured NO. Iverach, therefore, suggested that reactions such as those proposed by Fenimore may be important under fuel-rich conditions.

Bowman and Seery (*13*) went one step further in correlating their data on the formation of NO in shock-induced methane-oxygen-nitrogen combustion. Instead of assuming partial equilibrium, as Thompson *et al.* and Sarofim *et al.* did, they used a detailed methane reaction scheme (assuming no equilibration) with the Zeldovich reactions and found good agreement. In recent work (*19*) Bowman was able to obtain reasonable agreement between his reaction scheme and Fenimore's methane data under fuel-lean conditions. Bowman was not able to achieve good agreement under fuel-rich conditions even with the addition of the following reaction which most investigators feel is potentially important:

$$N + OH = NO + H \tag{14}$$

Lange (*18*) took the reverse approach and assumed hydrocarbon equilibration; he investigated NO formation reactions other than the Zeldovich pair to correlate this post-flat-flame experimental data. He found that if the rates for Reactions 15, 16, and 23 were increased substantially over the reported values, the results were reasonably predictable using the following reactions scheme:

$$N_2 \quad + O \qquad = NO \quad + N \tag{15}$$

$$N_2 \quad + HO_2 \quad = NO \quad + HNO \tag{16}$$

$$N_2 \quad + O + M = N_2O \quad + M \tag{17}$$

$$N_2 \quad + OH \quad = N_2O \quad + H \tag{18}$$

$$N_2 \quad + O_2 \quad = N_2O \quad + O \tag{19}$$

$$N_2 \quad + NO_2 \quad = N_2O \quad + NO \tag{20}$$

$$N \quad + O_2 \quad = NO \quad + O \tag{21}$$

$$N \quad + OH \quad = NO \quad + H \tag{22}$$

$$N_2O \quad + O \qquad = 2NO \tag{23}$$

$$N_2O \quad + O_2 \quad = NO \quad + NO_2 \tag{24}$$

$$N \quad + OH \quad = NH \quad + O \tag{25}$$

$$N \quad + H_2 \quad = NH \quad + H \tag{26}$$

$$N \quad + H_2O \quad = NH \quad + OH \tag{27}$$

$$NH \quad + OH \quad = NO \quad + H_2 \tag{28}$$

$$NH \quad + O \quad = NO \quad + H \tag{29}$$

$$NH \quad + OH \quad = HNO + H \tag{30}$$

$$NH \quad + O_2 \quad = HNO + O \tag{31}$$

$$HNO + M \qquad = H \quad + NO + M \tag{32}$$

$$HNO + OH \quad = NO \quad + H_2O \tag{33}$$

$$HNO + H \quad = NO \quad + H_2 \tag{34}$$

$$HNO + O \quad = NO \quad + OH \tag{35}$$

The adjustment in Reaction 15 is not unreasonable. The rate recently recommended by Baulch *et al.* (*20*) is only 30% lower than the adjusted value of Lange and hence lies well within the range of uncertainty given by Baulch *et al.*

Thus, there is no general agreement on which reactions are important in NO formation, possibly because different reactions may predominate depending on the experimental apparatus. Also, in flat, premixed flames, the high concentrations of O, H, and OH decay rapidly downstream of the flame; the residence time of N_2 in the flame zone of high radical concentration is often not long enough to cause the prompt NO to be a large portion of the total NO_x. However, the industrial flames responsible for the bulk of the national NO_x emissions are not premixed; they are diffusion. Further, there is no agreement on whether the hydrocarbon oxidation/NO formation coupling and prompt NO are more or less significant in diffusion flames. Therefore, the Combustion Research Section has initiated a program to define the chemistry of thermal fixation of NO under conditions typical of industrial furnaces and boilers.

One phase of this program, being conducted by Esso Research and Engineering (*21*), is directed at defining the significant combustion/NO formation reactions and reviewing the presently available rate data on each. Initially, a carbon-hydrogen-oxygen-nitrogen system survey considered methane and lower order species. Table II lists the 41 species considered; they represent over 300 reported reactions. As a first cut, reactions involving the 17 species indicated by asterisks were eliminated. It was felt that they would be of lesser importance for the coupling between NO formation and the combustion of methane and air at atmos-

Table II.   Species Considered in Combustion—No Formation Screening

^aC	H	N	O
CH	HN	NO	O_2
CHN	HNO	NO_2	$^aO_3$
CHO	HO	$^aNO_3$	
CH_2	HO_2	N_2	
CH_2O	H_2	N_2O	
CH_3	^aH_2N	$^aN_2O_4$	
$^aCH_3O$			
CH_4	$^aH_2N_2$	$^aN_2O_5$	
CN	H_2O		
CO	$^aH_2O_2$		
CO_2	^aH_3N		
$^aC_2$	$^aHCN_2$		
^aC_2H	$^aH_4N_2$		
$^?C_2H_2$			
^aC_2O			
$^aC_3$			

^{a} These species were eliminated during the initial period. *See* text for explanation.

pheric pressure and at temperatures between 1500 and 2500°K. The following types of reactions were also eliminated during the initial cut: three-body reactions of the exchange type, photochemical reactions, non-elementary step reactions. These considerations reduced the survey to a base group of 142 reactions.

Available literature was then reviewed; all known information on each of the 142 reactions was assembled in a computerized data bank. The report on this work will contain the following for each of the 142 reactions listed in the Appendix:

> Master species and reaction list
> Thermodynamic tables for each reaction
> Complete sorting of the reactions by species
> Kinetic parameters from experiments, calculations, and reviews
> "Best present rate" for each reaction
> References for the survey

Not all of the reactions listed in the Appendix have been studied experimentally or even estimated. Therefore, part of the EPA program is directed at developing automated estimation calculations based on group-additivity techniques. This work is being conducted at Stanford Research Institute (22). Once the literature survey is complete, parametric evaluations will be conducted in conjunction with experimental data analysis to define which of the 142 reactions are actually significant under industrial pollution-formation conditions.

As part of the experimental phase of the program, Esso Research and Engineering (21) is conducting combustion studies under a variety of conditions. The initial work (23) utilized a modification of the Longwell-Weiss reactor (24), termed a jet-stirred combustor (Figure 3). This

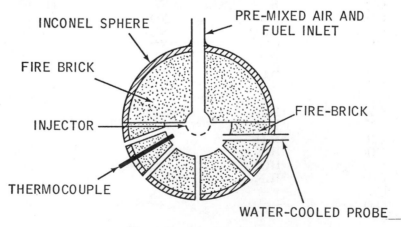

Figure 3.   Jet-stirred combustor

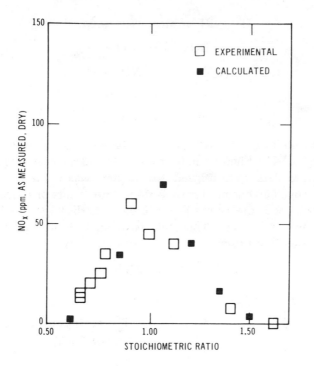

Figure 4. Emissions from hydrogen-air combustion in a jet-stirred reactor

device was selected because the combustion rates are limited by chemical kinetics rather than fluid dynamics (*25*). Also, in a jet-stirred reactor, residence time effects can be minimized by changing the fuel flow rather than the air flow.

Figure 4 shows the experimental data taken for hydrogen-air combustion. The solid squares are the result of a complete kinetic calculation (not assuming partial equilibration) (*26*), treating the jet-stirred reactor as a well stirred system and inputing measured reactor temperature or heat loss rates. The reaction scheme included the following:

$$OH + H_2 \qquad = H_2O + H \tag{36}$$

$$OH + OH \qquad = O \quad + H_2O \tag{37}$$

$$O \; + H_2 \qquad = H \; + OH \tag{38}$$

$$H \; + O_2 \qquad = O \; + OH \tag{39}$$

$$O \; + H + M = OH \; + M \tag{40}$$

$$O \; + O + M = O_2 \; + M \tag{41}$$

$$H + H + M = H_2 + M \tag{42}$$

$$H + HO + M = H_2O + M \tag{43}$$

$$N + O_2 \qquad = NO + O \tag{44}$$

$$O + N_2 \qquad = NO + N \tag{45}$$

$$N + OH \qquad = NO + H \tag{46}$$

(Note that the principal NO reactions, 44 and 45, are the Zeldovich Reactions 2 and 1). Figure 4 indicates that the agreement is quite good. Literature rate data were utilized; no attempt was made to adjust the rates to improve agreement. Figure 5 shows the results of a similar study with CO with good agreement. Figure 6 presents the experimental results with propane combustion. The theoretical analysis utilized the quasi-global initiation step to simulate the propane breakup.

$$2C_3H_8 + 3O_2 = 8H_2 + 6CO \tag{47}$$

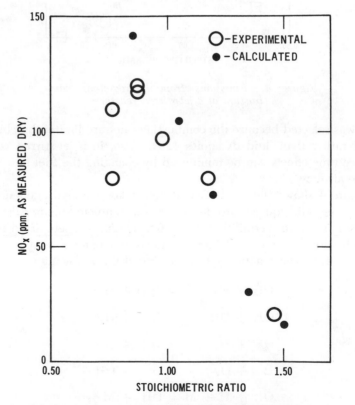

Figure 5.   Emissions from carbon monoxide-air combustion in a jet-stirred reactor

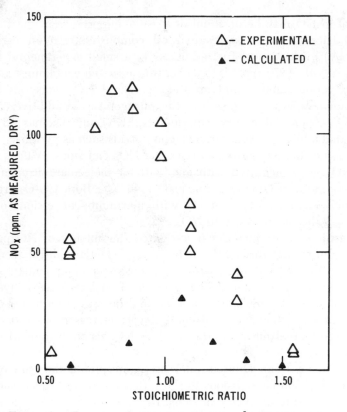

Figure 6.   *Emissions from propane-air combustion in a jet-stirred reactor*

Detailed finite rate calculations were used from CO and H_2 on as before: poor agreement was still observed. Poor agreement may be a result of the lack of a detailed hydrocarbon combustion mechanism or of other reactions with nitrogenous intermediates.

EPA is presently in the process of extending this work (21) by conducting detailed flame probing on premixed and diffusion flames in an axisymetric laboratory furnace burning CO, H_2, methane, and propane. The premixed burner and jet-stirred combustor data will be used in conjunction with detailed, finite rate plug flow and well stirred analyses to determine the chemistry of thermal NO_x formation during gaseous combustion.

Chemistry of NO_x Formation from Fuel Nitrogen Conversion

For many years it was assumed that NO was formed only by high temperature fixation of atmospheric nitrogen and oxygen; recent experimental studies have indicated that the conversion of bound nitrogen in the fuel to NO may be of equal or greater importance in the formation of NO_x during coal and residual oil combustion. In an early EPA (NAPCA) evaluation of fuel additives in a small experimental furnace, Martin et al. (27) noted that certain nitrogen-containing additives, notably various amines and nitrates, increased NO_x emissions through approximately 50% conversion of the nitrogen in the additive to NO.

In flat flame laboratory experiments, Shaw and Thomas (28) have shown that addition of fuel nitrogen compounds such as pyridines, amines, and cyanides to CO flames increases the NO_x emissions. Values to 1300 ppm NO_x were measured with and without molecular nitrogen during low temperature CO combustion (860-1145°K). Both $CO-O_2$-argon and $CO-O_2-N_2$ mixtures were studied with maximum conversions of about 40-50% of the fuel nitrogen to NO_x.

Martin and Berkau (29) investigated the amount of NO produced in an experimental furnace from burning a standard distillate oil (less than 0.01% nitrogen) doped with various nitrogen compounds (pyridine, quinoline, and piperidine). The fraction of fuel nitrogen converted to NO increased with stoichiometric ratio and decreased with fuel-nitrogen concentration, although the absolute levels increased with both. The percentage of fuel nitrogen converted to NO generally ranged from 20 to 70%.

Elshout and van Duuren (30) have interpreted the data of Smith (31) on large source emissions to show that the fuel nitrogen concentration was related to the NO_x emissions from boilers of a given size. Similar data are reported in the EPA (NAPCA)-sponsored Esso NO_x Systems Study (32).

Bartok et al. (12) examined the addition of a number of nitrogen compounds (including NO, NO_2, NH_3, $(CN)_2$, and CH_3NH_2) during methane-air combustion in a jet-stirred reactor. Under excess air conditions, essentially complete conversion (or retention) was observed; however, the fraction of the additive which oxidized to NO_x decreased sharply on the fuel-rich side.

Jonke (33) studied the NO emissions from a coal-fired, fluid-bed combustor operating at a bed temperature below 1300°K and observed 580 ppm NO emissions with both N_2-O_2 and argon-O_2. This corresponds to about 25% conversion of the fuel nitrogen.

Turner et al. (34) experimented with doped distillate fuels and residual oils in a package boiler and discovered that 40-80% of the fuel nitrogen, depending on concentration, is converted to NO during combustion under normal operating conditions. This conversion is further substantiated by the data from a West Coast utility shown in Figure 7.

Thus, based on the results of laboratory studies, it appears that fuel nitrogen is potentially important in the overall formation of NO_x. Unfor-

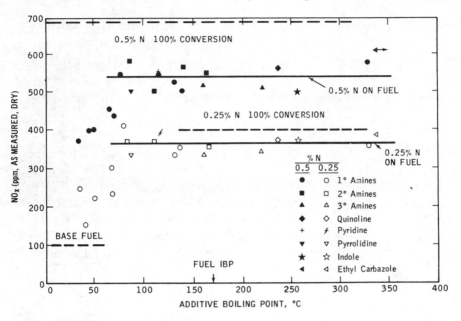

Figure 7. Effect of additive type and per cent N on NO_x emissions from a package boiler at SR 1.30

tunately, documented information on the level of fuel nitrogen normally found in coal and oil is very limited.

A table of coal properties compiled by Spiers (35) indicates that U. S. coals average from 1.15 to 1.74% nitrogen, corresponding to approximately 880-1330 ppm NO (dry) if 40% of the bound nitrogen is converted. Ball (36) reports that the average nitrogen concentration for U. S. crude oils in 1956 was 0.148% nitrogen. From this it is estimated that the average heavy oil would contain about 0.32% nitrogen, corresponding to about 220 ppm (dry) at 40% conversion.

The actual chemistry of fuel nitrogen conversion to NO is far from well understood; however, certain facts are discernible. First, it appears that the type of nitrogen compound present in fuel oil has little effect on the conversion. Martin and Berkau (29), investigating both unsaturated single-ring and saturated multi-ring compounds, observed only a slight effect. Turner (34) tested 20 nitrogen-containing additives including primary, secondary, and tertiary amines and hetrocyclics with similar results. As Figure 8 shows, except for the five additives with extremely low boiling points, the NO_x emissions for all compounds at a given N level were essentially the same. These data strongly indicate that the conversion of NO_x is essentially the same for most nitrogen compounds, irrespective of molecular type. They further suggest that the route from bound nitrogen in the fuel to NO may be through some common intermediate(s), such as NH_2, NH_3, N, or CN. Formation of large amounts of N atoms would seem unlikely because the bimolecular reaction

$$N + O_2 = NO + O \qquad (48)$$

is highly favored over the trimolecular reaction

$$N + N + M = N_2 + M \qquad (49)$$

Reaction 49 would predict much higher conversions than have been experimentally observed.

Second, there is considerable experimental evidence that increased oxygen availability results in increased fuel nitrogen conversion and higher NO_x emissions. The data of Martin and Berkau (29) (Figure 8) indicate that NO is proportional to $P_{O_2}^{0.21}$ for the system studied; Turner et al. (34) found similar results. Further, both investigators found little effect of bulk temperature on the formation of fuel NO_x.

Since the detailed chemistry of fuel nitrogen conversion is largely unknown at present, EPA recently initiated work at North American Rockwell's Rocketdyne Division to investigate the mechanisms of this conversion in heavy oil and coal combustion. The two-phase research program has elements in each phase running concurrently. Phase I, a theoretical analysis and an experimental study of fuel decomposition, includes: detailed identification of nitrogen compounds in actual coals and oils, experimental study of fuel decomposition paths and products, identification and concentration of products formed during decomposition. Phase II is a study of the reaction kinetics of the mechanisms identified in Phase I as being important in fuel nitrogen conversion.

Ultimately, it will be possible to define both the mechanism and rate of NO_x formation from thermal fixation and fuel nitrogen conversion. However, to be of value it must be coupled with an understanding of the combustion fluid dynamics because the latter are certainly as important as the chemistry. Current EPA programs in the area of fluid flow are aimed at analytically characterizing swirling flames, investigating the importance of recirculation zones, modeling furnace flows, etc. The initial combined chemistry/fluid-flow effort is a coordinated theoretical and experimental study of laminar- and turbulent-diffusion flames. The work is being conducted in the axisymetric laboratory furnace with controlled wall temperatures and complete two-dimensional probing capability. By comparing the diffusion flame data with premixed data from the same system it will be possible to better define the relationship of fluid dynamic parameters in NO_x formation.

Inputs from all of these programs will ultimately be used in the detailed analysis of point-wise species, temperature, and flow data pres-

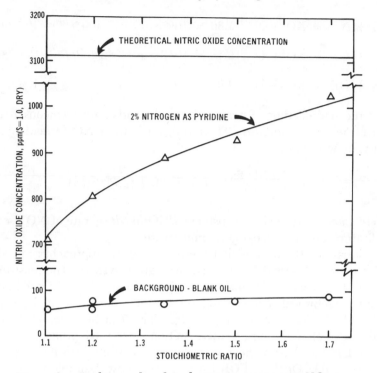

*Figure 8.   Background and fuel nitrogen conversion NO as a
function of stoichiometric ratio in an experimental furnace*

ently being generated on large scale experimental test furnaces burning
natural gas and coal. The results of these studies, together with the
chemical kinetics program just described, will be used to develop a complete understanding of NO formation and a mathematical model for
design and optimization of control technology.

Relationship of Pollutant Chemistry to Existing Combustion Modification Control Technology

Unfortunately, it is not possible to wait until NO formation is completely understood before attempts are made to control it. Therefore, it
is pertinent to summarize the present knowledge of the chemistry of NO
formation and consider how this has guided NO_x control technology. It
is important to remember that most existing control technology was originally developed empirically because the fundamentals (*i.e.*, the relationship of the chemistry, aerodynamics, etc., to NO_x formation) were not
well understood.

Thermal Fixation. The preceding sections have shown that during
natural gas combustion, NO results from the high temperature fixation
of atmospheric nitrogen according to the following reactions and coupled

$$O + N_2 = NO + N \quad 1.36 \times 10^{14} \exp\,(-75,400/RT) \quad \text{Ref. 20} \quad (1)$$

$$N + O_2 = NO + O \quad 6.43 \times 10^9 T \exp\,(-6250/RT) \quad \text{Ref. 20} \quad (2)$$

$$N + OH = NO + H \quad 4.0 \times 10^{13} \qquad\qquad\qquad \text{Ref. 37} \quad (14)$$

with the hydrocarbon system and possible other nitrogeneous reactions under fuel-rich conditions. Therefore, the rate of NO formation can be generally written as

$$\frac{d\text{NO fix}}{dt} = f\,(e^{-E/RT},\, P_{O_2}^\alpha,\, P_{N_2}^\beta,\, etc.) \qquad (50)$$

where α and β are positive constants, dNO fix$/dt$ = rate of NO formation by fixation, and T = local gas temperature.

Equation 50 indicates that there are several approaches to reducing the amount of thermal NO formed by a given system. The most obvious is to reduce local gas temperature. Since fixed NO is exponential with negative reciprocal temperature, significant reductions can be expected with reduced local flame temperature. This can be accomplished practically several ways, e.g., load reduction, increased primary stage heat removal, reduced air preheat, water or steam injection, or flue gas recirculation (FGR). Of these FGR is one of the most desirable from an operating standpoint because it does not significantly decrease overall plant efficiency. With FGR a portion of the flue products is cycled back to the combustion chamber where it enters with the combustion air. Figure 9 shows data (38) taken on gas-fired units under various levels of FGR; the data indicate that gas-fired units are quite effective with thermal NO_x.

Another way to reduce thermal NO_x is by reducing P_{O_2}. Practically this can be accomplished by dilution (e.g., with water or steam injection or FGR) or by reducing the overall excess air in the combustion zone. Low excess air (LEA) firing has been shown (39) to cause 15-35% reductions in NO_x, but is limited because excess air levels below a certain value drastically increase emissions of CO and unburned hydrocarbons and can cause severe slagging problems with coal combustion. LEA firing is somewhat anomalous, however, in that it also increases theoretical maximum flame temperature; this increase might be expected to outweigh the effect of P_{O_2} because of the exponential dependence on temperature. (This does in fact occur in premixed systems but not necessarily in diffusion flames, showing that, in addition to chemistry, the aerodynamics of the combustor must be considered before commercial systems can be fully understood.)

Fuel Nitrogen. During heavy oil and coal combustion, NO_x is formed not only by the fixation medium just described but also by the

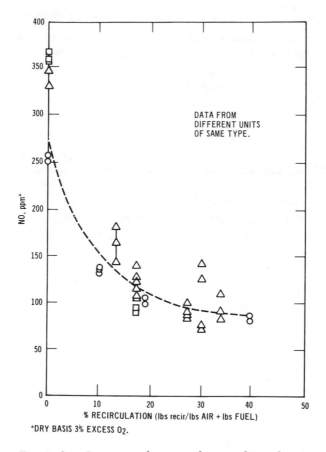

*Figure 9.   Gas recirculation with natural gas firing,
320 MW corner-fired unit*

conversion of bound nitrogen in the fuel. While no reactions can be confidently written, it is known that

$$\frac{dNO\,fn}{dt} = g\,(P_{O_2}^{\alpha},\,X_{N_2}^{\beta},\,\text{etc.}) \tag{51}$$

where the function g does not depend strongly upon local gas temperature, T, α and β are positive, $dNO\,fn/dt$ = rate of NO formation through fuel nitrogen conversion, and X_N = weight per cent nitrogen in the fuel.

Equation 51 indicates that the most obvious way to control fuel NO_x is by reducing the bound nitrogen content in the fuel. This reduction can be accomplished by fuel switching (from heavy oil or coal to light oil or gas) or by denitrification. Unfortunately, fuel availability limits both approaches.

The alternative is to decrease P_{O_2} through FGR, LEA, or staged combustion. Unfortunately, FGR has only a slight effect on fuel nitrogen conversion because it reduces P_{O_2} only slightly (Figure 10). LEA appears to be slightly more effective, but its utility is severely limited by operating problems with coal and heavy oil. By far the most powerful classical control technique is two-stage combustion (SC). SC usually involves admitting about 95% of the stoichiometric air through the burner throat and the remaining air through ports located above the burners. Staged combustion is effective because P_{O_2} is significantly reduced in the fuel-rich first stage; neither fixation nor fuel nitrogen species can compete effectively with hydrocarbon fragments for the limited O_2. By the time the secondary air is added, enough heat has been removed from the system to prevent substantial NO formation. Figure 11 shows the effectiveness of staged combustion even with coal firing (40). It should

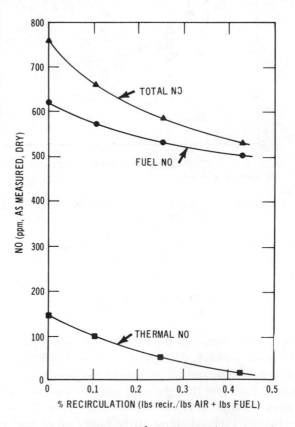

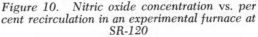

Figure 10.   Nitric oxide concentration vs. per cent recirculation in an experimental furnace at SR-120

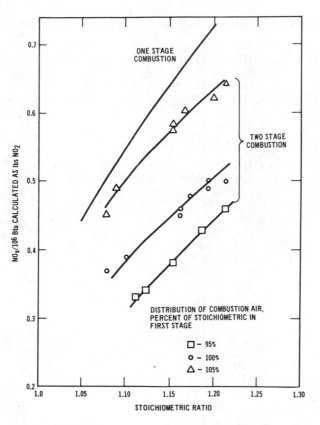

*Figure 11.   Two-stage combustion—500 lbs/hr coal-
fired boiler*

be cautioned, however, that the slagging and corrosion problems associated with staged combustion have not yet been fully evaluated.

At present, no completely satisfactory and universally applicable control technique is available, but several approaches (*e.g.*, flue gas recirculation, low excess air firing, and staged combustion) appear very promising. A better understanding of the chemistry of pollutant formation
should lead ultimately to optimization of these and other new techniques
for total control of NO_x emissions.

Appendix

Reactions Presently Included in Survey

CH	+ CHN	= CH_2	CN		CH	+ CO_2	= CHO	+ CO
CH	+ CHO	= CH_2	+ CO		CH	+ H	= CH_2	
CH	+ CH_2O	= CH_2	+ CHO		CH + H + M	= CH_2 + M		
CH	+ CH_3	= $2CH_2$			CH	+ HN	= CHN	+ H
CII	+ CH_4	– CH_2	+ CH_3		CH	+ HN	= CN	+ H_2

Reactions Presently Included in Survey (*Continued*)

$CH + HNO = CH_2 + NO$
$CH + HO = CHO + H$
$CH + HO + CH_2 + O$
$CH + HO = CO + H_2$
$CH + HO_2 = CHO + HO$
$CH + HO_2 = CH_2 + O_2$
$CH + H_2 = CH_2 + H$
$CH + H_2O = CH_2 + HO$
$CH + N = CN + H$
$CH + NO = CHO + N$
$CH + N_2 = CHN + N$
$CH + O = CO + H$
$CH + O + M = CHO + M$
$CH + O_2 = CHO + O$
$CH + O_2 = CO + HO$
$CHN + M = CN + H + M$
$CHN + CHO = CH_2O + CN$
$CHN + CH_2 = CH_3 + CN$
$CHN + CH_3 = CH_4 + CN$
$CHN + H = CN + H_2$
$CHN + HO = CN + H_2O$
$CHN + N = CN + HN$
$CHN + NO = CN + HNO$
$CHN + O = CN + HO$
$CHO + M = CO + H + M$
$CHO + CHO = CH_2O + CO$
$CHO + CH_2 = CH_3 + CO$
$CHO + CH_3 = CH_2 \ CH_2O$
$CHO + CH_3 = CH_4 + CO$
$CHO + CH_4 = CH_3 + CH_2O$
$CHO + H = CH_2 + O$
$CHO + H = CH_2O$
$CHO + H = CO + H_2$
$CHO + HNO = CH_2O + NO$
$CHO + HO = CH_2O + O$
$CHO + HO = CO + H_2O$
$CHO + H_2 = CH_2O + H$
$CHO + H_2O = CH_2O + HO$
$CHO + N = CO + HN$
$CHO + NO = CO + HNO$
$CHO + O = CO + HO$
$CH_2 + CH_4 = 2CH_3$
$CH_2 + HNO = CH_3 + NO$
$CH_2 + HO = CH_3 + O$
$CH_2 + H_2 = CH_3 + H$
$CH_2 + H_2O = CH_3 + HO$
$CH_2 + O_2 = CH_2O + O$
$CH_2O + H = CH_3 + O$
$CH_2O + HO = CH_3 + O_2$
$CH_3 + H = CH_4$

$CH_3 + HNO = CH_4 + NO$
$CH_3 + HO = CH_4 + O$
$CH_3 + HO_2 = CH_4 \ O_2$
$CH_3 + H_2 = CH_4 + H$
$CH_3 + H_2O = CH_4 + HO$
$CN + NO = CO + N_2$
$CN + O_2 = CO + NO$
$CO + HNO = CO_2 + HN$
$CO + HO = CO_2 + H$
$CO + HO_2 \ CO_2 + HO$
$CO + H_2O = CO_2 + H_2$
$CO + NO = CO_2 + N$
$CO + NO_2 = CO_2 + NO$
$CO + N_2O = CO_2 + N_2$
$CO + O = CO_2$
$CO + O + M = CO_2 + M$
$CO + O_2 = CO_2 + O$
$H + H + M = H_2 + M$
$H + HN = H_2 + N$
$H + HNO = HN + HO$
$H + HNO = H_2 + NO$
$H + HO = H_2 + O$
$H + HO + M = H_2O + M$
$H + HO_2 = 2HO$
$H + HO_2 = H_2 \ O_2$
$H + HO_2 = H_2O + O$
$H + H_2O = HO + H_2$
$H+ \ +N+ \ +M = HN + M$
$H + NO = NH + O$
$H + NO = NO + N$
$H + NO + M = HNO + M$
$H + NO_2 = HNO + O$
$H + NO_2 = HO + NO$
$H + N_2 = HN + N$
$H + N_2O = HN + NO$
$H + N_2O = HNO + N$
$H + N_2O = HO + N_2$
$H + O + M = HO + M$
$H + O_2 = HO + O$
$H + O_2 + M = HO_2 + M$
$HN + HN = H_2 + N_2$
$HN + HO = H_2 + NO$
$HN + HO = H_2O + N$
$HN + NO = HNO + N$
$HN + NO_2 = HNO + NO$
$HN + N_2O = HNO + N_2$
$HN + O = HO + N$
$HN + O + M = HNO + M$
$HN + O_2 = HNO + O$
$HN + O_2 = HO_2 + N$

Reactions Presently Included in Survey (*Continued*)

$HNO + M = HO + N + M$	$N + NO_2 = N_2 + O + O$
$HNO + HO = H_2O + NO$	$N + NO_2 = N_2 + O_2$
$HNO + NO = HO + N_2O$	$N + NO_2 = N_2O + O$
$HNO + O = HO + NO$	$N + N_2O = NO + N_2$
$HO + HO = H_2 + O_2$	$N + O + M = NO + M$
$HO + HO = H_2O + O$	$N + O_2 = NO + O$
$HO + HO_2 = H_2O + O_2$	$NO + NO = N_2 + O_2$
$HO + NO = HO_2 + N$	$NO + NO = N_2O + O$
$HO + NO_2 = HO_2 + NO$	$NO + NO_2 + N_2O + O_2$
$HO + O + M + HO_2 + M$	$NO + N_2O = NO_2 + N_2$
$HO + O_2 = HO_2 + O$	$NO + O + M = NO_2 + M$
$H_2 + NO_2 = H_2O + NO$	$NO + O_2 = NO_2 + O$
$N + N + M = N_2 + M$	$N_2 + O + M = N_2O + M$
$N + NO = N_2 + O$	$N_2 + O_2 = N_2O + O$
$N + NO + M = N_2O + M$	$O + O + M = O_2 + M$
$N + NO_2 = 2NO$	

Literature Cited

1. "Control Techniques for Nitrogen Oxide Emissions from Stationary Sources," Deptartment of Health, Education and Welfare, National Air Pollution Control Administration, Washington, D.C., Mar. 1970.
2. "Reference Book of Nationwide Emissions," Department of Health Education and Welfare, National Air Pollution Control Administration, Durham, N.C.
3. Bartok, W., *et al.*, "Systems Study of Nitrogen Oxides Control Methods for Stationary Sources," vol. II, Contract No. PH 22–68–55, Esso, 1969.
4. Zeldovich, Y. B., Sadovnikov, P. Y., Frank-Kamenetskii, D. A., "Oxidation of Nitrogen in Combustion," Academy of Sciences of USSR, Institute of Chemical Physics, Moscow-Leningrad (trans. by M. Shelef), 1947.
5. Zeldovich, Y. B., *Acta Physicochim.* (USSR) (1946) 21, 577.
6. Fenimore, C. P., *13th Intern. Symp. Combust.*, Salt Lake City (1970).
7. Harris, M. E., Rowe, R., Cook, E. B., Grumer, J., *Bureau of Mines Bull.* 653 (1970).
8. Sternling, C. V., Wendt, J. O. L., "Kinetic Mechanisms Governing the Fate of Chemically Bound Sulfur and Nitrogen in Combustion," Task Report, EPA Contract No. EHSD 71–45, May 1972.
9. Seery, D. J., Bowman, C. T., *Combustion Flame* (1970) 14, 37.
10. Edelman, R., Economos, C., *7th Propulsion Joint Specialist Conf.*, Salt Lake City, June 1971, paper 71–714 AIAA/SAE.
11. Marteney, P. J., *Combustion Sci. Technol.* (1970) 1, 461–469.
12. Bartok, W., Engleman, V. S., Goldstein, R., del Valle, E. G., 70th National Meeting, AICHE, Atlantic City, Aug. 1971, paper 37A.
13. Bowman, C. T., Serry, D. J., *GM Symp. Emissions Continuous Combust. Systems*, Warren, Mich., Sept. 1971.
14. Halstead, C. J., Munro, A. J. E., "The Sampling, Analysis and Study of the Nitrogen Oxides formed in Natural Gas/Air Flames," *Prepr., Shell Research, Ltd.*, Egham Research Labs, Egham, Surrey, England.
15. Thompson, D., Berr, J. M., Brown, T. D., *Nat. Meetg., AICHE, 70th*, Atlantic City, Aug. 1971, paper 37e.
16. Sarofim, A. F., Pohl, J. H., *14th Symp. Int. Combust., Proc.*, Aug. 1972.
17. Iverach, D., Basden, K. S., Kirov, N. Y., *14th Intern. Symp. Combustion*, Aug. 1972.

18. Lange, H. B., 64th Annual Meeting, AICHE, San Francisco, Dec. 1971.
19. Bowman, C. T. *14th Inter. Symp. on Combustion*, Aug. 1972.
20. Baulch, D. L., Drysdale, D. D., Horne, D. G., Loyd, L. C., "Critical Evaluation of Rate Constants for Homogeneous Gas Phase Reactions of Interest in High Temperature Systems," Dept. Phys. Chem., University of Leeds, England, Report No. 4, Dec. 1969.
21. "Definition of the Mechanism and Kinetics of the Formation of NO_x and Other Pollutants in Combustion Reactions," Environmental Protection Agency Contract No. **68–02–0224**, Esso Research and Engineering Co., Linden, N.J., Oct. 1971.
22. "Estimation of Combustion and Nitric Oxide Kinetics," Environmental Protection Agency Grant No. **800798**, Stanford Research Institute, Menlo Park, Calif., June 1972.
23. "Systems Study of Nitrogen Oxide Control Methods for Stationary Sources —Phase II," Environmental Protection Agency Contract No. **CPA 70–90**, Esso Research and Engineering Co., Linden, N.J.
24. Longwell, J. P., Weiss, M. A., *Ind. Eng. Chem.* (1955) **47**, 1634.
25. Hottel, H. C., Williams, G. C., Miles, G. A., *11th Inter. Symp. Combust.*, 1967 p. 771.
26. Engleman, V. S., Edleman, R. B., Bartok, W., Longwell, J. P., *14th Int. Symp. Combust., Proc., 14th*, Aug. 1972.
27. Martin, G. B., Pershing, D. W., Berkau, E. E., Environmental Protection Agency, Office of Air Programs Pub. No. AP–87, Sept. 1971.
28. Shaw, J. T., Thomas, A. T., *7th Intern. Conf. Coal Science*, Prague, June 1968.
29. Martin, G. B., Berkau, E. E., 70th National Meeting, AICHE, Atlantic City, Aug. 1971.
30. Elshout, A. J., van Duuren, H., *Electrotechnicals* (1968) **46**, 251.
31. Smith, W. S., "Atmospheric Emissions from Fuel Oil Combustion—An Inventory Guide." Environmental Health Series 999–AP–2, U.S. Public Health Service, Washington, D.C.
32. Bartok, W. *et al.*, "Systems Study of Nitrogen Oxide Control Methods for Stationary Sources," Final Report, NAPCA Contract No. PH 22–68–55, Nov. 1969, pp. 4–17.
33. Jonke, A. A., "Reduction of Atmospheric Pollution by the Application of Fluidized Bed Combustion," Monthly Reports No. 8 and 9, NAPCA Contract No. ANL–ES–CEN–F009, Mar. and Apr. 1969.
34. Turner, D. W., Andres, R. L., Sieginund, C. W., "Influence of Combustion Modification and Fuel Nitrogen Content on Nitrogen Oxides Emissions from Fuel Oil Combustion," Esso Research and Engineering Co. Report, Linden, N.J. 1971.
35. Spiers, H. S., "Technical Data on Fuels," 6th Ed.: The British National Committee, World Power Conference, 1962, pp. 297–298.
36. Ball, J. S., *API Proceedings* (1962) **42** (VIII).
37. Campbell, I. M., Thrush, B. A., *Trans. Faraday Soc.* (1968) **64**.
38. Bagwell, F. A., Rosenthal, K. E., Teixeina, D. P., Breen, B. P., Bayard de Volo, N., Hehro, S., *J. Air Pollut. Contr. Ass.* (1971) **21**, 702–708.
39. Bartok, W., Crawford, A. R., Cunningham, A. R., Hall, H. J., Manny, E. H., and Skopp, A., *Proceedings, Clean Air Congress*, Academic Press, New York, 1971, pp. 801-818.
40. McCann, C. R., Demeter, J. J., Dzubay, J., Bienstock, D., 65th Meeting, APCA, Miami Beach, June 18–22, 1972.

RECEIVED February 15, 1972.

INDEX

The text of this book is set in 10 point Caledonia with two points of leading. The chapter numerals are set in 30 point Garamond; the chapter titles are set in 18 point Garamond Bold.

The book is printed offset on Danforth 550 Machine Blue White text, 50-pound. The cover for the hard bound edition is Joanna Book Binding blue linen.

Jacket design by Norman Favin.
Editing and production by Spencer Lockson.

The book was composed by the Mills-Frizell-Evans Co., Baltimore, Md., printed and bound by **The** *Maple Press Co., York, Pa.*